Understanding Each Other After 9-11

Acclaim for

Dr. Kirk Heriot's

UNDERSTANDING EACH OTHER AFTER 9-11

"*Understanding Each Other After 9-11* contains a wealth of information about the origins, beliefs, and practices of the world's most significant religions. Dr. Heriot has given us new depth in our understanding of the important principles that religions share. Anyone interested in learning more about the world's religions will want to read this valuable new resource."

— C. David Lundberg, author of *Unifying Truths of the World's Religions: Practical Principles for Living and Loving in Peace*

"*Understanding Each Other After 9-11* should be read and discussed vigorously by all who want to do what is right in the world but find themselves fearful of, and alarmed by, those whose beliefs are differently placed around the great circle of religious tradition. An important book for patriots who long for a future in which everyone thinks spiritually and acts accordingly!"

— Reverend Wanda Windsor, United Methodist Minister

"A delightful invitation to augment our knowledge of the world's major religions. Each chapter traces the origin, historical highlights, and essential features of one faith. Kirk Heriot's research and elucidative skills bring these religions into sharp focus. Written in clear, compelling language, *Understanding Each Other After 9-11* is must reading for anyone who seeks a better understanding of religion."

— Ruth Hoppin, author of *Priscilla's Letter: Finding the Author of the Epistle to the Hebrews*

"There is much ignorance, misunderstanding, and bias among believers of different religions. There are also areas of common ground that can serve as a place to open a dialog with one another. Dr. Heriot is to be commended for his efforts at facilitating mutual understanding."

— Rev. Dr. James T. Stout

UNDERSTANDING EACH OTHER AFTER 9-11

What Everyone Should Know About the Religions of the World

KIRK HERIOT, M.D., PH.D.

LOST
COAST
PRESS

Understanding each other after 9-11

What Everyone Should Know Abou-t the Religions of the World

Lost Coast Press
155 Cypress Street
Fort Bragg, CA 95437
(800) 773-7782
www.cypresshouse.com

Cover and book design: Mike Brechner / Cypress House

Library of Congress Cataloging-in-Publication Data

Heriot, Kirk, 1955-
Understanding each other after 9-11 : what everyone should know about the religions of the world / Kirk Heriot. -- 1st ed.
p. cm.
Includes index.
ISBN 978-1-882897-98-8 (casebound : alk. paper)
1. Religions. I. Title.
BL80.3.H47 2010
200--dc22 2008039010

First edition

Printed in China

2 4 6 8 9 7 5 3 1

Dedication

To the sacrifices of my mother, Mary,
the memory of my father, Henry,
and the promise of my children,
Adam and Neil.

Acknowledgments

On an immediate level, I am indebted to Dr. Richard McCaughey for his comments on the Christianity section, to Dr. Mohammed Shafiq for his comments on the Islam section, and to Dr. Michael Dobkowski for his input into the portion on Judaism. Doctors Jena Gaines and Donald White read every word of the manuscript and offered many constructive comments. On a larger level, I am indebted to my parents for instilling in me a love of learning, to my wife for her love and support, and to my sons for providing an incentive to understand each other and the breathtaking diversity of humanity in their world.

CONTENTS

ILLUSTRATIONS

Prologue

OUT OF ONE, MANY

WE ARE A YOUNG species, only about 200,000 years old. All of us come from one source and share one destiny, yet from our commonality emanates a bewildering array of cultures, civilizations, religions, and beliefs. Profound diversity has emerged from our unity. American coins say, *E Pluribus Unum* (Out of Many, One), but the history of humanity says, *Out of One, Many.* We have slowly and painfully learned that we are vastly more alike than different, and that the differences we see in others are far less than we had initially thought. It has been a triumph of humanity that our sense of difference, or otherness, is slowly diminishing. This sense of diminishing difference is the continuing great experiment of our species.

In this survey of today's major religions, I invite you to explore with me a portion of our diversity, in the hope that understanding diversity may help us find our way back to a greater measure of unity. Understanding other religions, and their similarities to our own, enhances our sense of belonging by enormously expanding the community to which we can belong. I hope this work connects us to the past on a scale that is deeper and broader than is possible by understanding just one religion. It is wonderful for a Jew or a Christian or a Muslim to feel connected to his past, and indeed he or she should, but I hope this work allows us all to connect *to each other and to our collective past,* and to come together in unity as we face our collective future. I hope the reader finds connections to the other people with whom we share our lives and our planet, and to the past from which we derive our heritage. Through these connections, the study of religion offers a link to the future through which all of us can continue our shared destiny.

No attempt is made in this book to discuss each religion comprehensively. In particular, many of the daily activities and ceremonies of these religions, and many of their esoteric philosophical concepts, are not discussed. The tensions between different cultures and different religions that we are experiencing in the aftermath of 9–11 do not stem from a lack of *detailed* knowledge. They stem from a lack of *basic* knowledge. This was tragically evident September 15, 2001, when Balbir Singh Sodhi, a Sikh, was shot and killed by a man so ignorant that he thought all Muslims were responsible for the 9–11 attacks and that anyone wearing a turban was Muslim. This work provides the basic knowledge that is necessary and sufficient to allow us to understand each other and to live in harmony.

Religions are the kindling of conflict, but also the doorway to understanding. I hope this study of the religions of the world diminishes our sense of difference, expands the reader's view of life, and augments his or her personal experience of life by the experience of the billions of colleagues, of different faiths, beliefs, and knowledge, with whom we share our planet.

UNDERSTANDING EACH OTHER AFTER 9-11

Chapter 1

ORIGINS OF RELIGION

A RELIGION IS A SET of beliefs in a higher reality, a greater truth, or an ultimate power that comforts us and helps us cope with our lives. Any religion, as actually practiced, is a complex set of religious, social, philosophical, and cultural beliefs. Religion is set apart from other areas of thought by its ubiquity in all of our activities and thinking, our perception of it as the source of final answers, and its ability to govern our behavior in an immediate and forceful way. Religion encompasses the best and the worst of thought, but at all times is the most complex system of beliefs in any culture.

Societies, like individuals, develop along substantially predictable pathways, and like individuals, they achieve foreseeable milestones in a predictable order. One such milestone is a belief in a force or forces greater than themselves. All societies independently develop one or more sets of complex religious beliefs even before they achieve civilization (which is generally characterized by the presence of cities, specialization of labor, a writing system, and well-developed agriculture). Indeed, traditional or "primitive" societies that have not attained the hallmarks of civilization still have well-developed religious beliefs. Religions are never static. Once they develop, they continue to transform, changing as other areas of the society change and as other cultures and belief systems are encountered. At all times, religion forms the foundation of the society.

It is therefore essential that anyone attempting to understand history understand religions.

To my mind there are two reasons for the development of religion. The first is that we humans are inherently curious and need to understand our world. For most of our history, we have lacked the ability to understand or control our environment and had no idea that our progress would culminate in any understanding of the world, so supernatural deities seemed the only way to explain mysterious events. The second reason is the search for inner peace. We need to believe our lives have meaning and purpose. In a world filled with mysterious and sometimes hostile forces, the presence of deities comforted people and gave them a sense of belonging.

Archeological evidence and early writings suggest that the earliest religions shared certain characteristics. These often included the worship of the sun, which all cultures recognized as the ultimate giver of life. Other natural occurrences, such as wind, water, earth, fire, the sky, and the sea were also widely worshipped. People recognized their dependence on these phenomena and conceived of them as living entities, the worship of which created the first deities and began religion.

Initially, many deities were conceived as animal-like. These are called *theriomorphic* deities. Theriomorphic deities were superseded by gods with human attributes, in behavior as well as in appearance. These are called *anthropomorphic* deities. Some gods had both animal and human features, such as a human head on an animal body, or vice versa — perhaps a sort of transition form (one thinks, for example, of the jackal-headed Egyptian god Anubis).

The advantage of anthropomorphic gods is that they are more comprehensible, and therefore more accessible. There are two theories why people began to envision gods in anthropomorphic terms. First, as people gained some control over their environment, they became secure and confident enough to conceptualize the processes of the world as being under the control of beings resembling themselves. The second reason pertains to the increasing stratification of society that accompanies civilization. It has always been the curse of civilization that it is accompanied by greater stratification of society. It is thought that cultures, before attaining civilization, generally contained a limited hierarchy, with a small number of priests or chiefs having hegemony over an otherwise substantially equal populace. With the advent of cities and civilization, stratification became more pronounced and more complex. Difficult public works projects, such as irrigation, required leaders whose power exceeded that of other people. Now people could see *other people* with vast amounts of power and influence. Still unaware of their own ability to uncover the mysteries of nature and improve their lot, people began to envision deities in human form. The great adventure had begun.

Venus of Willendorf

The Venus of Willendorf was found in 1908 near the town of Willendorf in Austria. It is a small (just over 11 cm, or about 4.5 inches) figure dated to about 24,000 BCE. The Venus was not created with facial features, and it is not clear if she is wearing a hat or has braided hair wrapped around her head. Since the discovery of the Venus, other statues of similar design, with enlarged abdomens and enlarged breasts, have been found, many of which are older than the Venus. The purpose of these Venus figurines — if they had a purpose — is not clear. Because of the enlarged breasts and abdomen, there is speculation that they might represent fertility, but this is not established. Is she pregnant, or simply obese? Why is her face not depicted? Is this even a votive or religious work? Whatever its purpose was, the Venus is the most famous work of the Stone Age and has found its way into pop art and jewelry, as is shown here.

Chapter 2

RELIGIOUS BELIEFS OF INDIGENOUS PEOPLES

The term "indigenous" refers to societies that lack the hallmarks of civilization alluded to in our consideration of the origins of religion. The term "primitive" is occasionally used for these societies, but is avoided here because of its unwarranted connotations about the collective wisdom of the culture and the intellectual level of its members.

Developed nations tend to accept absolute realities and to apply black-and-white thinking in many areas, while indigenous societies are more likely to see shades of gray. The shades of gray that permeate the beliefs of indigenous people may seem strange to Westerners, but the study of history and of other cultures allows us to learn new ways of thinking that augment and complement our strengths. To the Westerner, the beliefs of indigenous people may seem almost childish, but this impression is a mistake. Indigenous beliefs are fully mature, but in a way not generally appreciated in developed cultures.

While each society has its own unique set of religious beliefs, there are similarities in the beliefs of all indigenous peoples. Their religions have little or no scripture. In its place, these religions rely on oral tradition and *activity,* and in general are *more participatory* and *less analytical* than those of developed societies. Whereas the West seeks laws of nature and unchanging aspects of reality, indigenous societies are more likely to strive to live in harmony with nature, and their religions seek to *interact* with the world. Indigenous people see themselves as one with the world and attempt no detached explanation of it. Indigenous religions almost universally lack a belief in humanity's right to dominate the world.

Indigenous people generally believe in a world beyond the visible one. Spirits, many of whom are evil, inhabit that world. Though there are variations among cultures, most indigenous religions allow for interaction with these spirits in one or both of two ways. The first is through spirit possession, in which spirits commandeer a body, often necessitating an exorcism. The second mode of interaction is through shamans. Sometimes called "medicine men," shamans are actually intermediaries to the Spirit World. Shamanism is a more active interaction wherein a shaman engages in rituals to enter the Spirit World. Then he can either control evil spirits or elicit the assistance of benevolent ones. In addition to rituals, masks are important in interacting with the Spirit World, and hallucinogens may also be used. Interestingly, those who are helplessly possessed by spirits tend to be women, whereas those who have some control over spirits, such as shamans, tend to be men.

African Mask

African masks are now valued works of art, but their origin lies in religious expression. A person known as a Shaman wore a mask during celebrations or times when special requests were made. The masks represent a spirit that possesses the Shaman and allows him to communicate with deities or ancestors. The Shaman enters a trance-like state during which his utterances — often "translated" by others during the ceremony — represent messages from ancestors or gods.

As examples of the religious beliefs of indigenous peoples, we will examine the beliefs of the Yoruba people in Nigeria and make some general observations about Native American religions. Many Africans, including the Yoruba, believe that the world is made from force (*Àshe* in the Yoruba language), not from matter. Moreover, force moves the world and shapes events. The supreme god, Olorun, conveys force to all living creatures, after which it can also be conveyed from one creature to another. Force can also be present in works of art. Because force is more fluid and variable than matter, this view of the world regards change as a natural part of life and accepts it much more readily than the Western view does. One of the sharpest dichotomies between Western and non-Western societies is their view of change, and one of the greatest lessons we can learn from other societies is that change is normal and is not to be feared.

Olorun is considered so remote that he is worshipped only indirectly through Orishas, which are aspects of the supreme spirit that manifest as the guardian spirits that every person has (one can also think of the Orishas as lesser gods and Olorun as their father).

In contrast to the Western mind-body dichotomy, the Yoruba believe that a person consists of four, not two, elements. These are the *Ara,* which is the body, the *Emi,* which is the life principle (understood as breath), the *Ori,* which is the inner head (personality) and *Ese,* which are the legs (movement). There is communication among the Oris so that our destinies are linked. In one account, the Ori is constructed by an Orisha named Ajala and determines the destiny of the person. Each individual can choose a head and a destiny prior to birth. Olorun usually respects these choices. The problem is that Ajala often makes heads that are flawed, which accounts for problematic people. In another account, the guardian spirit of a person goes to Olorun and requests a particular destiny. That guardian spirit then lives inside the person's head. By either account, African thought is distinguished by a choice of destiny; however, this destiny can be thwarted by not observing proper behavior or making the appropriate sacrifices. Certain medicines or results of witchcraft may also change a destiny. Likewise, proper behavior may improve a destiny.

One of the attributes predetermined by the Ori is the time of death. If people die prematurely, they become ghosts until the time they were supposed to die, at which time they can have a normal afterlife. The belief that most events are predetermined makes divination an integral part of Yoruba thinking. The *Ifa* divination system scatters palm nuts on a board, after which their arrangement, as interpreted by an Ifa priest, determines which portion of a long oral text to consult for the particular problem (we shall see a similar method of divination in the *I Ching* when we examine Chinese religions).

In Yoruba culture, the word "person" has a secondary meaning as an individual who is worthy of respect because he or she actively participates in and contributes to the culture. In this sense, one is not born a person, but rather attains this designation through experience and proper conduct. Being a person means fulfilling one's role in society. The Yoruba believe that the qualities that make a person cannot be written, nor can one obtain this designation in isolation, because morality means participating in functions that are sanctioned by and of benefit to society, such as family life, working, honoring ancestors, seeking the good of the tribe, etc.

The Yoruba believe in reincarnation, and have a unique view of it. Ancestor spirits exist in the ancestral world, but simultaneously wish to be with their family, so they return as new members of the family. Deceased ancestors are regarded as integral parts of the family, as indicated by their reincarnation. Occasionally, people have names that mean "father returns" or "mother returns." I find this a lovely way to look at death and birth.

Many of us do not realize how frequently elements from different religions are blended as cultures encounter each other. We see this in Chinese religious thought, for example, as Buddhism, Confucianism, and Daoism traded ideas. Hinduism incorporated concepts from Buddhism. Christianity and Islam built on Judaism, and Judaism may have incorporated elements of Zoroastrianism. In Africa, there has been some blending of indigenous religion with Christianity and Islam, and some traditional African deities are equated with Catholic saints.

All moral codes view the individual as having obligations to other individuals and to the community. A characteristic of American Indian thinking is that the community to which the individual has obligations is enlarged to include nature. In keeping with this embracing of a larger community, we find less black-and-white thinking than in industrialized societies. This means that time is thought to be cyclical, that reason is not the only way to understand, and that there is no dichotomy between the material and the spiritual. Native Americans believe in a Great Spirit that permeates and gives life to everything, including objects that Westerners would regard as inanimate. This Great Spirit is not thought of as anthropomorphic. Because it gives life to all things, all things are manifestations of the Great Spirit, and are not as different as the West would believe. Even gods are manifestations of the Great Spirit. All creatures have consciousness, though the nature and manifestation of consciousness may vary from creature to creature. The Native American John Lame Deer expressed this view with his statement that "All creatures have stories to tell."

Native Americans view themselves as caretakers of the natural world, as opposed to the Western concept of being its masters. Native Americans believe that animals agree to be hunted, and this is why they must be well treated and must be given thanks after a successful hunt. The bones of the animal must be returned to its native habitat. Native Americans believe in reincarnation for people and animals, and believe that the bones provide the basis for this transition.

Native Americans view land as a living entity to be shared and enjoyed by all. It is anathema to them to enclose land or for any individual to claim ownership of part of it. Such claims prevent the energy of the land from flowing freely among all living creatures. Private ownership of land is to them what walling off a space and claiming ownership of the air inside it would be to us. Circles are important to Native Americans. They believe that each person is the center of a circle that intersects with other circles. The natural world consists of circles within circles.

To Native Americans, the merging of the material and the spiritual implies that all things are sacred. Native Americans think of dreaming and waking as continuous, and believe that wisdom can come equally from either. Rituals reinforce this continuity. Because reason is not the only means of understanding, shamans use non-rational means. A shaman often has a special relationship with a particular animal, which he should therefore not hunt.

It is a hallmark of Western thinking that people have the individual freedom to determine their actions. Indigenous societies have also struggled with this question, and while accepting some degree of free will, generally believe that our lives are largely predetermined. Native

Americans believe in an integral association with nature that predetermines much of who we are, but individuals are still held responsible for their actions.

Now let us consider the religions of "developed" societies, keeping in mind not only their similarities to each other, but also their similarities to the beliefs of "undeveloped" societies, with whom we share far more than we realize.

Chapter 3

HINDUISM

THE WORD "HINDU" IS a Western word that simply refers to the people Westerners found living near the Indus River. Some prefer the term "Brahmanism" to "Hinduism" since the latter term has many connotations and cultural overlays. Some have suggested abandoning the term "Hinduism" entirely. Though I am sympathetic to this argument, I use the term "Hinduism" because of its familiarity.

More than any other religion, except possibly Judaism, Hinduism is culture-based. Though there are 15 million Hindus in Pakistan and Bangladesh, and about 18 million in Nepal (the world's only officially Hindu state since India is officially secular), the history and practice of Hinduism is inextricably bound to India, and the vast majority of the world's 700 million Hindus live in that country or have direct roots to it. For this reason, the statement "I am a Hindu" tells us much more about a person than the statement "I am a Christian."

The story of Hinduism begins with the Indus Valley civilization, now more often called Harappan, which was in bloom by 2,500 BCE.*

---

* Throughout this work, the term "BCE," referring to Before the Common Era, will be used in place of the term "BC." The term "CE," referring to the Common Era, or Before the Christian Era, will be used in place of the term "AD." This is a

The native Harappan civilization, brought to light by the excavations of Mortimer Wheeler after WWII, left us physical structures, but attempts to read their language have brought only frustration. About 1,700 BCE, people speaking a language from the Indo-European family migrated into the Indus Valley and mixed with the native people. These newcomers were once called Aryan invaders, but historians no longer use the term "Aryan" because of its association with Nazi Germany. Likewise, these people are no longer called invaders because there is no evidence of a military conquest. For the Indo-European settlers, the frustration is reversed: hymns in their Vedic language have survived, but they did not leave anything tangible.

The precise interaction between the native people and the Indo-European migrants is not clear. The Harappan civilization was in decline before the Indo-Europeans arrived, and the contribution of the latter to the final demise of the native culture is unclear. Likewise, it is debatable how much of a contribution the native Harappan civilization made to Hinduism, and the matter is almost irresolvable because we cannot read their language. However, Hinduism seems to have arisen from a merging of the two cultures, and depending on how one interprets certain archeological finds, some rudimentary aspects of the religion may have been components of Harappan civilization. The contribution of the Indo-Europeans to Hinduism is more direct and obvious. Indeed, after a long period of oral transmission, the Hindu holy books were finally written in Sanskrit, which is derived from the Indo-European Vedic language.

The earliest form of Hinduism is based on the Vedas (*veda* means "wisdom" in Sanskrit), which are thought to be primarily the work of the Indo-European settlers. For this reason, this early form of Hinduism is sometimes called "Vedic religion" to distinguish it from mature Hinduism, which developed centuries later.

---

newer terminology that is intended to be less Christian-centered. However, the birth of Jesus remains the distinction between BCE and CE. A date of 100 BCE is the same as 100 BC, and the date of 100 CE is the same as AD 100. The new terminology also remains Christian-centered because it assumes that Christianity is "common" throughout the world. The newer terminology may be slightly less Christian-centered in that it makes no reference to Jesus, but it is fundamentally reflective of the fact that currently, economic power in the world is primarily found in Christian nations.

There are four Vedas, the foremost of them the *Rig Veda,* which is primarily a collection of hymns to gods. The *Sama Veda* consists of chants, the *Yajur Veda* is a collection of formulas used in sacrifices and rituals, and the *Atharva Veda* contains popular incantations and lore. The last three Vedas are largely supplements to the Rig Veda. The four Vedas were recited by priests and were transmitted orally by them. Each Veda apparently had its own class of priests.

The main text of each of the four Vedas is accompanied by commentary and wisdom literature. Specifically, each Veda has four sections: *Samhitas* (hymns; the main text; also called the mantra section, dating to about 1400–900 BCE); *Brahmanas* (ritual texts and priestly manuals, dating to 800–600 BCE); *Aranyakas* (forest treatises, dealing with reflections on the meaning of rituals, dating to c. 600 BCE); and *Upanishads* (philosophical and wisdom literature, 800–200 BCE). The Samhitas and Brahmanas are collectively known as the *karmakanda* (ritual section) and describe a cosmology based on a transcendent Supreme Being and a system of worship through ceremony and chanting. The Aranyakas and Upanishads are collectively called the *jnanakanda* (knowledge section) and discuss the journey of the soul in philosophical terms. Whereas each collection of Samhitas is associated with one or a small number of Brahmanas and Aranyakas, it is associated with numerous Upanishads. For example, the Rig Veda consists of the Rig Samhita, a small number of Brahmanas and Aranyakas that are uniquely associated with the Rig Samhita, and a larger number of Upanishads that are also uniquely associated with the Rig Samhita. Likewise for the Sama Veda, Yajur Veda, and Atharva Veda.

The canonical terminology can be confusing. Often, when one speaks of the Rig Veda, he or she actually means the Rig Samhita, the first portion of the Rig Veda. In addition to speaking of four Vedas, one can also speak of "the Veda," the combination of all parts of all Vedas. Upon hearing the term "Veda," we must rely on the context to indicate whether the speaker is referring to one or all of the Vedas, or whether he or she is referring to just the Samhita portion or the entire Veda.

The Samhita portion of the Rig Veda is the oldest active collection of religious writing. It is believed that the godsof the Indo-European settlers revealed the Rig Samhita to special people called Rishis in the very distant past. The Rishis did not write the Samhitas; they only transmitted the word of the gods (we shall see the concept of revelation, as opposed to writing, again in the Torah and the Koran).

Until the Upanishads — those marvelous philosophical works that we will consider in a moment — the Samhitas were the backbone of the Vedas. The Samhitas are not a narrative story comparable to what we might find in the Old Testament, but are concerned primarily with rituals and were probably intended to be recited during sacrifices. Indeed, the accounts of creation that do exist in the Samhitas are often contradictory. Likewise, there is no consensus in the Samhitas about what happens after death. Some passages envision a happy afterlife, while others indicate that there is no afterlife. Vedic religion held that the breath was the manifestation of the soul, which was called *Atman,* but it was not until the Upanishads that the concept of Atman would be fully developed. There are occasional passages in the Rig Samhita that call for a degree of introspection. One passage, for example, says "truth is one, but the wise call it by various names." However, the focus of the Rig Samhita was rituals, not introspection. Importantly, the Rig Samhita makes no mention of reincarnation. This would not become a major tenet until fully developed Hinduism.

The roughly thirty-three gods mentioned in the Rig Samhita are not the gods of fully developed Hinduism. Indra was primary among these gods. Others include Agni, Varuna (the custodian of Rita), Rubra, and Soma, who produces ecstatic experiences through an unknown plant that is thought to be his embodiment. The Samhitas speak of creation as divided into three levels: earth, mid-space, and the home of the gods and the ancestors, which is called *Svarga.* They speak of an ultimate reality called *Brahman,* which was distinct from the many separate gods that are mentioned. The Samhitas also speak of an organizing force called *Rita,* which keeps the universe in harmony and brings about order. Even the gods are subject to Rita. In contrast to the God of Judaism, Christianity, and Islam, Hindu gods are not omniscient or omnipotent, nor are they lawgivers. They did not create the world, but rather were created after it and are subject to its laws. The wisdom of the Samhitas is thought to predate even the creation of the world and to supersede even the power of the gods.

The Rig Samhita refers to a light-skinned people conquering a dark-skinned people. The society of the newcomers was already stratified at the time of their arrival into the Indian subcontinent. In Vedic times, the highest class, consisting of priests and teachers, were the *Brahmins* (this class may also be spelled *Brahman,* in which case it is not to be confused with Brahman, the supreme reality and the composite of all the gods in mature Hinduism). The *kshatriyas* (or *ksatriyas*) were warriors and administrators, followed by the merchants and artisans. Initially, the lowest classes were the farmers called *vaishyas,* but the later Vedic writings mentioned a class called *sudras,* people of the land, who may have been the indigenous people. It was thought that these classes, which eventually became known as castes, came from the sacrifice and dismemberment of the primordial human called the *Purusha,* whose various parts became the different castes.

The father performed many rituals in the early Hindu home. Even today, the home is the center of Hindu worship, and almost all Hindu homes have some sort of shrine. An individual called an *Atharvan* performed shamanic rituals for the purpose of healing or to influence life passages. The text for these rituals is found in the Atharva Veda. *Srauta* rites were much more complex and only occasionally performed. Performers of Srauta rites had to be Brahmins with special training. Their principal job was to chant Vedic hymns perfectly.

All religions have their philosophical and metaphysical component, and for Hinduism, this is found in the Upanishads. They were composed during what Karl Jaspers referred to as the "Axial Age," the period from 800 to 200 BCE, when many cultures began to ponder the individual, and many religions, including Judaism, Jainism, Hinduism, Buddhism, Confucianism, and Daoism, either formed or moved toward their contemporary expression. It was during this time that questions of introspection, the afterlife, and the relationship of the people to all that was around them would come to the fore. In Hinduism, these questions were posed in the Upanishads, most of which were probably composed in the seventh and sixth centuries BCE. The Upanishads are part of the Vedas, and conclude them, but here again, a cautionary note on nomenclature is in order. Scholars agree that the Upanishads are the concluding portion of the Vedas. Indeed, the Upanishads are sometimes called the *Vedanta,* meaning "end of the Vedas" (though "Vedanta" may also refer to a religious practice based primarily on the Upanishads). However, some practitioners distinguish between the earlier portions of the Vedas and the later Upanishads because of the very different content and tone of the latter.

There is no agreement on the precise number of Upanishads, but usually it is said there are 108 of them. Each Upanishad is associated with one of the four Vedas. The Upanishads are primarily in the form of a dialogue between teachers and students, and in fact, the word refers to a sitting down beside (a teacher). They were to be chanted, and were transmitted orally for centuries prior to being written down.

The Upanishads completed the Vedas, reinvented Hinduism, and transformed it into the form we know today. The Upanishads demonstrate more concern for the individual self than the older literature did, and also express more concern about death. They are more philosophical and metaphysical than the existing writings had been. Even more important, however, is that before this time Hinduism, like other religions of the period, was primarily concerned with the maintenance of the cosmic status quo, with little regard for the individual. But the Upanishads redirected Hinduism toward *individual* harmony, transformation, and actualization. While the Samhitas stress ritual, the Upanishads emphasize meditation.

The Upanishads also consider Brahman — the ultimate reality — in much greater detail than did the Samhitas, and transformed it into a power of powers that the human mind cannot comprehend. The Upanishads say that Brahman is beyond the senses and is without qualities. This is what the Upanishads say about Brahman:

> *Without moving, it is swifter than the mind. Standing still, it overtakes those who run.*
> *It is within all and it is outside of all. It is the thread that strings together all creatures.*
> *That truly whence kings are born, that by which they lived once born, and that into which on deceasing they enter.*
> *It is far different from what is known and it is farther than the unknown.*

The Upanishads also transformed the concept of *Atman*. Though the essence of the self — what we might call the soul, and which Hinduism calls the Atman — was equated to the breath in the Samhitas, by the time of the Upanishads this was seen as overly simplistic. Moreover, the breath clearly does not survive the body, but the Atman must. The Upanishads concluded that the nature of the Atman, like that of Brahman, was beyond description or understanding. The Atman is not a soul in the Western sense, but a *collective soul* or self that is an all-pervasive, everlasting, unchanging, invisible reality that is found in all of us and that is identical in all of us. Because all of us come from and return to the same substance, we are all deeply connected even if we do not know each other. We are all of and from the same substance. While the Upanishads do not all agree on the nature or physical manifestation of Atman, they do agree that Atman is never born and never dies and does not have a specific bodily or physical correlate. It does not reside in either the breath or in the mind. The Atman makes possible the *Jiva,* which is the individual soul or self. Our individual selves occasionally emerge from the Atman in the same way that individual drops of water may occasionally be discerned in a giant flowing river. If Westerners believe in a soul, they see it is a separate and distinct entity, preserving individuality, and that its immortality is not guaranteed. But the Atman has always been and always will be, no matter what form an individual transmigration takes.

Then, in a revolutionary opinion that is unique to Hinduism, the priests who wrote the Upanishads made the leap that the external world, Atman, the Vedic gods, and Brahman are all manifestations of a single reality. This is *Upanishadic Monism,* which fully develops a long-standing idea in the Rig Samhita and holds that Brahman and all of creation are inseparable and are different manifestations of the same entity. Unlike the Old Testament religions of the West, Upanishadic Monism holds that the Creator and the created cannot be separated, that the creator is found in all things and in all creatures, and that what appear to be discrete entities are actually parts of a giant whole. All things are part of the total reality. Moreover, what appear to be opposites or dualities are illusions. It is ignorance about this monism that leads to the perception of unique selves. This in turn leads to hostility, dogmatism, feelings of superiority, and conflict.

Upanishadic Monism requires a different concept of individualism. Individualism is very real, but that which makes us individuals is dispersed throughout the cosmos, intertwined with ultimate reality and merged with the individualism of others. This unity of Atman and Brahman, and its implications, form the foundation for the path of wisdom. One must give up traditional individualism. Anything that encourages individuality or connotes a sense of specialness must be eschewed. One Upanishad cautions against the use of the words "I" and "my." Another Upanishad teaches that when all desires that cling to the heart are surrendered, a mortal becomes immortal.

Mature Hinduism, as elaborated in the Upanishads, views the universe as a living entity, every part of which — every tree, rock, and person — is the universe in microcosm. Mathematically inclined readers will recognize this as essentially a fractal view of the universe, wherein the whole is composed of repeating units, each of these units is itself composed of smaller repeating units of the same structure, and each of those smaller units is composed of still smaller units of the same structure, in a continuing process. In fully developed Hinduism, the Creator brought the universe forth from its own essence, and all that has been created is depicted as a living, changing entity that *cannot be differentiated from the Creator*. Even the Creator will change.

In current times, with most contemporary religions having some concept of an afterlife, we assume that the belief in life after death has always been an integral part of religious thought, but this is not true. With occasional exceptions, such as the eternal life of the Egyptian Pharaoh in the Old Kingdom, most religions of early antiquity either had no conception of an afterlife, or thought of it as a shadowy, rather unpleasant place. Some possibility of an afterlife was extended to commoners in later Egyptian history, but the concept of an afterlife as a pleasant and attainable experience for everyone came into several religions more or less simultaneously during the Axial Age.

The Upanishads made a belief in an afterlife integral to Hinduism, and did so in a unique way. All religions that originated in India believe in some sort of transmigration of the soul (called *Samsara;* usually called reincarnation or rebirth in the West), whereby the soul takes a new body. The origin of the Hindu concept of transmigration is not clear. Such a belief is not in the Samhitas, making an Indo-European origin unlikely. It may have originated from the indigenous Harappan people, or it may have been imported. Whatever the origin of the basic conception, the Upanishads transformed the doctrine of transmigration of the soul and fused it with *karma,* which is the accumulated consequences — good and evil — of actions in previous lives. A unique contribution of the Upanishads is that the rebirth is determined by karma.

As expressed in the Upanishads, the soul can experience six possible fates after the cremation of the body. The first of these is to be unified with Brahman. This is the happiest possibility, called *Moksha.* The other five fates involve rebirths: as a lesser god, as a human, as a ghost, as an animal, or as a spirit in Hell. Hell is a real concept in Indian religions, but it is realized through Samsara. In fact, though a person may be reborn as a god, the gods themselves are subject to the reincarnation cycles, and they themselves will eventually come back as people or even as lower animals.

Westerners often think of reincarnation as something good, an opportunity for immortality, but to Hindus, reincarnation is a burden because it constantly postpones the ultimate goal — union with Brahman. Samsara forces an individual to continually live life, with all of its frustration and suffering, rather than to achieve bliss through union with Brahman. Samsara postpones Moksha for so long (the time scale involved is millions of years) that it is rendered remote and effectively unachievable. *Samsara is not thought of as continual births, but as continual suffering and deaths,* and it is considered tragic. Even being reborn as a god is only a temporary solution, as additional rebirths will follow. It would be much better to bring the cycle to an end by becoming one with Brahman. Moksha, another contribution of the Upanishads, is not being reborn as a god. *Rather, it is not being reborn at all.*

Hinduism is a particularly difficult religion for Westerners to grasp because of the inherent cultural differences between East and West, in particular the cyclical thinking and lack of simple cause and effect that characterizes the East. Westerners believe that history is linear, progressive, and directional — that it is going somewhere — and this is readily seen in the Western religions of Judaism, Christianity, and Islam, which have a linear vision of time wherein our life is lived only once, and then our unique soul lives forever in an unchanging eternity. But Eastern religious thought holds that history is cyclical, without a specific direction, and that the journey of both humanity and the universe is a circle without beginning or end. Westerners are puzzled by this cyclical view of time, but a cyclical view is quite reasonable because our lives consist of cycles. The sun rises and sets every day. Children grow up and have their own children, who in turn grow up, etc. The real puzzle is not why

Eastern religions are cyclical, but why Western religions are not.

Three characteristics of the quest for knowledge emerged from the Upanishads. First, the quest must be for the unity of all knowledge. Second, the quest is not purely intellectual. Third, this knowledge will permit the conquest of death. In contemporary terms, the Upanishads admonish us that knowledge is a reflection of all aspects of being human, we are composed of more than just rationality, and all knowledge is an affirmation of life.

There is a tendency in the West to believe that because the Upanishads became an integral part of the Veda*s*, the philosophy they espouse must be an integral part of Hinduism for every practitioner of that religion, but this is not true. Though the Upanishads revolutionized Hinduism, not every Hindu followed the new course. After the Upanishads brought Hinduism to maturity, it became possible to identify a group of Hindus with heterodox beliefs. As we shall see, some of these differing opinions would become the new religions of Buddhism and Jainism, but what concerns us now is that most Hindus preferred a less abstract, less philosophically demanding form of Hinduism. They wanted a form that was more concrete, less contemplative, and had more definable deities, perhaps with images that would help in their worship. In the Upanishads, Brahman is too mingled with the whole of reality to be a distinct object of worship. Many Hindus wanted a deity that was distinct enough from the rest of creation to be approachable in times of trouble or anxiety.

To accommodate these people, and to make Brahman more knowable and approachable, the many gods and goddesses that had always been part of Hinduism were conceived of as manifestations of Brahman. Devotion to any of these manifestations constitutes devotion to Brahman and thereby brings the practitioner into essential conformity with the Upanishadic view. These manifestations of Brahman became more familiar and comfortable to people than the Upanishadic view of Brahman as an unapproachable, incomprehensible entity that cannot be separated from common reality. This is why Hindus today tend to worship one of the manifestations of Brahman rather than Brahman himself.

Though early Vedic religion refers to a supreme entity called Brahman, it makes no connection between Brahman and the thirty-three gods mentioned in the Rig Samhita. Early Vedic religion was polytheistic, but mature Hinduism is monotheistic — Brahman is the one god, with many manifestations. Most Westerners believe that Hindus recognize many gods, but what we perceive as different gods are perceived in mature Hinduism as different manifestations of one deity. The apparent discrepancy is a reflection of the Indian, and indeed the Eastern, belief in multiple manifestations of reality where Westerners see singleness. It is integral to Hinduism that opposites, dualities, and discrete entities are an illusion of our perception. It is not a question of the number of gods, but a question of the number of manifestations of one God that humans are capable of understanding. Brahman (spelled with an "n" at the end) is the ultimate unknowable reality. Though Brahman is typically thought of in the West as having three manifestations — *Brahma* (without the "n"), *Vishnu,* and *Shiva* — *all* of the many individual deities in Hinduism are manifestations of Brahman. All of the different manifestations of the Supreme Being, and all of the subtleties of Hinduism, can be thought of as lenses through which one sees a slightly different picture of the same reality.

Shiva (or Siva) is commonly thought to be the destroyer of the universe, but actually he destroys so that there can be further creation. Hinduism is a religion of continuous destruction and re-creation, and by destroying, Shiva makes it possible for Brahma, the creative aspect of Brahman, to create a new universe. In the Hindu concept of time, a day in the life of Brahma is called a *kalpa,* which lasts 4.32 billion years and is followed by a night of equal length. A year is 360 of these day-night combinations. A *maha kalpa* is one hundred of these years, and is the lifetime of Brahma. At the end of a maha kalpa, Shiva will dissolve the universe and a new Brahma will form. Though a maha kalpa is an unimaginable length of time, it is noteworthy that even Brahma will not live forever. Christians cannot conceive of any limit to the lifetime of their God.

Of the several prominent images of Shiva, one of the most familiar is the *Nataraja,* depicting the four-armed Shiva's cosmic dance in which he disperses the ignorance of the night. In his upper right hand, he holds a drum with which he sounds the world into existence. In his upper left hand, he holds a flame, with which he will destroy the present universe for the next creation. His other right hand is upright, indicating that the viewer need have no fear, while the other left hand points down to his upraised foot, telling the viewer that he will find refuge. His planted foot crushes the demon of ignorance. The surrounding ring of fire represents Samsara.

Shiva

Hinduism blurs the line between creation and destruction. Though Shiva is said to be the aspect of Brahman that destroys, he actually destroys so that there can be creation. This is a *Nataraja* (dancing) image, in which Shiva's cosmic dance disperses the ignorance of the night. In his upper left hand, he holds a flame, with which he will destroy the present universe for the next creation. His lower left arm points down to his upraised foot, indicating a place of safety. In his upper right hand, he holds a drum with which he sounds the world into existence. His lower right hand is upright, reassuring the devotee, while his planted foot crushes the demon of ignorance. The surrounding ring of fire represents Samsara.

Vishnu is the *sustainer* of the universe between successive cycles of creation and destruction. Vishnu does appear in the Samhitas and is said to be the younger brother of Indra. Hindus believe that nine bodily incarnations, or avatars, of Vishnu have so far appeared. Two of these are Rama, the main character in the epic poem the *Ramayana,* and Krishna, the principal figure in the *Bhagavad Gita,* which we will examine in a moment. Interestingly, the ninth avatar of Vishnu was Buddha, testimony to the respect Hindus have for Buddhism. The tenth avatar will appear when the universe comes to the end of its present cycle.

In iconography, Vishnu may be depicted as any of his ten avatars, but when shown as himself, he usually has blue skin and appears with a mace in one hand (symbolizing divine knowledge and the power to destroy evil), a lotus in a second hand (symbolizing purity and fertility), a sharp, spinning disk in a third hand (symbolizing a purified mind), and a conch shell in the fourth (representing the primordial sound that gave rise to creation). In some depictions, a ball, symbolizing the earth, may replace the lotus. The *Gita Govinda* is the story of Vishnu's loves and is deeply erotic. These stories, and the works of art that depict Vishnu or his lovers, are understood as parables of love and devotion to Vishnu.

Vishnu

Vishnu, the preserver of the universe, is usually depicted with blue skin as an indication that he is divine, despite his portrayal in human form. In one hand, he holds a mace (symbolizing knowledge). In his other hands, he holds a water lotus (a symbol of purity and fertility), a disk (a symbol of power), and a conch shell (representing the primordial vibration that gave rise to creation).

Other gods are the boy god *Karikeyya,* the monkey god *Hanuman,* and the elephant-headed *Ganesh,* remover of obstacles. Westerners perceive Hindu deities as masculine, particularly since Hindu art usually depicts a deity as a single male. But Hindus generally perceive deities as an integrated combination of masculine and feminine aspects. Just as there are multiple male aspects of the Supreme Being, some of which we have considered, so there are multiple female aspects. These are collectively called the *Mother Goddess, Devi,* or *Maha Devi.* All female deities are considered to be different forms of Devi, who manifests either as separate goddesses or as consorts to male aspects of Brahman. The consort to Brahma is *Sarasvati;* the consort of Shiva is *Parvati;* that of Vishnu is *Lakshmi* (or *Laxsmi*). Some of Vishnu's avatars have consorts, such as *Sita* (married to Rama) and *Radha* (consort of Krishna). Unlike the male gods, goddesses rarely appear on their own. The prominence of female deities in Hinduism is unique among the world's major contemporary religions. Female deities are present as far back as the Samhitas, and may have been a component of indigenous Harappan civilization. *Shakti* is the life-giving principle that is associated with the goddess. Devotees of the Goddess are called "Shakta," and worship of the Goddess is called "Shaktism."

The male principle of the deity is considered to be passive. Goddesses have power, and male gods cannot attain power without goddesses. All forms of the Goddess, in turn, require the gods to restrain their raw energy and give it useful form. The independent goddesses do not have sufficient male restraint and are angry and evil, while the married goddesses are loving. Also, gods are seen as celestial and goddesses as terrestrial.

Vaishnavas worship Vishnu, *Shaivas* worship Shiva, and *Shaktas* worship primarily the Goddess Devi. Most Hindus are primarily devoted to Vishnu or Shiva (the preferred God is often designated by markings on the worshipper's forehead). The result of these diverse approaches is that like any religion, Hinduism is a family of related beliefs, not a single set of beliefs. Indeed, most Indians do not call themselves Hindus or claim to practice a religion of that name. They simply see themselves as primarily devoted to one manifestation of God and adhering to a set of accompanying beliefs and traditions. Most people called Hindus by Westerners call themselves Vaishnavas or Shaivas, but are fully aware of and respect other legitimate manifestations of Brahman. This is why Hinduism may initially appear to a Westerner as a polytheistic religion, but it is monotheistic, with a conception of God as having multiple manifestations and being inextricably merged with his creation into a single entity from which we all emerge and to which we all return.

Lakshmi

Lakshmi is the consort of Vishnu. She is depicted in red clothing (symbolizing her vitality and activity) with gold embroidery (indicating prosperity). Her four arms demonstrate that her presence extends in all directions. Her four hands represent the four goals of life — dharma, kama, artha, and eventually, Moksha. The coins falling from one hand assure her devotees that she will provide for them. Her open right front hand bestows blessings. The lotus flowers in her back hands symbolize spiritual purity.

An immediately clear way to see how much more comfortable most people were with this modification of the Upanishadic view is that the Upanishads championed Brahman as the divine manifestation of ultimate reality to whom people should pray, but by the early medieval period, worship of a single manifestation of Brahman became common, and today, so few Hindus worship the Upanishadic conception of Brahman that there is not a single temple to Brahman himself in all of India.

At the same time, however, Hindus wanted to be sure that their conception of these manifestations of Brahman were not completely human. Thus the images of Vishnu have blue skin, those of Shiva have four arms, those of Ganesh have the head of an elephant, etc. The god is welcome to inhabit the image if he or she desires, but the image is not understood to be the actual god, only a potential temporary home for him or her. At the end of certain festivals, the image might be destroyed because the god no longer lives there.

The Vedas were the oral tradition of the priestly class and are therefore not necessarily reflective of the beliefs or daily practices of the common people. Indeed, the vast majority of Indians have never read any of the Vedas. For them, other writings are a much more important guide in daily life. The literature of Hinduism, like that of Judaism, is comprehensive and consists of a set of texts that is considered to be infallible because they are of divine origin, and an additional set that is revered, but not divinely inspired. The term *Sruti* refers to the tradition that is *revealed* by Brahman, and is therefore infallible. To some, this means the entirety of the Vedas, including the Upanishads, while to others, it refers only to the Samhita portion of the Rig Veda.

The second group of works is called the *Smriti*. The term "Smriti" refers to the tradition that is remembered, but not revealed. More specifically, it refers to a collection of ancient Sanskrit texts: the two *Itihasas,* the *Puranas,* the six *Vedangas* (not to be confused with the *Vedanta,* the end of the Vedas), and the four *UpaVedas.* Chief among the Smriti are the Itihasas (Sanskrit for "so it was"). These include works of epic history, and describe a hero whose exploits reveal the religious, philosophical, and cultural beliefs that are to be conveyed. The two most important Itihasas are the *Mahabharata* and the Ramayana. While the Smriti is not quite as authoritative as the Sruti, it is more familiar to most Hindus and a more practical guide to daily life.

The Mahabharata is the longest epic poem in the world (about 100,000 lines) and was written between the fifth century BCE and the third century CE. The Bhagavad Gita is part of the Mahabharata, and is a treasured and familiar work in its own right. The Ramayana is an allegory of the triumph of virtue over evil, and is attributed to a man named Valmiki. These two epics and the Puranas are the major parts of the Smriti.

The Puranas were written in the *Gupta* period (fourth century CE) and deal with the creation of the gods and their lives, rules of living, rituals, and hymns. They are works containing ethical and cosmological teachings relative to gods, man and the world. There are eighteen major Puranas, dealing primarily with five subjects: primary creation, secondary creation, genealogy, cycles of time, and history.

The Vedangas are post-Vedic works. Four Vedangas govern correct chanting of the Vedas. These are *Shiksha* (phonetics), *Çhandas* (meter), *Nirukta* (etymology), and *Vyakarana* (grammar). The two other Vedangas are *Jyotisha Vedanga* (astronomy-astrology) and *Kalpa Vedanga* (procedural canon). The *Kalpa Vedanga* includes a number of *Shastras* (a Shastra is any sacred or religious writing or a collection of writings on a given subject), such as the *Shrauta* and *Shulba Shastras* (ritual codes), *Dharma Shastras* (social law) and *Grihya Shastras* (domestic codes).

The Smriti also includes the *UpaVedas*, meaning "Secondary Vedas," which are texts on sacred sciences, composed by *rishis*. Rishi is a general term for an enlightened being, though seven particular rishis, called the *sapta-rishis,* are mentioned in the Rig Samhita and said to still guide mankind. The UpaVedas amplify and apply the Vedic knowledge. The four prominent UpaVeda*s* each consist of several texts and are concerned with a particular subject. These are: *Arthaveda* (statecraft), *Ayurveda* (health), *Dhanurveda* (military science), and *Gandharvaveda* (music and the arts). The *Sthapatyaveda* (treatises on architecture) and the *Kama Shastras* (texts on erotic love) are also sometimes classed as UpaVedas.

Also generally included in the Smriti are the founding *sutras* of six ancient philosophies. In Hinduism, a sutra is an aphorism that could be preserved orally and is often accompanied by commentary. Reciting sutra texts from memory is a daily ritual for many Hindus.

Darshana refers to seeing or feeling the presence of the Divine. Any sensory experience is a Darshana if it allows the person to connect with a divine presence. Even beholding a photograph can be a form of Darshana.

Among the hundreds of Hindu Darshanas are six classical philosophical systems, collectively called *Shad Darshana,* which are attempts to describe truth and the path to it. The six components of the Shad Darshana are *Nyaya, Vaisheshika, Sankhya, Mimamsa, Yoga,* and *Vedanta.* The first four of these systems deal with what Westerners regard as conventional branches of philosophy, such as logic, epistemology, and metaphysics. The fifth system is yoga, which uses both physical practice and philosophical study to attain self-realization by ceasing unnecessary thought. As we shall see, there are several types of yoga, but most Westerners mistakenly believe that yoga is only a physical discipline. Yoga was codified by Patanjali about 200 BCE in the *Yoga Sutras.* The sixth system of the Shad Darshana, Vedanta, is the study and practice of the Upanishads, and the remarkable monism that it espouses.

The Bhagavad Gita *(Song of God)* merits special attention because it is the most famous and influential work of the Hindu canon. The Bhagavad Gita was a late addition to the Mahabharata. Its precise date is unclear, but most estimates range from about 150 BCE to the first years of the Common Era. While the Bhagavad Gita did not fundamentally redirect Hinduism in the way that the *Upanishads* did, it did present the main tenets of the religion in a form that most people could understand, and has therefore become the primary source of Hindu ethics and virtually a handbook of the religion.

The Bhagavad Gita is written in verse and was intended to be sung. It narrates a battle between two families over the succession to a throne. The story takes place at a site that has been identified and is a common destination for pilgrims. The main character is Arjuna, a reluctant warrior who surveys the enemy army before the battle and sees his cousins, friends, and former teachers. He does not want to fight people he loves and respects, and he wonders if victory would have any meaning at the cost of such destruction.

To understand the Bhagavad Gita, we must first understand the concept of *dharma,* a term used in all religions of Indian origin. It cannot be precisely translated because of its metaphysical component and its foundation in Eastern philosophical thought. The one-word English translation of "duty" is often used. This is reasonably accurate, but is a Western simplification of a larger concept. More completely, dharma refers to justice, righteousness, and the natural order of the universe.

Dharma holds that there is a natural order, intrinsic to reality and not dependent on human action, which carries with it a set of responsibilities for each individual. These responsibilities depend on the person's station and situation in life. Dharma refers to the proper way to act vis-à-vis the harmonious principles of nature. The difficulty that Arjuna faces is not only a conflict between dharma and his feelings, but also a conflict between two kinds of dharma — the dharma that he faces as a warrior and the dharma that he faces because of his responsibilities to his family. The Bhagavad Gita illustrates that the quandaries of life are not between good and evil, but between two goods.

Arjuna's charioteer is Krishna, an avatar (incarnation) of the god Vishnu, whose advice to Arjuna constitutes the majority of the story. Krishna points out that Arjuna should perform his duties without regard to their consequences. One should be oblivious to traditional success or failure and to the immediate consequences of actions. The karma of an action is not determined by the action itself or its consequences, but rather by adherence to dharma. Krishna further says that the way of *Bhakti* — devotion — makes actions justifiable. If an action is undertaken from dharma and for the love of God, one need not fear either its immediate consequences or subsequent karma. In an interesting cultural parallel, Krishna's counsel to Arjuna foreshadows the debate that would be waged in the West many centuries later over whether an action should be judged on its consequences or its intent.

Krishna explains that Arjuna's enemies will not really die because their human existence is temporary anyway. Krishna states that the ultimate consequences of Arjuna's actions are actually unknowable in the long scheme of eternity, with the innumerable rebirths that his opponents will face, but the dharma requiring war is direct and immediate. This realization instills a sense of love and devotion in Arjuna. He understands that he is an inseparable part of the universe and not a distinct entity. This recognition removes the conflict between desire and duty, and provides a pathway to union with God.

Krishna then discusses detachment. He asks Arjuna to detach himself from all consequences, positive and negative, of the actions he must take. He asks Arjuna not to feel bad about what he must do, and likewise not to seek personal glorification from his duties. Krishna teaches the value of asceticism and study to bring about this detachment from the consequences of action. Though the Bhagavad Gita is not the origin of the caste system, Krishna does refer to different classes and enumerates the various requirements of dharma for each.

Arjuna then asks Krishna to show himself in his full glory, which Krishna does. He is likened to a thousand suns rising in the sky at the same time. Krishna gives Arjuna a third eye with which Arjuna sees not only the true form of Krishna, but also the universe as it really is. He sees his cousins being devoured by Krishna. Krishna then tells Arjuna again that he does not have to worry about his actions if he loves and is devoted to him and has good intentions. Krishna tells Arjuna to kill his opponents because "they are already killed by me." "Be just my instrument."

Krishna movingly describes the immutability of the soul and how its everlasting presence renders earthly actions inconsequential. To help Arjuna achieve wisdom, Krishna recommends yoga; in particular, *karma yoga,* a type of yoga that focuses the mind so that action can be taken. In describing yoga, Krishna uses the analogy of "a lamp unflickering in a windless place."

The Bhagavad Gita does not tell us that Arjuna's cause is the just one; this is irrelevant. Nor does it tell us who ultimately wins the war. This too is irrelevant. As we ponder the Bhagavad Gita, imagine the enormous contrast since Vedic times, when every rite and ritual had to be performed precisely. Now, Krishna teaches that rituals are less important than dharma and devotion. The Bhagavad Gita teaches that anyone, regardless of his or her status or education, can achieve attachment to God from the performance of the duties that are appropriate to that person's situation.

The Bhagavad Gita ponders the conflict of duty versus desire in our lives — a universal question that transcends all cultures and times. Though Krishna's advice is sound for the many situations in which our hands are truly tied, where is the line between the wonderful sense of acceptance that Krishna offers Arjuna and our responsibility for independent thought and action when adherence to duty hurts other people, particularly for those who do not believe in Samsara? Devotion to duty is the double-edged sword of humanity. It is the basis of an organized society, but it can also be society's greatest danger.

What then, are the larger lessons of the great poem beyond Hinduism and the duty/desire conflict? The battle is a metaphor for the struggle within each individual. Ultimately, the Bhagavad Gita is about understanding what truly matters in life and making appropriate choices based on this understanding. Our task is not necessarily to do what is most expedient, but rather to make choices based on the values and ideals that matter in the long run. Moreover, once we have identified what we need to do, we must throw ourselves into the task with the devotion of Arjuna, and perform it to the best of our ability. I believe the Bhagavad Gita teaches us that we should never be dependent upon the external world for our peace or happiness. True peace lies within us, and is not contingent upon circumstances. The disciplined mind, the mind that has studied and is learned and devoted, can rise above the difficulties and enigmas and humdrum of daily life.

There is a common misconception among Westerners that Hinduism created the caste system. Though Hindu scriptures may occasionally allude to different classes, they do not create or officially sanction a caste system, which is a political and historical institution, not a religious one. Indeed, as we have seen, the society of the Indo-European settlers was already stratified before it mixed with the indigenous population and before Hinduism formed. Hinduism and the caste system matured together, and because religious and political thinking are always intertwined in any society, the caste system has become incorporated into the expression of Hinduism. Some Hindus who subscribe to a caste system find justification in sacred texts. The rationale is either that those of lower standing deserve their status because of misdeeds in a previous life, or that the situation will even out or be reversed in another life. But the caste system did not originate from the religion.

The word "caste" was originally Portuguese. Hindus use the term *Varna* (color) for caste. They also use the term *Jati* (earth group) for subgroups within a caste. Traditionally, marriage must be within the same caste and preferably within the same Jati. The differences between the castes are based on spiritual purity and dharma. The concept of dharma evolved concurrently with the maturation of castes, and the two concepts are inextricably linked, so each caste has duties shared by no other. Dharma became the guide to behavior and is discussed in the *Dharmashastras,* the best known of which is the *Marvadharmashastra* (also called the *Laws of Manu).* Manu (not to be confused with Mani, the founder of the now-extinct religion called Manichaeism) is an apocryphal person, and his laws are of undetermined date. Most scholars believe they were written in the first or second century CE, probably based on work that dates to about 500 BCE. Manu's Laws assigned different dharmas to each caste, and thereby gave form to the perceived differences in spiritual purity among them.

There are four castes in the Varna system: the Brahmins (intellectuals and priests), Kshatriyas (warriors and temple rulers), Vaishyas (merchants, farmers, and artisans), and Sudras, or Shudras, (laborers and peasants). Each man of one of the upper three varnas is born with three debts. The first is the debt to the sages, which he repays by learning the Vedas. The second is his debt to the gods, which he repays by performing sacrifice. The third debt is to his ancestors, and it is repaid by having children, specifically sons. These three castes are known as "twice-born" because they undergo a second ritual birth as children when they undertake to learn the Vedas. The fourth class, the Sudras, does not have such a ritual and are called "once-born."

The Untouchables are completely outside of the caste system. They are also called "outcasts" or "children of God," and refer to themselves as the "oppressed ones" (*Dalits*). They are considered so impure that no act of purification can cleanse them. Indeed, even to touch them is to become unclean, and there is some feeling that they can pollute a cleansing body such as the Ganges River. They are considered the sink into which flow the impurities of the world. This perception compels them to perform work that cleanses others. So far removed are the Dalits from Indian society that many Indians do not even consider them to be Hindus. Many people of higher castes insist that even laying eyes upon Dalits is equivalent to touching them and is therefore to be avoided at all costs. Dalits traditionally often live outside of towns and are banned from public facilities, though the advocacy of Gandhi, and subsequent government policy, have somewhat mitigated these strictures. Untouchability has been officially illegal throughout India's independence and is banned by its constitution (the constitution does not abolish the caste system, but contrary to tradition, incorporates Dalits into it, making them part of the Sudras, and it forbids discrimination on the basis of caste). The Indian government is attempting to institute what Americans would call affirmative action to benefit Dalits, but faces huge resistance from tradition and business interests.

Under no circumstances may an individual perform work associated with a higher caste. In some circumstances a person can perform work associated with a lower caste, but such work should be on a short-term basis only. This mandate is part of the Hindu philosophy that if everyone adheres to the dharma specific to his or her station, universal harmony will prevail. The general belief, prevalent since the time of Manu, is that failure to adhere strictly to caste-appropriate behavior and dharma leads to chaos. Enforcement of appropriate caste behaviors comes from relatives, fellow caste members, and specific caste councils. The caste system has led to astonishing stability over the centuries, indeed millennia, of Indian society, but it also teaches us that stability is not necessarily the most admirable characteristic of a culture.

The caste system seems unduly harsh to most Western observers, but we must remember that in the West we have an unofficial caste system, based on money, race, gender, or other criteria. Indeed, the caste system offers hope for eventual escape from unpleasant circumstances in another lifetime. As we will see, all of the world's currently practiced major religions subscribe to a fundamental egalitarianism relative to earlier religions, but that egalitarianism may be expressed differently among the great faiths. Hinduism offers the downtrodden a greater degree of hope through Samsara than they had previously known. When judged by the standards of the time and place of its origin, and compared to comparable practices in other cultures, the caste system reminds us that societies and religions are more alike than different.

Some form of vegetarianism is historically preferred in Hinduism because of the belief in transmigration, meaning that the soul of an animal may have once been human. Among the lower castes, however, especially in the north, vegetarianism is not always strictly practiced. Cows enjoy a unique status in Hinduism, partly because they are the symbol for all animals and partly because of their contribution to humanity, making them in effect symbols for all mothers.

Manu also stipulated the *ashramas,* or stages of life, for both men and women. For men, the first, or student stage, starts at age seven for Brahmins and at older ages for the three other upper castes. This first stage of celibacy and learning begins with an initiation rite and an apprenticeship under a master. Absolute dedication and devotion to the master is required, and many behaviors that Westerners regard as normal for childhood are forbidden. The boy's natural birth is, in effect, replaced by a second birth by way of men, giving rise to the term "twice-born." Only twice-born men can learn the Vedas. Thus, as in many religions, including Christianity, the maternal physical birth is superseded by a paternal spiritual birth. Learning a career is important in the student stage. The boy also receives a sacred mantra, which he is to repeat every morning.

The student stage is followed by the marriage stage, and then by the householder stage. While dharma is still important in the householder stage, attaining necessary material possessions is also important. Families are usually raised in the householder stage. Children, especially sons, are essentially mandatory, and only sons can perform the funeral rite of a parent.

The next stage is called "forest dweller," and it is in this stage that one should become more reflective and more aware of the ultimate reality. The forest-dweller stage is appropriate only after the householder stage. Soul searching and introspection should not come before one has fulfilled his obligation to society and family.

The final stage is that of complete renunciation of all mundane aspects of life, even of name and family. In this stage, the devotee should give up his house and beg for food. He even renounces dharma and some rituals that had previously been important. After the necessary familial obligations are met, the elderly person is finally in a position to fully understand and live a life without a sense of individualism. The aim is supreme freedom. Though only a minority of men accept this stage, they are still occasionally seen, dressed in orange robes. A wandering Hindu holy man is called a *Sadhu,* and some Sadhus are fulfilling this stage.

The Laws of Manu also specified stages of life for women. Manu stipulated that women are to be honored by men, but at the same time completely dependent upon them. Indeed, it was this dependency that established the three traditional stages of a woman's life. The first of these is when she is a daughter, in which case she is being raised for the family of her future husband. During this stage, she is dependent upon her father.

Marriage is the next stage of a woman's life. Because of a woman's dependency, marriage is roughly comparable to the young man's student stage, but it is also equivalent to a man's householder stage because a man and a woman live together in the house. A red dot on the woman's forehead indicates that she is married. It shows that her status is auspicious and life giving. The woman has obligations to God, ancestors, and tradition, as does the man, but as a wife her obligations to her husband overshadow all of these. A married son lives in his parents' house until their death, but a married daughter lives in the home of her husband's parents, where she is subject not just to her husband, but also to her mother-in-law.

Traditionally, marriages are arranged. The rationale is that decisions on marital partners are made by more mature people who are able to see past immediate attraction and exercise the necessary objectivity. It is possible that arranged marriages have less of the immaturity and poor judgment that often characterize Western marriages, and many arranged marriages appear to work very well. But even the best of them entail significant trauma as a teenage girl moves from a familiar and loving parental home to the home of a husband she barely knows, as a lower member of a new family, not all of whose members necessarily welcome her.

The final stage of life for many women is widowhood, a stage in which a woman has lost much of her status because it came strictly through her husband. This is a stage of dependency on sons. Widows were often viewed as outcasts. They were given difficult household assignments, were expected to shave their heads, were expected to wear white (the color of mourning) indefinitely, and were discouraged from remarrying. In theory, widows who threw themselves on their husband's pyre — a practice called *sati* — did so voluntarily, but this was probably not always the case. A number of people in contemporary India are trying to improve the status of the country's 30 million widows, but like all social reformers, they face religious and cultural obstacles. Moreover, much of India's population lives in rural villages, away from any realistic mechanism to introduce change. Here, illiteracy, poverty, and lack of technology hinder the dissemination of new ideas. Interestingly, traveling theater groups are taking on this challenge.

While there clearly are many aspects of classical Hinduism that Westerners would regard as sexist, as is the case for any religion, we must judge Hinduism in the cultural context in which it arose and is maintained. In fact, Hinduism, like Islam, conveyed to women a higher status than they had previously known. The study of religion teaches us that any misogynist overtones we associate with a religion are due to one or more of three reasons: the overlay of the patriarchal culture in which it arose; the failure of the religion to keep pace with changing times; or our misunderstanding of the religion. No major contemporary religion affords women less than what they were accorded at the time and place of that religion's origin.

Life has four goals, called *purusharthas.* The first of these is *artha,* the seeking of necessities (luxuries are discouraged, but the need for necessary possessions is accepted). The second is *kama,* which is pleasure or love. Sensuality and sexuality were never prohibited in Hinduism, but they need to be between members of the same caste, and alcohol is forbidden. The *Kama Sutra* is a famous text on sensuality that is familiar to many Westerners.

The third goal is dharma, which pertains to laws and obligations. This encompasses civil law and religious law, and also professional and family responsibilities. *Stri dharma* is the dharma of women. Women are central to the dharma of men even though they have a subordinate role. For example, even in Vedic times, women were required for rituals to be effective, though they had no direct role in those rituals, and only a married man could perform a sacrifice. The third obligation of men in the upper three varnas, to produce children, also requires the participation of women. These first three goals — artha, kama, and dharma — are the foundation of the path of correct action, called *Karma-marga.* Ritual, festival, and pilgrimage are also key aspects of *Karma-marga.* Gandhi created a new manifestation of Karma-marga with his interpretation of dharma as nonviolent political action. The fourth goal is Moksha itself, but for most Hindus, Moksha is too far off to be a goal of this life, and the first three goals — in an attempt to obtain a better rebirth — are the focus of daily life.

There are three pathways, or *margas,* to Moksha. These are collectively called the *Trimarga.* The first of these three pathways is the *Karma-marga,* the path of correct action, discussed above. What we do in life should be a combination of sensible possessions, reasonable sensuality, and adherence to duty. The other two pathways to Moksha involve how we think. The second pathway to Moksha is the *Jnana-marga,* or way of wisdom, knowledge, or insight. The way of wisdom is a reflection of the shift from ritual and sacrifice to introspection during the Axial Age (800–200 BCE). The Upanishads are the source book for the path of wisdom. The third pathway to Moksha is the *Bhakti-marga,* the way of devotion. Some combination of these three pathways of the Trimarga is desired, and no single pathway can bring about Moksha.

Each of these three pathways is associated with a form of yoga. The word "yoga," from the Sanskrit word for "to join," refers to the practice of uniting the mind with the universe through physical and mental discipline. Sanskrit texts refer to yoga as "the stopping of the whirlpools of the mind." There are a number of types of yoga in Hindu practice, and all are designed to assist in the margas. For example, *Karma yoga* focuses the mind so that it can take action. It is a yoga that brings about the detachment that permits duty and service to others to prevail. This is the type of yoga that Krishna recommended to Arjuna. *Jnana yoga* is the yoga of wisdom and scholarship. *Bhakti yoga* revolves around devotion. *Raja yoga* stresses meditation. *Tantra yoga* is yoga of ritual and chanting, often involving mysticism. The West does not grasp the full significance of the yogas, nor does it perceive the mental component of the practice. The most common form in the West is *Hatha yoga,* which is a series of exercises.

Bhaktas have primarily chosen the bhakti pathway, as opposed to the jnana or karma pathways, to reach Moksha. The path of devotion, called Bhakti, is based on a deep love of God. There are two orders of Hindu Bhaktas. *Saguna Bhaktas* believe that God can have a face and a form, such as the typical image of Krishna. However, *Nirguna Bhaktas* believe that it is impossible to ascribe a form to God. Nirguna Bhaktas are also called "Sants." Sants reject the caste system and emphasize the internal experience of religion over the use of dogma or ritual. Sants are tolerant of Islam and in fact see themselves as neither Hindu nor Muslim. Indeed, as we shall see, Nanak was a Sant who combined elements of Hinduism and Islam into the new religion of Sikhism. Kabir (c. 1440–1518) was a Sant poet and philosopher who is revered by Hindus, Muslims, and Sikhs.

There is no specific Sabbath in Hinduism. There are temples, and there may be collective worship as for other religions, but Hindus usually worship alone. Most Hindus practice some sort of daily worship, called the *Puja.* The Trimarga and all of its components form the basis of the Puja. Following a cleansing bath, the Puja usually takes place before an image of a manifestation of God, because an image facilitates focusing on God. The image is considered a representation of God, and worshippers may feed and clothe it, but the image is not an incarnation of God. The use of images should be approached cautiously, lest they convey the idea that God is a simple, discrete being. Care of images is one form of Bhakti.

Most religions have celebrations at the major passages of life, and there is much to be learned about a religion by how it views the stages of life. In Hinduism, these celebrations are called *Samskaras.* One of these commemorates the second birth and the initiation into being a student. Another is the funeral passage. While cremation is by far the rule, children younger than fifteen, wandering ascetics, and occasional members of an unusual sect may be buried rather than cremated. In addition, poor people who cannot afford cremation may be buried. Ideally, the body is given a final purifying ritual bath before cremation. Though cremation is a very important passage, it is always handled by Dalits. After the cremation, family members take a purifying bath without looking at the pyre. The ashes are placed in a sacred place, usually in a body of water. Rituals for the benefit of the deceased occur after the death.

Festivals are more frequent and more important in Hinduism than in most other religions. The major festivals in Hinduism are *Holi* (in March, celebrating the triumph of Vishnu over a demon and the return of spring), *Diwali* (celebrating Rama's return from exile), and *Dusserah* (celebrating the Ramayana in southern India, but with a different meaning in other places). Perhaps the most common festival is Holi. Many religions have festivals or holidays that celebrate both an event in that religion's history and an occurrence in nature (this is particularly common in Hinduism and Judaism). Holi's dual celebration of Vishnu's triumph and the return of spring is an example of this convergence of religion and culture. Holi is a time of great levity and one of the few times when people from different castes can mix. Those in power are subjected to playful humiliation. The intent is to relax conventions for a short time.

Any site of pilgrimage is really a place where people's spirits can cross upward into heaven and where heaven can cross down into earth. Pilgrimages are very important in Hinduism, but unlike Islam, there is no one specific destination. Varanasi (also called Banaras or Kashi) is a sacred city that is as close as Hinduism gets to Islam's Mecca, but India is filled with sacred places. All rivers are perceived as having divine origin, and are considered a manifestation of the life-giving force of the Goddess. Rivers are therefore life giving, and are excellent both for pilgrimages and as final resting places for the deceased. Some will move near a river in their final days so that they can be cremated and their ashes placed in the river. One will occasionally see pictures of Shiva with the rivers spouting from his head in the form of a Goddess. The Ganges is especially revered and is a common pilgrimage destination. One of the most popular Hindu myths concerns the descent of the Ganges from heaven to earth.

Tantric Hinduism is an unorthodox form that attempts to find liberation by acquiring supernatural power. The Tantric texts date from the seventh to eleventh centuries CE, but are thought to incorporate much older ideas. For the most part, Tantra developed within Saivism, the worship of Shiva, and its texts are in the form of a dialogue between Shiva and the Mother Goddess. For followers of Tantra, its canon even supersedes the Vedas.

Most Hindu tantra is "left-handed." Left-handed tantra uses rituals, mantras, mysticism, and gurus. Tantrism is associated with its own form of yoga, but other forms of yoga must first be mastered. Left-handed tantra occasionally permits practices that are normally forbidden in Hinduism, such as eating meat, drinking wine, and having extramarital intercourse. Marriage outside of caste may also be possible. These are permitted because in certain circumstances they can facilitate Enlightenment. Their casual use is not part of Tantra. Tantric rites are practiced under the supervision of a guru in a sacred place and are highly ritualized. Participants begin by bathing, dressing, and applying cosmetics. Male and female participants then form a circle around the guru, with the women sitting to the guru's left (hence the name). Meat and wine are consumed, after which the participants may engage in sexual intercourse if the guru deems it appropriate, but the purpose of this sex is not orgasm, but rather an ecstatic embrace that allows the participants to achieve greater awareness of reality. Each of these activities is associated with a specific mantra. The women are perceived as the Goddess and are worshipped. One of the aims of tantra is to break down dualities. The ritual sex is a reenactment of the union of Shiva and the Mother Goddess that empowered both deities. So-called "right-handed" tantra is more conventional, with worship of Shiva or Vishnu, but still uses a mantra. The Muslim invasion all but removed Tantrism in the north, but it survives in the south and has been especially influential in Tibetan Buddhism.

We close our consideration of Hinduism with the effects derived from the British occupation of India. The occupation brought about several different interpretations of traditional Hindu literature, resulting in a more liberal view in some cases and a conservative backlash in others.

Ironically, it was the British occupation that planted the seeds of Indian nationalism. Other Western ideas the British brought into India include nonviolent defiance (which Gandhi received in large measure from Tolstoy) and egalitarianism (the relative egalitarianism of the Bible was very influential to Indians). Now we examine two religions that sprang from the rich variety of Hinduism.

Chapter 4

JAINISM

THERE ARE ONLY ABOUT 4 million Jains in the world, almost all of whom are in India. The Jains are followers of master teachers called *Jinas* (also *Tirthankaras* or *Arhats*), humans who are considered to possess the highest level of understanding. Jains believe that time is infinite and consists of cycles of upward and downward movement, during which humanity correspondingly ascends or descends. Forty-eight Jinas appear in each cycle.

Jains believe that their religion and its truths have always been present. The religion has no founder and it has no place or time of origin. They believe that Mahavira (c. 599–527 BCE), commonly considered by Westerners to be "the founder" of Jainism, was simply the most recent Jina who has taught the religion. In practical terms, however, Jainism, like Buddhism, almost surely began as a modification of Hinduism, probably under Mahavira's influence.

Mahavira was a shadowy figure about whom little is known. Like Buddha, he arose in that marvelous period of questioning and prosperity of the sixth century BCE, a time when people dared to question the Vedas and introduce new ideas into classic Hinduism. Mahavira is reputed to have come from a wealthy family and to have had a wife and children prior to embracing the extreme asceticism that would characterize Jainism. The *Kalpa Sutra*, an account of the life of Mahavira, is important to Jains.

Like Buddha, Mahavira placed emphasis on self-reliance over deities and sacred texts, and offered a simple, more egalitarian approach that people could understand. Though neither Jainism nor Buddhism is anti-theistic, neither is particularly theistic, nor was either founder ever considered a god. Like Buddhists, Jains may believe in one or more gods, but these are not central to the religion. A common Jain deity is the goddess *Ambika,* who was an exemplary Jain laywoman who, after leaping into a well with her two sons to escape her wrathful Brahmin husband, was reborn a Goddess.

Jinas occupy the highest of the five spiritual levels in Jainism. Next to them are *Siddhas,* who have achieved liberation. Then come those who instruct monks and nuns in spiritual ways, followed by those who instruct them in scripture. Monks compose the fifth group.

There is no priesthood in Jainism, and the monastic order is not as well demarcated from the laity as in other religions. Monks will often live among laypeople. Monks and ascetics take the great vows of Jains, the *Mahavratas.* These vows are nonviolence, truthfulness, celibacy, not taking anything that is not given freely, and detachment from all material possessions. Fasting after nightfall is also customary. The vows that laypeople take are called *anuvratas* (lesser vows), which include vegetarianism and the rejection of deliberate killing (unintentional killing, though regrettable and a cause of unfavorable karma, is not a violation of the vows).

Jains also believe in *samsara* and *karma,* but their conception of *karma* is not the simple cumulative "cause and effect" of Hinduism and Buddhism. Unlike Buddhists, who believe that there has to be intent for adverse karma to result, Jains believe that even unintentional harmful acts generate such karma. Whereas Buddhists believe in not harming only those that are sentient, Jains do not believe in harming any living creature. This is why Jains often sweep the ground in front of them as they walk to avoid accidentally injuring any being. They believe that all living creatures, and even inanimate objects, have a soul, the *Jiva.* Jains believe that inanimate objects and lower animals may have only one sense, but will develop additional senses as they evolve toward becoming human. The *Tattvartha Sutra,* an important text for Jains, enumerates fourteen stages of spiritual growth, though most Jains aspire only to the first six.

A division occurred among Jains in about the fourth century CE, resulting in the *Digambaras* and the *Shvetambaras.* The Digambaras believe that all possessions are to be shunned, even clothing (this is for men only; women are still clothed). Life without clothing is an indication that a man has overcome sexual urges and his sense of shame. Digambaras also believe that women cannot attain liberation until they are reborn as men. Shvetambaras disagree, believing it unnecessary to forgo clothing in order to attain the mental focus that leads to purification. They also believe that liberation can come to women. The two groups also disagree on the authority of certain texts.

Jains celebrate an eight to ten-day day period called *Paryusana-parva,* in which the *Samvatsari,* a festival observed by the Shvetambaras, is celebrated. At the end of Paryusana-parva, confession is made. Since there are no priests, confession is made to ascetics or to family members. Jains ask pardon with the following statement:

> *I ask pardon of all living creatures. May all of them pardon me. May I have a friendly relationship with all beings and unfriendly with none.*

Purification, discipline, and meditation are vital to Jainism. A common method of meditation is the *Samayika,* which lasts for forty-eight minutes. It starts by forgiving and asking forgiveness from all living things. The following prayer is then uttered:

> *Friendship to all living forms, delight in the qualities of the virtuous ones, unlimited compassion for all suffering beings, equanimity toward all who wish me harm, may my soul have these dispositions now and forever.*

During worship, Jains often gaze at and adorn the image of a Jina, a master teacher. Jinas may not directly assist a person because they have been completely liberated from the world, but concentration on an image of a Jina may help one achieve purification.

The symbol of Jainism is the open palm. A simple open palm may be used, but there is often a wheel in the palm. The wheel symbolizes the dharma, used in its broader sense of living harmoniously with nature. In the center of the wheel is the word "ahimsa" (harmlessness). As an example of their reverence for all living creatures, Jains operate a bird hospital in Delhi.

Ahimsa

The open palm is used in iconography of Lakshmi and Shiva, where it indicates reassurance and blessing. The open palm is the symbol of Jainism, and again indicates a benevolent spirit. There is often a wheel, symbolizing dharma, in the palm. In the center of the wheel the word "ahimsa" (harmlessness) may be written.

Chapter 5

BUDDHISM

MORE THAN ANY OTHER religion, the roots of Buddhism are simple. Buddha preached perhaps the simplest message ever delivered, and in doing so he made his religion accessible to the masses. He also gave people hope that peace and happiness could be found without severe deprivation or a deity. This simplicity is one of Buddhism's great gifts to the world. The other is that it lacks a fundamentalist expression or a history of violence.

Buddha is traditionally said to have been born in 563 BCE, but most scholars would place the date closer to 490 BCE. The Buddha's actual name was Siddharta Gautama. He is also called Shakyamuni, *the* Buddha (as opposed to *a* Buddha), and Gautama. Buddha was born in what is now southern Nepal, but preached in the Ganges region of India. The word "Buddha" is usually translated as the "Enlightened one," but is better translated as the "Awakened one." This work uses the terms "Enlightened" and "Awakened" and "Enlightenment" and "Awakening" synonymously.

While the precise details of Buddha's life and teachings are closed to us, we can be reasonably assured that he accepted the basic tenets of Hinduism, but taught that the Vedas were not inviolate and that Hindu authorities could be questioned. He also rejected the paramount importance of sacrifices and rituals. Indeed, one of the sharpest lines of distinction between Buddhism and Hinduism is that the former abandoned the emphasis on sacrifice in favor of the ability of the practitioner to control his own thoughts. Nor did Buddha recognize the caste system. He offered egalitarianism, which Hinduism did not (for this reason, many Dalits have converted to Buddhism). Finally, Buddha did not accept the idea that following a god or a guru was the way to end suffering. Rather, Buddhists must follow the power within themselves.

While Buddha was undoubtedly an innovative thinker, he was probably also responding to and developing ideas that were in the air during the time in which Hinduism was being transformed. Indeed, the Upanishads, which redirected Hinduism toward ideas that would become central to Buddhism, were written over a long period that included the Buddha's lifetime. Great religious leaders are great precisely because they respect the sacred works and ideas of their time, yet simultaneously absorb and develop other ideas. Great religious ideas, like those in the sciences, are usually the product of an anonymous and largely forgotten group of people, of whom one or a small number stand out and are remembered.

Before Buddha, Moksha — the release from Samsara, the perpetual cycle of birth and death — could only be achieved by extreme asceticism. After a youth of privilege, Siddharta briefly followed an ascetic pathway. Legend has it that Siddharta's father tried to protect him so that he would not choose that path. We are told that the father appeared to be successful and that the son integrated into society, was married, and had a child. But it is said that one day, the future Buddha had four visions: of a sick person, an old person, a dead person, and an ascetic. These images showed Siddharta how sheltered his life had been and how much suffering there was in the world. His visions overcame his father's wishes, and Siddharta became an ascetic and a wandering monk, begging for food. One day, however, a woman gave him some rice pudding that enticed him away from extreme asceticism and into a more moderate path. It is said that the future Buddha compared extreme asceticism to tying knots in the air. Siddharta found peace on the middle path between privilege and deprivation.

The addition of the middle path to his philosophical departure from the Vedas marks the beginning of Siddharta's contributions. It is said that at this time he sat under the lotus tree and achieved Enlightenment, becoming the Buddha and defeating the demon *Mara* (symbolized in iconography by Buddha's right hand touching the ground).

Many people found the middle path and the simplicity of the Buddha's message more palatable than Hindu asceticism. Part of Buddha's popular appeal was his refusal to deal with abstract philosophical questions. He did not offer him himself as an authority, but rather invited people to explore for themselves. Instead of authority or philosophy, he offered simplicity and inquiry.

Buddha's first teaching after his Awakening was of the Four Noble Truths. These are simple concepts that, without asceticism, can permit escape from the cycle of constant birth and death. The first Noble Truth is the existence of suffering (*Dukkha*). Suffering may be the best single word in English, but we need not have experienced pain or a distinct, profound loss. Suffering also refers to any feeling of unhappiness, encompassing anxiety, craving, boredom, etc. Suffering can also be caused by change or the fear of change, even if the new circumstances are not intrinsically painful. Pleasant moments or good memories can be causes of suffering if we become addicted to them and are unable to accept change. Another kind of suffering comes from having false goals or desiring possessions and accomplishments that are not true to the self. This form of suffering emanates from the failure to know oneself. Sadness and disappointment are perhaps the best terms to use in thinking of suffering in Buddhism.

The second Noble Truth concerns the cause of suffering, which is desire or craving. Craving takes two forms. The first is the craving for what we have never had. This form of craving arises from confusion between the concepts of want and need. It is reasonable to recognize legitimate needs and seek to fulfill them, but invariably, the fulfillment of legitimate needs leads to additional desires for things that are less urgently needed, the pursuit and attainment of which is distracting and counterproductive. We form the impression that more will make us happier, and we come to believe that something is needed when it is actually only wanted. Paradoxically, the way in which we try to be happy or to avoid suffering — acquiring something we believe will give us pleasure — is the cause of much of our suffering.

A problem with craving is that it comes in deceptively small, insidious steps. We crave just a little more and then just a little more and then just a little more. No single craving is particularly harmful, but collectively they form a persistent pattern that carries us inexorably down the pathway of insatiable desire. Craving derives from believing that there is always something "wrong," that something must be improved. Buddhism asks us not to think in terms of "if only": if only this were true, if only that were not, if only I had this. Our desire for achievement and possessions may appear to be the pathway to happiness, but it is actually the pathway to suffering because it places us on a never-ending treadmill of wanting more and more.

The second form of craving is a desire to return to a past moment or for the perpetuation of the present moment. It seems odd that this is a form of craving, but nothing is permanent, and failure to realize this will lead to suffering. We must be careful not to yearn for a fictitious life constructed from the best moments of our past.

The causes of suffering are inextricably linked to the Buddhist concepts of impermanence and *no self.* Buddha pointed out that impermanence is a quality of our lives, and that this is observable over very short as well as very long periods of time. Life changes even when it seems to be the same, just as a flowing river seems constant, but the water rushing past is different with each moment. If we accept this change, we will crave less.

Because of this constant change, we do not have fixed, permanent identities that we must be concerned about or that we should require others to respect. This absence of a fixed, permanent identity is the doctrine of no self. This concept is troublesome to most Westerners because we are accustomed to thinking of our identities as unchanging throughout our lives. Indeed, Christianity and Islam stipulate that our individual selves will persist for eternity, but Buddhism holds that because the self is not truly separate from the rest of the world, it makes little sense to promote the self at the expense of the rest of the world. Likewise, because we are all different manifestations of the same essence, it is desirable to wish others well, and futile to compete with them. No self therefore permits us to let go of ambitions, competitiveness, and attachments. In conjunction with the acceptance of impermanence, no self helps us accept the disappointments in life. Insistence on permanent, unchanging circumstances and a distinct self are leading causes of craving and desire.

The third Noble Truth is simply that there is a way to be released from suffering. Elimination of craving, and the suffering it causes, is possible. We can accept reality and cease to desire.

The fourth Noble Truth tells us how to eliminate suffering. It illuminates the Eightfold Pathway, by which we can focus our minds so as to eliminate craving and the suffering it causes. The Eightfold Pathway can be written in English in the following manner:

Right understanding (or Right views): This pertains to the optimal understanding of the above situation, namely that there is unhappiness, that it comes from desire and dissatisfaction with what is, and that there can be relief. Right understanding refers to exceeding a simple awareness of the Four Noble Truths and the Eight-Fold Path, and completely understanding the concepts. This means not accepting the teaching as dogma given by a master, but as truths that are verified by one's own experience. Buddhists believe that only by verifying the Four Noble Truths and the Eightfold Path through one's own experience can they be truly understood and made a part of daily life.

Right intent (or Right thoughts): This is the determination to place the tenets of Buddhism foremost in our minds and to not be distracted by the superficialities of the world.

Right effort: This pertains to a conscious attempt to behave according to the tenets of Buddhism. We must always be on guard against craving.

Right conduct (or Right action): This is behaving with kindness and charity. Buddhists are taught five precepts related to proper conduct. These are:

> *I will refrain from harming.*
> *I will not take what is not offered.*
> *I will not engage in inappropriate sexual behavior or sexual misconduct.*
> *I will not engage in false speech. This precept refers not only to lying, but also to content, tone, appropriateness, swearing, gossiping, idle chatter, raised voices, etc.*
> *I will refrain from intoxicants. This refers not only to alcohol but also to anything that dulls the senses or inhibits the ability to think clearly.*

Notice the substantial similarity of these five prohibitions to many of the Ten Commandments of Western religions. Buddhists do not view a failure in any of these areas of conduct as a sin, as a Christian might. They have a more forgiving attitude among themselves when a mistake is made in one of these categories.

Right speech: This is not only speaking the truth and speaking charitably, but also examining why we have spoken unkind or false words.

Right livelihood: This is engaging in an occupation that promotes kindness, charity, and life. An integral part of right livelihood is to avoid professions that make it more difficult for other people to follow the Eightfold Path. For example, Buddhism frowns on a profession centered on alcohol or animal slaughter, even if the individual does not partake of its products.

Right concentration: These are the physical and mental exercises that focus the mind, remove superficialities, and see the truth. Meditation is specifically encouraged.

Right mindfulness: This is taking the awareness that comes from meditation and study and integrating it into daily life. Buddhism believes deeply in the power of the mind. It advocates extensive self-examination to achieve self-awareness. More than this, right mindfulness is being aware of and attentive to all of reality, just as it is, without craving or aversion.

The Eightfold Path can be reduced to three categories: behavior, concentration, and wisdom. To summarize: the Four Noble Truths are that there is suffering, craving for more is the cause of this suffering, there is a way to obtain relief, and this way is the Eightfold Path. Through the Four Noble Truths and Eightfold Pathway, Buddhism strives for a middle path that rejects both extreme asceticism and decadence. By understanding the Noble Truths and following the Eightfold Pathway, we can finally be released from the eternal frustration of infinitely repeating births and deaths and become one with all of creation. This state is *Nirvana.*

In Nirvana, the individual self is merged with and inseparable from all consciousness. It is a blending of the self into the universe, after which there is no more longing or desire, no more painful death and rebirth. Enlightenment and the Nirvana that it leads to are similar to the Hindu concept of Moksha, but there are two important differences. First, whereas Moksha is conceived as a union with Brahman, Nirvana is not directly tied to union with a deity (though this difference is blurred by the fact that Hindus do not make a sharp distinction between Brahman and creation — to merge with Brahman is to merge with all of creation). Second, Nirvana places greater emphasis on life in the present. The Enlightened individual is not just released from the cycle of rebirths, but also has the opportunity to live more happily in the here and now.

Achieving Nirvana is difficult because it requires sacrifice, a new way of thinking, and a lifestyle that initially appears uncomfortable. Nirvana occurs in two stages. Upon experiencing Enlightenment, the fortunate Buddhist no longer generates karma but still has to contend with preexisting Karma. This is called Nirvana with remainder, which occurs when an individual is free of craving. Freedom from craving will lead to release from suffering, but karma from past lives remains. At final Nirvana — called Nirvana without remainder, or *Parinirvana* — all karma is dispersed. Only then is Samsara escaped. Nirvana with remainder can be realized in life, but Nirvana without remainder can only be achieved at death.

Some Buddhists believe that Nirvana can be obtained without any deities, while others believe that one or more deities are required (we will see more about this when we discuss *Mahayana Buddhism*). Buddha is not, however, considered a god to either group.

Buddhism arose in the midst of a powerful and deeply held caste system and took the radical position that people of all castes were equal and equally capable of Enlightenment. Buddhism not only offered a simpler way of life than competing religions, but also, as Christianity would later do, appealed to the common person. It held that ordinary people, in ordinary life, could reach the same state of Enlightenment as ascetics. The simple message of the Buddha and the universal appeal of the Four Noble Truths have much to offer all of us, whatever our religion.

Because Buddha's ideas arose from Hinduism, Hindus have welcomed Buddhism as a heterodox philosophy within Hinduism, but have not accepted it as an orthodox manifestation of their religion. Buddhists may continue to worship Hindu gods, though these gods are considered independent of the basic Buddhist tenets. Likewise, Buddha is considered an incarnation of Vishnu, and as such can be worshipped by some Vaishnava Hindus.

As we have seen, the word "dharma" has a broad meaning in Hinduism and is roughly translated as duty. Buddhism and Hinduism share some terminology, but the shared words often have different meanings. In Buddhism, dharma (*dhamma* in Pali, a vernacular form of Sanskrit spoken in northern India in Buddhist times) more often refers to the teachings of Buddha. For example, since a wheel with eight spokes (representing the

Eightfold Pathway) is a symbol for Buddhism, the Buddha's teaching of the Four Noble Truths is sometimes referred to as the First Turning of the Wheel of Dhamma or as the First Discourse, and it is sometimes said that his teachings set in motion the Wheel of the Dhamma.

Wheel of Dhamma

The Wheel of Dhamma (or Wheel of Dharma) is also called the Dharmacakra or Dhammacakka. The Buddha's teaching of the Four Noble Truths is sometimes referred to as the First of the Wheel of Dhamma (or the First Discourse), and set in motion the Wheel of the Dhamma. The roundness symbolizes the perfection of the Dhamma (used here as the teachings of Buddha). The eight spokes represent the Eightfold Pathway. The hub symbolizes discipline, and the rim represents mindfulness and concentration. Mahayana Buddhists, depending on their precise beliefs, recognize one or two additional turnings of the wheel.

After the death of the Buddha, his disciples gathered to create an authoritative compilation of his teachings, which were preserved orally. A monk named Ananda is said to have recited the Buddha's doctrinal teachings, which became the *Sutta-Pitaka.* A monk named Upali recorded the rules and regulations, which became the *Vinaya-Pitaka.* Subsequently, a reflection on the Buddha's teachings, the *Abhidhamma-pitaka,* was added. These collections were not written until several centuries after the death of the Buddha because it was felt that oral transmission afforded the teachings greater respect and prevented their transmission to people who were not ready to receive them. The first written versions of these three compilations were in Pali, and together they constitute the *Pali Canon* (also called the *Pali Tripitaka).*

The *Dhammapada* is an excerpt from the Pali Canon, and is the Buddhist text most familiar to Westerners. The 423 verses of the Dhammapada are the earliest collections of Buddha's teachings and present life from a tranquil Eastern perspective. Every Westerner should read the Dhammapada. It is a small work whose pages truly sing of the simple truths that are the basis of happiness. From the first verse:

We are what we think
All that we are arises with our thoughts.
With our thoughts we make the world.
Speak or act with an impure mind
And trouble will follow you
As the wheel follows the ox that draws the cart.
Representative excerpts from subsequent verses include:
Your worst enemy cannot harm you as much as your own thoughts unguarded. But once mastered, no one can help you as much, not even your own mother or father.
It is better to conquer yourself than to win a thousand battles.
How easy it is to see another's faults, but how hard to face your own. Dwelling on another's faults multiplies your own.
Resist the desire to hurt until the sorrows vanish.
Hate never dispels hate; only love dispels hate. A Master never returns evil for evil.
Speak the truth, give whatever you can, never be angry.
The fragrance of virtue travels even against the wind.

Asoka (or Ashoka) was the king of India's first great empire, the Mauryan Empire, in the third century BCE. He converted to Buddhism and through his conquests and missionaries greatly increased the reach of the religion, changing it from a local to a regional religion. In addition, Asoka expanded trade with foreigners, which Hinduism had discouraged. These trading contacts undoubtedly facilitated the spread of the new religion.

Stupas began as burial places for royalty before Buddhist times. While maintaining a basic structure, these stupas came to have different forms and different names in different cultures. Buddhist stupas are raised structures marking a holy place and believed to contain relics of the Buddha. The origin of Buddhist stupas is said to be an instruction from Buddha to his followers to take his bones after cremation and bury them in a mound. Many of these stupas are attributed to Asoka. The stupas became sites of pilgrimage because it is believed that the Buddha left behind some of his power in the objects that he used. Buddha is not thought to be present in relics or in images that have been made of him, and Buddhists do not worship him. Rather, they seek his strength and wisdom. Buddhist stupas also have regional names. In Southeast Asia, for example, *pagoda* refers to more elaborate, tiered stupas (and occasionally used for tiered secular buildings) that may be entered.

The earliest representations to the Buddha are aniconic; that is, they represent the Buddha only by symbols or by objects associated with his life. Examples of these symbols are stupas, the tree of Enlightenment, and the wheel with eight spokes. Buddha may also be represented simply by his absence, such as an empty throne. It is not clear if this aniconic period represents an absolute prohibition against his representation, or artistic and cultural preferences.

Images of Buddha appear near the beginning of the Common Era. Images in the Mathura style, in which the Buddha was depicted as large, even obese, were most common. This was typical of the representation of all human figures in India at this time. Some of these representations are remarkable for showing the stability of the Buddha while simultaneously conveying unexpected buoyancy. The Gandhara style, named for the region on the border of Pakistan and Afghanistan, shows Greek influence dating to the conquest of Alexander the Great. The muscles are much more evident and there is more detail in the clothing. These two styles came together in the Gupta style in the fourth through sixth centuries

CE. In this style, the Buddha is more slender and graceful, with a serene smile and, again, delicate robes. The giant statues of Buddha that were destroyed in Afghanistan early in 2002 were in the Gupta style.

Buddha

As described in the text, images of Buddha have undergone variation over the centuries, reflecting the influence of the many cultures that Buddhism came into contact with. In addition, images of the Buddha vary depending on which of the 32 major attributes are emphasized. While images may depict a standing figure, most are of a seated Buddha, with folded legs. He wears simple monastic robes. A serene facial expression is always shown. A number of hand gestures, called mudrā, may be shown, each with a specific meaning. In this image, the Buddha has an open right hand, symbolizing benevolence and charity, and inviting the viewer to partake of the wisdom that is offered.

Buddhist monasteries were originally places for monks to rest from their wanderings during the rainy season, when roads were impassable. Subsequently, they became year-round abodes. By the fifth or sixth century of the Common Era, the monasteries had also become places for secular learning. Buddhist monks not only preserved secular knowledge, but also actively taught it. By concentrating Buddhism in a relatively small number of places, however, monasteries made the religion more vulnerable when Muslims from Afghanistan invaded India in the eleventh and twelfth centuries. This is a major reason why there is so little Buddhism in India today.

Divisions within Buddhism became evident soon after the death of Buddha. The second Buddhist Council took place about one hundred years after Buddha's death and dealt with some divisions within the movement. There were conservative and liberal factions that did not recognize each other. These would eventually grow into eighteen different sects and would lay the foundation for the differences between Mahayana and *Theravada Buddhism.*

The original form of Buddhism, as currently practiced, is Theravada Buddhism. Theravada Buddhists consider the *Sutta-Pitaka,* the portion of the Pali Canon that is said to be a recitation of Buddha's actual words, sacred. Given the changes that have occurred in Hinduism and Judaism in the past 2,500 years, Theravada Buddhism is arguably the oldest relatively unchanged religion in the world.

Mahayana Buddhism grew out of Theravada Buddhism and became prevalent about the beginning of the Common Era. Mahayana means "greater vehicle," and it maintains that many traditions in Theravada Buddhism are preliminaries to a deeper understanding. In addition to the texts of Theravada Buddhism, Mahayana Buddhism makes use of texts that are called sutras. The word "sutra" is not specific to Buddhism. We have encountered it before in Hinduism, where it refers to a short, memorable aphorism. In Buddhism, a sutra is a text thought to be derived from the Buddha's teachings. Mahayana Buddhists believe that Buddha revealed the teachings of the sutras only to a small number of people who were capable of understanding them. The teachings were then concealed for several centuries until the world was ready to receive them. Sutras are not presented as writings of Buddha himself, but as the recollections of a close disciple, based on his personal observations. Most sutras begin with the phrase "This is what I heard."

The common thread of the sutras is that Buddha's simple message, forming the basis of Theravada Buddhism, was actually only a preliminary one, and needed to be elaborated and developed into the Buddha's complete teachings. To present the concept that what had appeared to be a complete set of teachings was actually only preliminary, the sutras use the concept of expediency. In this concept, which is most fully developed in the *Lotus Sutra,* Buddha presented to the masses a simplified form of his complete teachings because this version could be understood by most people in that time and place. The analogy — presented in several parables in the sutras — is that of a teacher or parent telling a child only what is immediately needed to attain a required action, knowing that the child cannot and need not understand the entire situation. The most famous parable of this nature is the parable of the burning house, found in the Lotus Sutra, in which children ignore their father's pleas to leave a burning house, so he lures them out of the house with the promise of a special toy for each. The father used this subterfuge as an expedient to achieve the immediately necessary goal, after which he could further teach or enrich them. According to Mahayana Buddhism, the requirement for expediency is past and the time is now right for the revelation of the entirety of Buddha's teachings, via the sutras.

Additional concepts of the sutras — and again, we see this well developed in the Lotus Sutra — is that the Buddha actually achieved Enlightenment many eons ago, long before his actual time on earth, and that anyone who has patience and is of a pure mind can eventually achieve Enlightenment over the course of many lifetimes and great amounts of time.

In contrast, Theravada Buddhists do not recognize the sutras as containing additional teachings that emanated from Buddha. In addition, whereas all Buddhists recognize the First Turning of the Wheel of Dhamma as the teaching of the Four Noble Truths, Mahayana Buddhists, depending on their precise beliefs, recognize one or two additional turnings of the wheel. Today, Mahayana Buddhism is found in China, Japan, and Tibet. It is also common in Vietnam (but not in other Southeast Asian countries). Theravada Buddhism is practiced primarily in the rest of Southeast Asia.

Theravada Buddhism is occasionally called *Hinayana* ("lesser vehicle") Buddhism, but this is an inappropriate and derogatory term. There is nothing lesser about Theravada Buddhism. It is relatively simple and conservative, and is concerned with individual Enlightenment. Theravada Buddhists seek to become Arhats, meaning that they seek individual Enlightenment through the assistance of the Buddha's teachings. In Jainism, Arhat is another name for a Jina, a master teacher. In Buddhism, an Arhat (also spelled "Arahat" or "Arhant" when used in the Buddhist sense) is a person who has experienced Nirvana during his or her lifetime, as did the Buddha. The difference between an Arhat and the Buddha is that the Buddha achieved Enlightenment alone and made it possible for others to follow, whereas an Arhat requires the teaching of the Buddha. Some of the Buddha's disciples were Arhats, and Theravada Buddhists seek to follow in their path.

Theravada Buddhism stresses withdrawal from the world, including from the family, often resulting in monastic life. Pursuant to the importance of monasticism, meditation is important. Though no Buddhist sees the Buddha as divine, Theravada Buddhism sees him as a single, unique individual with a unique message. Mahayana Buddhism is more abstract and philosophical, and its adherents believe that there have been many Buddhas in addition to the known one, and that many more will come.

Mahayana Buddhism stresses the interconnectedness of all creatures and emphasizes compassionate works, in large part because acts of kindness underscore this unity. Mahayana Buddhism is concerned not only with individual Enlightenment, but also with the Enlightenment of all living creatures. Compassion is an integral part of all Buddhism, but universal compassion for all living creatures is more characteristic of Mahayana than Theravada Buddhism. Mahayana Buddhists believe that all sentient beings will eventually become Buddhas.

A major contribution of Mahayana Buddhism is the concept of a *Bodhisattva* (from the words *bodhi,* meaning "awakening" and *sattva,* meaning "purity and intelligence"). Though not all Mahayana Buddhists conceive of a Bodhisattva in precisely the same way, we can generally think of a Bodhisattva as an awakened individual who has left the world, but rather than proceed to Nirvana, which he has earned, he has instead returned to this world to awaken others. A Bodhisattva has not renounced Nirvana and will eventually achieve it and become a Buddha once his work on earth is finished. A Bodhisattva does not just seek Nirvana like the Theravada Buddhist does; because of his more global view of interconnectedness, he wishes to help others. In keeping with the emphasis on compassion, the ultimate goal of the Mahayana Buddhist is to become a Bodhisattva, not an Arhat.

The Bodhisattva ideal — the essence of Mahayana Buddhism — is the set of behaviors to which Mahayana Buddhists aspire. The ideal is achieved by a pathway, divided into stages, by which one can become a Bodhisattva. One account gives six stages: generosity, moral conduct, patience, courage, mental concentration, and wisdom; another account gives ten stages. Whereas Theravada Buddhists seek Nirvana as individuals by becoming Arhats, the Bodhisattva ideal of Mahayana Buddhism guides its followers toward altruism. Bodhisattvas foster wisdom and compassion, and they encourage people not only to be wise, but also to act. This emphasis on acts of compassion and action is more evident in the Mahayana than in the Theravada tradition, and reflects its greater connectedness to the larger world.

Bodhisattvas can be, and often are, laypeople, and it is a major tenet of Mahayana Buddhism that these people need not be monks or nuns. Mahayana Buddhism has monasteries, but there is less withdrawal from the world and more interaction with it than in Theravada Buddhism. Once a person becomes a Bodhisattva, he or she can continue to participate in daily life. You may find a Bodhisattva on the golf course or in the office, but they always apply the Four Noble Truths in a way that fosters wisdom and compassion. The Bodhisattva ideal made Buddhism more accessible to people because the idea of a righteous person actively involved in ordinary life made the religion seem less foreign. Theravada Buddhism was based in monasteries, and remote from most people. Mahayana Buddhists believe their form opens the religion to laypeople and gives it an expanded context that is more applicable in daily life. In general, Mahayana Buddhists regard Arhats as selfish because they do not teach or try to get others into Nirvana. At the same time, Theravada Buddhists believe that their version concentrates on the Four Noble Truths, whereas the elaborate complexities of Mahayana Buddhism may cause the simple foundations to be missed. Theravada Buddhists regard Bodhisattvas as superfluous.

Because Mahayana Buddhism so greatly expanded the scale and scope of the religion, it is possible to believe that some Bodhisattvas have ascended from Earth and live in the heavens. These were at one time people on earth, though no celestial figure is thought to have lived in historical times. They are called "celestial Bodhisattvas," who are supernatural beings, but not gods in the Western sense (Buddhism is fundamentally non-theistic and has no position with regard to the God of Judeo-Christian-Muslim tradition).

An example is *Avalokiteshvara,* the celestial Bodhisattva whose reincarnation is envisioned in the Dalai Lama (contrary to popular belief, the Dalai Lama is not considered a reincarnation of the Buddha, but rather of Avalokiteshvara, though the current Dalai Lama has indicated that he prefers to be considered simply as a human being and a Buddhist monk rather than the reincarnation of any specific entity). It is said that Avalokiteshvara can assume thirty-three different manifestations, so that any audience can conceive of him in a familiar and comforting form. In China, Avalokiteshvara is worshipped as *Kuan-yin,* who is female.

Kuan-Yin

In Chinese Buddhism, Kuan-Yin (or Guanyin) is considered to be a female manifestation of the celestial Bodhisattva Avalokiteshvara. Kuan-Yin is the Bodhisattva most closely associated with compassion. She is depicted in a flowing robe, usually with one or more necklaces. Her left hand holds a willow branch. Her right hand is often shown holding a water jar containing pure water. The crown often contains an image of the celestial Buddha Amitabha, considered to be Kuan-Yin's teacher and mentor before she became a Bodhisattva.

These celestial beings are thought to have once been people on Earth and to have brought the Bodhisattva ideal to such a high level of development that they now reside in the heavens, where they are available to help people reach Enlightenment. Avalokiteshvara, for example, can be invoked by a specific chant that often appears in religious imagery.

Maitreya is another celestial Bodhisattva. He is venerated throughout the Buddhist world, including in Theravada countries (he is the one celestial Bodhisattva generally recognized by Theravada Buddhism). Mahayana Buddhists believe that Maitreya will be the next Buddha (the historical Buddha was the twenty-fourth Buddha in the present stage of the world. When the world declines, Maitreya will come as the next Buddha). Maitreya has not yet visited Earth as a Buddha, but he has occasionally been to Earth as a Bodhisattva, and is depicted in China as a laughing, chubby Buddha. Many statues from China that Westerners believe to be of the Buddha are actually of Maitreya.

In addition to celestial Bodhisattvas, Mahayana Buddhism also believes that there are celestial Buddhas, who reside in special places (Buddha lands) that people reach just before Nirvana. *Amitabha* is a celestial Buddha whose name means "infinite life." Because Buddhas are removed from the world, they are more capable of helping people in the final stages of Nirvana than in the initial, or day-to-day stages (Bodhisattvas fill this function), but Amitabha is perhaps an exception. When he was a Bodhisattva, he vowed that he would establish a special place where anybody — even someone in the very early stages of Enlightenment — could go and achieve Nirvana by chanting his name with true faith. This place is called "the Pure Land," and devotion to Amitabha is sometimes called "Pure Land Buddhism." One of the features of the Pure Land is that all fantasies, provided they come from pure thought, are immediately fulfilled. In the Pure Land, Amitabha will appear before and teach anyone who sincerely invokes him. According to the long form of the *Pure Land Sutra,* the Pure Land is achieved by adhering to the Buddhist ideals, believing in Amitabha, and meditating. This is a visual meditation in which the meditator focuses on and visualizes the Pure Land. In the short form of the Pure Land Sutra, all that is required is belief in Amitabha and in the Pure Land, and keeping his name in mind. A moral life and adherence to the doctrines of Buddhism in general are not mentioned in the short form of the Pure Land Sutra. Devotion to Amitabha is important in Chinese and Japanese Buddhism, and Amitabha (*Amida* in Japan) is nearly worshipped by some Pure Land Buddhists.

The importance of celestial Bodhisattvas and celestial Buddhas is that they afford people assistance in becoming enlightened. The Buddha taught that anyone could reach Nirvana, but Mahayana Buddhism teaches that it is possible to get help from benevolent celestial entities. Unlike Theravada Buddhism, the individual need not go it alone. In particular, the assistance of these beings is very helpful in making a commitment and taking the first steps. Mahayana Buddhism opens up the religion to common people and makes its benefits available to all. Indeed, many Chinese who are not even Buddhist believe in the Pure Land and perceive it as heaven (as we shall see, there is also another conception of heaven in Chinese folk religion that is run by secular figures).

Mahayana Buddhism believes that after the death of the Buddha, there were three 500-year periods characterized by increasing corruption. In the first, the Perfect Age of the Dharma (Dharma here is used in the Buddhist sense, referring to the teachings of the Buddha), people were able to reach Enlightenment on their own. In the second, the Dharma Semblance Age, they required help from a Bodhisattva. The third was the Degenerate Age of the Dharma, and was a time of blatant corruption in which people needed all the help they could get to reach Nirvana. Pure Land Buddhism was so popular in the Tang Dynasty because people knew they were living in the third 500-year period.

A major contribution of Mahayana Buddhism is the concept of Emptiness. All religions have a metaphysical component that is elusive and initially strange, and which appears after the religion is relatively mature (for example, in Christianity, it is the concept of the Trinity). The concept of Emptiness is perhaps the most difficult aspect of Buddhism. It can be thought of as an extension of the concept of no-self. Hinduism believes in a collective self, the Atman, and in an individual self, the Jiva, but believes that both emanate from Brahman and will ultimately be integrated into him. Though neither Theravada nor Mahayana Buddhism believes in a distinct and permanent self in the Western sense, they differ in their views of reality and the self. All Buddhists believe that reality is based upon fleeting moments, which combine to give the illusion of reality. Theravada Buddhists believe that what appears to be a distinct self and a perceivable reality is really a momentary illusion caused by the flow of these fleeting moments, but they believe that these moments are real. The Mahayana took the Theravada thinking a step further and denied the existence of even these ephemeral moments. What we perceive as reality is not even composed of real moments, but of instants that are themselves illusory. In Emptiness, what we believe to be reality is an artifact caused by the fleeting perceptions of our senses. This means that there is no absolute reality. Reality is actually empty of absolute meaning. Space and time are therefore without meaning. Every place is any place and every time is any time. This emptiness — this lack of a tangible, firm reality — is the nature of all things and all thoughts. In fact, to Mahayana Buddhists, our very existence is illusory.

Mahayana Buddhists believe that because there is no absolute reality, there can be no absolute duality; that is, there can be no difference between any two apparently different concepts. Even Nirvana and Samsara cannot be differentiated. This means that Nirvana is *now, this moment,* not sometime in the future. Moreover, Samsara, the dreaded reincarnation that was a stark contrast to Nirvana, actually *is* Nirvana. Emptiness also means that the duality we perceive between ourselves and our loved ones is artificial. By removing absolute reality, Emptiness removes cause and effect. In a major departure from Theravada Buddhism, the Mahayana believe that because cause and effect are disrupted, we can no longer rely on the traditional teaching that Samsara comes from our mistakes. Rather, Enlightenment is everywhere. We just have to recognize it. If we understand Emptiness, we are already enlightened.

Emptiness holds that a full appreciation of the illusory nature of reality requires us to divest ourselves of our ordinary conceptions of reality, especially dualities and cause and effect, in order to achieve a true understanding of existence. This expression of Buddhism most sharply contrasts with the Western view that existence is absolutely real, as is our uniqueness. Paradoxically, however, the West has been the one place that actual evidence for something like Emptiness has been found in quantum mechanics, where neither duality nor cause and effect is valid in certain situations.

I believe the best way for most Westerners to look at Emptiness is not as a Mahayana Buddhist would, but rather as additional evidence for the ebb and flow of the universe and the constant changes in our lives. We are real and unique individuals, and we have a true reality, composed of fleeting, but real, thoughts and moments. But we must accept and be at peace with the fact that our reality constantly changes and is unpredictable. Embracing the essence of Emptiness might help us do this. The concept of Emptiness can help us understand the insignificance of most of life's difficulties.

Differences over the details of Emptiness led to major schools of Mahayana Buddhist philosophy. The first of these is the *Madhyamika* (also spelled *Madhyamaka),* founded by *Nagarjuna* in the second century CE. The second major division of Mahayana philosophy is the *Yogachara* (also *Yogacharya* or *Yogacara),* founded by *Asanga* in the fourth century. The details of these schools need not concern us, but pertain to the nature and perception of reality and knowledge — what Westerners call metaphysics and epistemology. Nagarjuna, for example, systematized the study of a collection of important sutras called the *Perfection of Wisdom Sutras.* These schools, and their way of viewing knowledge and reality, would have profound influence on the subsequent expression of Mahayana Buddhism.

India was not only the original birthplace of Buddhism, but also the birthplace of most of its variations. The Tantric version of Buddhism, the last major form, emerged in the sixth century CE in India. The word "Tantric" has several meanings. It can refer to a body of texts that are central to this form of Buddhism, to the teachings that are transmitted from teacher to student, or to power. The Tantric tradition is also called the "*Mantrayana,*" meaning "the vehicle of mantras" (sacred chants). Tantra is found in many of India's religions. Hinduism, Jainism, and even Indian Islam have some Tantra. It is debatable whether Tantric Buddhism is a form of Mahayana Buddhism or is a completely separate form that stands alongside Mahayana and Theravada Buddhism. Those who feel that Tantric Buddhism is a separate type refer to it as "*Vajrayana.*"

Tantric Buddhism uses chants, rituals, and mysticism, all of which are a heritage of Hinduism. Tantric Buddhism extends the idea of Emptiness, in particular its expression of non-duality. Because of the doctrine of non-duality, serenity and passion are not perceived as different. A Tantric writing says that a thorn removes a thorn and passion removes passion. Tantric Buddhism seeks to remove the appearance of opposites. The Tantric tradition resolves opposites and varieties, helping the practitioner understand that everything is a unified whole from which no distinctions can be drawn. The Buddha is often thought of and depicted as angry in Tantric Buddhism because undesirable emotions can be removed most effectively by expressing and acknowledging them and then channeling this expression into more constructive avenues.

A Tantric teacher is called a *guru,* and in Tibetan Buddhism, a *lama.* Tantric Buddhists believe that these teachers are indispensable to understanding their discipline. Symbolism is important in Tantric Buddhism because it assists the practitioner in understanding the philosophical concepts. Much of this symbolism is male-female. Because of Emptiness and the absence of dualities, there is no difference between the sexes.

The mandala, the most important symbol in Tantric Buddhism, is used in rituals and meditation. A mandala is essentially a circle, often made from colored sand, and can be thought of as separating the ritual space inside it from the mundane space outside it. The mandala can also be conceived as a middle ground between mundane daily life and the macrocosm, another union of apparent opposites. Mandalas have five points — east, west, north, south, and center. One of Mahayana Buddhism's numerous Buddhas is found in each of these points. In a ritual, mandalas serve as temporary domiciles for these Buddhas. In the Tantric tradition, following from Emptiness, there is no separation between an individual and the Buddha, so the mandala facilitates the unification of an individual and the Buddha. The mandala can also represent a portion of the cosmos. For example, Tibet can be depicted as a mandala, and pilgrimages to Tibet can be recreated by walking around the mandala. After the ritual is completed, the mandala is swept away (this may strike us as tragic destruction, but to practitioners of Tantric Buddhism, it is simply another illustration of the inescapable impermanence of life).

Mandalas can also be used in conjunction with texts. For example, in the *Tibetan Book of the Dead,* mandalas guide the soul to the afterlife and assist the surviving loved ones. The *Mahavairochana Sutra* is also important in Tantric Buddhism. It discusses the way of obtaining the wisdom of Buddha, and teaches that the cause of wisdom is the desire for Enlightenment, the foundation of wisdom is compassion, and the way to wisdom is skillful practice. This sutra teaches the student to look inward to obtain wisdom, and describes details of Tantric practice, such as rituals, gestures, mantras (magical formulas), and mandalas.

Beginning about the year 1000 CE, two centuries of devastating raids from Afghanistan destroyed many Buddhist monasteries, effectively ending the practice of Buddhism in India. By 1200, Indian Buddhism had come to an end. It continued in Tibet, however, and today, the Buddhism of Tibet, Nepal, Mongolia, and Bhutan, though unique and heavily Tantric, is substantially a preservation of Indian Mahayana tradition.

Although Buddhism did not survive in India, it sought converts more than other Eastern religions of its time and was the first major Eastern religion to spread beyond its land of origin. Buddhism entered China in the second century CE, but its adoption was not automatic. There were linguistic and philosophical differences to be overcome. This was during the era of Han-Confucianism, and Confucianism's emphasis on rituals differed from the Buddhist approach. Buddhism in China also had to reconcile with the Confucian view of family. Families were the bedrock of Chinese society, but a major tenet of Buddhism was that they should be looked upon with detachment. There was also potential incompatibility between the ideas of reincarnation and ancestor worship. If one believes in the former, how does one participate in the latter? Yet another reason that Buddhism was slow to catch on in China is that it was centered in monasteries, which were uncommon in China.

However, as we will see, Daoism was more similar to Buddhism than Confucianism was. Unlike Confucianism, Daoism advocated contemplation and withdrawal, held that reality was ultimately inexpressible, and believed that we cannot assume a simple cause and effect that may at first be apparent — all ideas that fit well with Buddhism. An additional characteristic of Daoism that facilitated the acceptance of Buddhism was its tenet that every situation brings unexpected results, quite often good, and that inaction is often the best action. Daoism was Buddhism's entry point into China. In fact, Dharma, the teaching of the Buddha, was translated as the *Dao,* the cosmic force that ensures stability. One of Daoism's influences on Buddhism was to make it more pragmatic and less abstruse. It also made Buddhism more concerned with nature and with natural ways of living. In addition, Daoism made Buddhism more amenable to sudden rather than gradual Enlightenment. Buddhism's emphasis on compassion and the social disruption at the end of the Han Dynasty also created opportunities for the religion.

Chinese Buddhism reached its height in the Tang Dynasty. Chinese Buddhism adhered to the Mahayana view that Samsara is Nirvana, and that Nirvana was not a distinct entity at the end of Samsara. In Chinese Buddhism, the Bodhisattva Kuan-yin (*Cannon* or *Kannon* in Japan) is an important Bodhisattva. Kuan-yin is often depicted as female, though she arose from the male celestial Bodhisattva Avalokiteshvara. One of the indigenous Buddhist schools that existed in Tang times was called *T'ien T'ai* (Heavenly Terrace; also called *Tiantai*), founded by Chih-i in the sixth century CE. Chih-i reconciled occasional discrepancies in Mahayana Buddhist literature by recognizing the Lotus Sutra as the most authoritative source. Another indigenous school was *Hua-Yen* (Flower Garland; also called *Huayan*), founded by Fa-Tsang. This school was not based on the Lotus Sutra, but rather on other Sutras. Hua-Yen favored a more sudden Enlightenment.

A third indigenous Chinese Buddhist school was *Ch'an* (Meditation). Ch'an is the only indigenous form of Buddhism to survive in China; the other schools were suppressed in the ninth century. The influence of Daoism is evident in Ch'an Buddhism. For example, paradoxes and a desire for direct person-to-person transmission are characteristics of Ch'an Buddhism that are traceable to Daoism. Ch'an would give rise to the Zen school in Japan. A dispute over leadership crisis in the Ch'an school is documented in the *Platform Sutra of the Sixth Patriarch,* the first extensive exposition of Zen Buddhism.

Buddhism entered Tibet in the seventh century CE in what is called the First Diffusion of the Dharma. This was about the time Tantrism was becoming integrated into Indian Buddhism, and the schools of Tibetan Buddhism are all substantially Tantric. The time of the First Diffusion was also when Tibet began to unify as a coherent political and military entity. According to tradition, the king of Tibet dreamed that Tibet rested on the back of a female demon and that Buddhism could not take hold in the country until this demon was restrained. Tibetans therefore built a series of temples around the country, each of which restrained a part of the demon's body. Finally, a temple that pinned down her heart was constructed in the center of Lhasa, the capital city. This temple, the *Jokhang,* is the most important Buddhist temple in Tibet. It is a site of pilgrimage and the site of one of the most famous statues of Buddha, the *Jobo Rinpoche.*

The First Diffusion came to an end about 836, traditionally from the anti-Buddhist practices of King Langdarma, after which Buddhism waned in Tibet. Buddhism was reintroduced in the eleventh century in the Later Diffusion of the Dharma.

Tibetan Buddhism used to be called Lamaism because of the centrality of the lama. There are four major schools of Tibetan Buddhism: *Nyingma, Kagyu, Sakya,* and *Geluk.* Only Nyingma predates the Later Diffusion. It considers itself the direct heir of *Padmasambhava* (c. 730–805 CE), a Tantric practitioner who helped build the first Tibetan monastery. The Nyingma School is substantially based on texts called *termas,* supposedly left by Padmasambhava himself. It is felt that not all such texts have been found, so the canon of Tibetan Nyingma Buddhism is not closed. Indeed, many of the historical leaders of the Nyingma School, such as Jigme Lingpa (1730–1798 CE), have supposedly found new termas.

The Kagyu School traces its origin to *Marpa,* a lama who lived in the eleventh century, and whose most famous disciple was Milarepa. The Sakya School emerged in the eleventh century under the leadership of Drogmi. When the Mongols invaded Tibet, many eventually converted to Buddhism, largely because of the influence of this school. The Geluk School emerged in the fourteenth century under Tsongkhapa (1357–1419). After the death of Tsongkhapa, leadership of this school passed to the lineage of the Dalai Lama, the incarnation of the celestial Bodhisattva Avalokiteshvara. Tenzin Gyatso, the current Dalai Lama (the title means "Ocean of Wisdom") is the fourteenth such leader of the Geluk School, the latest in a line of incarnations that goes back to the fourteenth century. One of the most important Dalai Lamas was the fifth, who lived in the seventeenth century. He built the Great Palace (also called the Potala Palace), which is a pilgrimage destination and was, until the Chinese invasion of Tibet in 1949, the residence of the Dalai Lama.

The current Dalai Lama has taught that we should all consider every person to have been our mother in a previous life. He also recommends putting yourself in the position of other people and letting yourself feel their anger toward you. He expresses gratitude to the Chinese for teaching him patience and allowing him to meditate on compassion. Few people living today offer us more than the Dalai Lama, and his great lesson — that we can look upon enemies as teachers — illustrates that Buddhism, like all religions, has much to teach us about wisdom, peace, acceptance, and dealing with anger and frustration.

Buddhism entered Japan in the sixth century CE. Just as Daoism was the entry point for Buddhism in China, so Shinto was the point of entry of the new religion in Japan. Shinto is the indigenous practice of spirit and nature worship in Japan. In Shinto, a deity is any entity outside of our normal experience that inspires awe or has power over us. These deities are known as *Kami*. The most important Kami is the Sun Goddess *Amaterasu*. However, ancestors and the emperor are also Shinto deities. After the introduction of Buddhism, the Bodhisattvas and Buddhas of Mahayana Buddhism and the Kamis of Shinto were often considered different manifestations of the same deities. Many practitioners of Shinto accepted Buddha as another Kami, while Mahayana Buddhists regarded their celestial Buddhas and Bodhisattvas as compatible with Shinto Kamis.

Buddhism actually entered Japan from Korea, but the influence was Chinese Buddhism. Prince Shotoku (573–621) provided a constitution for Japan that included elements of Buddhism and Confucianism. The emperor Shomu gave prominence to Buddhism during the Nara period (710–784), when it became the de facto religion of Japan. Shomu built a huge wooden temple, Todai-Ji, which contains a statue of Buddha called Dainichi.

At the end of the Nara period, the capital was moved to Kyoto, and the Heian period (794–1185) began. During this period, two important Buddhist schools arose in Japan. One was the *Shingon* School, founded by Kukai (also known as Kobo Daishi). The other was the *Tendai* School, founded by Saicho (also called Dengyo Daishi). The Tendai School was particularly influential in Japanese Buddhism. It is the Japanese version of the T'ien-T'ai School from China, which was founded by Chih-i and which stressed the Lotus Sutra. Kuya, a tenth-century member of the Tendai School, introduced elements of the Chinese Pure Land School, advocating the praise of the celestial Buddha Amitabha (called *Amida* in Japan).

In the Kamakura period (1192–1333), the capital shifted from Kyoto to Kamakura. The Kamakura period was a time of social unrest, during which the familiar Buddhist teachings seemed ineffective. This caused people to reconsider the little-remembered idea of the Degenerate Age of the Dharma, which held that people were becoming more corrupt. Honan (1133–1212) was a Pure Land Buddhist who split from the Tendai tradition and taught his followers simply to chant the name of Amida

Buddha, saying that the practice would supersede all previous Buddhist practices. This was a simple and attractive idea in a difficult period. Religions are vehicles of hope in all circumstances, but in particularly difficult times, religions are often simplified, or people focus on a part of a religion, to provide a single, simple act that miraculously cleanses the perceived evil.

Shinran was a follower of Honan. His version of Buddhism, *Jodo Shinshu,* was based on Pure Land, and is today the most popular form of Buddhism in Japan. It is also the form practiced in the United States by the Buddhist Churches of America.

Another reformer in the Kamakura period was Nichiren (1222–1281). Nichiren was trained in the Tendai School, but came to believe that the Lotus Sutra was the only means for salvation. Nichiren believed that Buddha himself had written it. The Mongols were menacing Japan at the time, and Nichiren preached that unless Japan converted to complete reverence for the Lotus Sutra, it would be swept away. He also cast himself as a prophet, maintaining that only he could point the way to Japan's salvation.

Japan also indirectly received Buddhism in the late sixteenth century, when it began to embrace Neo-Confucianism, a form of Confucianism originating in China and incorporating elements of Buddhism and Daoism.

Zen Buddhism arose in Kamakura Japan. Its origins are in Ch'an Buddhism of China and the meditative tradition of Indian Buddhism. Two of the people that gave Zen its start were Eisai (1141–1215) and Dogen (1200–1253). Eisai began in the Tendai tradition, but became disenchanted with it and traveled to China to study Ch'an. He returned a Master in the *Rinzai* tradition, a form of Zen Buddhism that believes in sudden Enlightenment. To achieve sudden Enlightenment, the Rinzai School emphasizes startling a student. *Koans* (or *Kong-ans),* which are riddles intended to elicit a sudden awakening regarding Emptiness, are the principal way of doing this, but a Rinzai master may even physically lash out at a disciple. Spontaneity prevents dwelling on previous thoughts or actions, and this is one of the purposes of the Koan. There is no one right answer to a koan — the answer is the moment of understanding that the Zen master wishes to convey.

Dogen too began his career as a practitioner of Tendai Buddhism and also went to China. When he returned, he established the *Soto* School of Zen Buddhism, which emphasized meditation and gradual Enlightenment. He differed with Eisai in thinking that koan practice too sharply contrasted Enlightenment and ordinary experience. Dogen believed that koans actually interfered with Enlightenment because they sent the practitioner down a pathway that was too esoteric. Rather, he emphasized the practice of *Zazen,* which is sitting meditation.

The Rinzai and Soto Schools use slightly different approaches to Zen, but the central point is that Zen believes that Enlightenment is all around us, and can be achieved by replacing the focus on the mundane with reflection and contemplation. The everyday world is not something that has to be avoided or escaped from through Nirvana, nor is Nirvana a state that can only be achieved in the far future. If we focus on the present moment with calmness and contemplation, we will see that Nirvana is this moment.

Zen postulates that Nirvana is right here, right now, right in the middle of mundane daily life, if we can see it. In Zen, an enlightened person might easily be found on any street. Zen teaches that Enlightenment is not an intellectual experience, to be understood from a text. Rationality is not a complete guide to life. Rather, the calm, contemplative mind grasps Enlightenment and opens the door to Nirvana. The enlightened person simply knows who he or she is and is at peace with himself. In simple terms, the gift of Zen is to enjoy life in the present moment.

The essence of the Zen is that all beings possess Buddha nature. This means that we do not need to strive to become Buddhas, but rather need to recognize that we already are. The extension of this is that we already have whatever it is that we desire. We do not need to acquire anything or to divest ourselves of anything to attain self-esteem, tranquillity, peace, and happiness. The only difference between Buddhas and us is that they have recognized their nature. As soon as we recognize ours, the process is complete.

Pursuant to its belief that Enlightenment is all around us and is made inapparent by the mundane affairs of daily life, Zen discourages talking. A Zen koan says, "Open mouth already a mistake." A Zen garden is a quiet place for meditation, but the maintenance of the garden is itself a form of meditation. The Zen emphasis on the present moment and on general tranquillity and understanding, rather than particular tasks, has made it influential in the arts. Much Chinese and Japanese art demands that the viewer contribute to the experience, so colors and details are often sparse. As an example of how Buddhism has influenced the arts, consider the comments of the Japanese philosopher Nishitani Keiji (1900–1990) about arranged flowers. He commented that the flowers appear from nothingness and float in emptiness. He also said that they change the space around them and interact with that space even if there is nothing in the space. The flowers appear to have abandoned all attachments. They are cut out and detached from everything, yet are part of everything. They communicate through silence. We can apply Keiji's comments to any work of art.

Zen is also evident in Japanese poetry. An example is the poems of Matsuo Basho (1644–1694), one of which is:

Old Pond,
Frog Jumps In,
Sound of Water.

A common interpretation is that the pond is the meditative mind, the frog represents something that facilitates Enlightenment, and the sound of water is a sudden Enlightenment. But as is always the case with works of art, multiple interpretations are possible. Is the sound of the water an Enlightenment made possible by the frog, or are the frog and the splash it makes distractions that must be set aside to return to a contemplative state that makes Enlightenment possible?

Thus the ideas of the Buddha have expanded over the centuries to become one of the world's greatest and most diverse religions. In Buddhism, the term *Sangha* (or *Samgha*) can refer to a congregation of at least four people with common views or to the Buddhist monastic community, but is more generally used by Buddhists to refer to all practitioners of Buddhism. Buddhists say that they take refuge in the Buddha, in his teachings (Dharma), and in the community of Buddhism (Sangha). Though Buddhism is still largely a religion of Asia, it has entered the West in increasing numbers, beginning with European colonialism.

We close our discussion of Buddhism with a portrait of a remarkable contemporary practitioner of that religion. Aung San Suu Kyi (b. 1945) was the daughter of the man who spearheaded the independence movement in Myanmar (formerly Burma) during and after World War II. She was living in Oxford in 1988 when she returned to Myanmar to visit her mother. Because she was a noted pro-democracy activist, she was placed under house arrest shortly after her return. Despite this, her party won a major victory in 1990, but the military nullified the election and imprisoned opposition leaders. Aung was eventually released from confinement, but her house arrest was reinstated in 2004 and extended in 2007. At this writing, she has spent ten of the past sixteen years in some form of detention, but has never been silent, and her simple but powerful words resonate around the world. In her speech *Freedom from Fear,* she says that it is not power that corrupts, but fear. People who have power are corrupted by the fear of losing it, and people who do not have power are corrupted by the fear of having that power used against them. She goes on to say that we must not let fear dictate our actions. Buddhists of all forms, and all of us, can be proud that one such as this still speaks with a strong and steady voice.

Chapter 6

SIKHISM

THERE ARE APPROXIMATELY 20 million Sikhs in the world today, making it the fifth largest religion, after Christianity, Islam, Hinduism, and Buddhism, with slightly more followers than Judaism. The word "Sikh" means "learner" or "disciple." Guru Nanak (1469–1539) was the founder of the Sikh tradition in the sixteenth century. He was a Sant (a Hindu who has chosen the Bhakti pathway of devotion to reach Moksha) living in a time of conflict between Hindus and Muslims. He rejected the strict dogma of Hinduism and Islam, and sought to return to the simple will of God by combining aspects of both religions: from Islam a discrete God who created everything and is separate from that creation; and from Hinduism the concept of Samsara until union with God. To him are attributed the words: "There is no Hindu or Muslim ... I shall follow the path of God." Sikhs believe that Guru Nanak received direct revelation from God.

Nanak was followed by nine additional gurus. The fifth guru, Arjun, compiled the *Adi Granth,* a collection of hymns of the first four gurus, in 1604. The Adi Granth (meaning "first book" in Punjabi) was the first Sikh holy book. It is also sometimes called the *Guru Granth Sahib,* but these terms are not synonymous because the Guru Granth Sahib is a more complete version of Sikh writings that includes the Adi Granth as well as compilations from the last five gurus.

The *Japji* (in Punjabi, *Jap* means to recite; the suffix "Ji" conveys a special respect), composed by Guru Nanak, appears at the beginning of the Guru Granth Sahib. The Japji (also called Japji Sahib), consists of an opening verse called the *Mul Mantra* (also spelled *Mool Mantra*), followed by thirty-eight hymns and a closing verse called a *Salok*. The Japji reverberates with the oneness, love, and generosity of God. These are the most reverent verses in Sikhism, and Sikhs recite them every morning.

The Mul Mantra is said to be the essence of Sikhism, and it is said that the rest of the Guru Granth Sahib is an elaboration of the Mul Mantra, which addresses the qualities of God and is the basic profession of faith in Sikhism. In English translation, this brief but infinitely complex passage is as follows:

One Universal Creator God, The Name Is Truth, Creative Being Personified, No Fear, No Hatred, Image Of The Timeless One, Beyond Birth, Self-Existent, By Guru's Grace.

Sikhs do not assign a gender to God and do not use a pronoun in the Mul Mantra. If we were to translate with a masculine pronoun, for clarity, the Mul Mantra might read something like this:

There is only one God. His name is truth. Present in all beings, Creator of everything, He is without fear or hate. He is timeless, beyond birth and death. Self-existent, He is known by the Guru's grace.

The following thirty-eight hymns of the Japji describe the way in which the follower can be transformed and become able to comprehend reality. One hymn says God "never stops giving, the takers get tired."

In the closing Salok of the Japji, the follower understands the need to perform good actions along with his or her increased understanding. The Japji allows the Sikh to understand something of God, receive His teachings, and use that understanding to behave righteously in the world.

The tenth guru, Gobind Singh (1666–1708), was particularly influential in Sikh history. Unlike his predecessors, Guru Gobind Singh did not appoint a successor. Rather, he let it be known that the Adi Granth would be his successor, and he added to it works from later authors, resulting in the final Sikh holy book, the Guru Granth Sahib (roughly translated as "the great book that guides"). A copy of the Guru Granth Sahib is in every *gurdwara* (Sikh temple). Sikhs also revere the poetry of Kabir (c. 1440–1518), as do Muslims and Hindus, and many of his poems appear in the Guru Granth Sahib.

Gobind Singh also founded the *Khalsa* ("pure") community in response to persecution against Sikhs, and initiated the Khalsa baptism ceremony still used today. The Khalsa is undertaken as part of a personal spiritual journey when the Sikh is ready. In the ceremony, five Khalsa Sikhs (who have completed the Khalsa) and the Guru Granth Sahib must be present. The initiate drinks *Amrit* (sugar water stirred with a dagger) and receives instructions, including not removing any body hair, refraining from alcohol, tobacco, and other intoxicants, not eating meat from an animal slaughtered in the Muslim manner, and not committing adultery. The initiate is required to follow the Khalsa Code of Conduct, part of which stipulates that men will adopt the surname *Singh* ("lion"), and women will adopt the surname *Kaur* ("princess"). Alternatively, they may use these designations as their middle names, followed by the surname "Khalsa" (recently, to avoid duplication of names, Sikhs will occasionally use Singh or Kaur as a middle name and the name of their village as a surname). Sikhs strive to learn Punjabi and to wear the physical symbols of a Khalsa at all times. These symbols are the five Ks. Men wear their hair and beard uncut (*Kesh,* symbolizing submission to God's will); they carry a comb (*Kangha*) in their hair; they wear short undergarments (*Kachh*); they carry a steel dagger or sword (*Kirpan*); and they wear a steel bracelet (*Kara,* symbolizing their bond to God and to the ten gurus). A turban is also characteristic. Sikhs who have undergone Khalsa are accepted into the Khalsa community. All Sikhs are expected to be Khalsa or to be working toward that achievement.

Sikhs respect other religions, but believe that their rituals allow the focus to drift toward ceremony. Sikhs reject most Hindu rituals such as fasting, obligatory vegetarianism, pilgrimages, yoga, forced celibacy, and the worship of images. Other than the Khalsa, ceremony and ritual in Sikhism is minimal. Sikhs believe in a single God, without gender or body, who predated creation, was distinctly responsible for all creation, and is not subject to Samsara. They do not accept the Hindu conception that God has multiple manifestations, nor do they recognize the divinity of the Vedas. Sikhs reject any manifestation of the caste system, and believe in the equality of women. There is no priesthood in Sikhism. Sikhs do not recognize the four stages of Hinduism and do not at any time in their lives renounce the world, as the last stage of Hinduism stipulates. Rather, they seek to be at peace with God in their everyday lives.

Five K's

The Kesh refers to uncut hair and beard, symbolizing submission to God's will. The Kachh are loose fitting undergarments originally intended to provide the wearer with freedom of movement during battle, as the early Sikh community had conflicts with Muslims. Today, it is worn for traditional purposes, to remind the practitioner of the sacrifices of the early Sikh community. In men, the Kachh may occasionally be worn as an outer garment. The Kirpan is a dagger or short sword and is also worn to remind the Sikh of early conflicts, not for use. The Kangha **is a comb serving to keep the hair orderly under the turban and is a symbol of cleanliness and orderliness. The Kara is a steel bracelet symbolizing the Sikh's bond to God and to the ten gurus.**

There are no avatars in Sikhism, but God is manifest in the Gurus and in the Guru Granth Sahib. Sikhs do not believe in a simple heaven or hell, but rather believe in rebirth. Freedom from rebirth and unification with God (called *Sachkhand* in Sikhism) can be obtained if the individual becomes enlightened. The sinner (*manmukh*) is characterized by the five vices: *Kam* (lust), *Krodh* (anger), *Lobh* (greed), *Moh* (worldly attachment), and *Ahankar* (pride). A person goes through five stages in moving from manmukh to *gurmukh* (devotee of the gurus).

Today, a Sikh is someone who believes in one god and the ten Gurus and their teachings, believes in the Guru Granth Sahib, has faith in the Amrit (the holy, sweetened water used in the Khalsa ceremony), and follows no other religion.

The *langar* is the serving of free vegetarian meals in the gurdwara and is a Sikh tradition. In the langar, food is prepared and eaten together in a sense of egalitarianism. This is a reflection of the Sikh desire for service, and reinforces the Sikh rejection of caste.

Every religion has a group of practitioners who seek to restore its lost purity. The *Singh Sabha* arose in the late nineteenth century and sought to purify Sikhism by a return to old ways. The Singh Sabha also sought to remove what they believed to be idolatry and superstition from Hinduism, and thus bring the two religions closer. In the 1920s, the Singh Sabha acquired a political agenda (ousting foreign powers) and became the *Akali* movement. The political party of Sikhs, called the *Akali Dal*, successfully campaigned for a Punjabi-speaking state (founded in 1966). Some Sikhs are separatists and seek an autonomous state to be called Khalistan. Friction in India between some Sikhs and some elements of the government came to a head in 1984, when the Golden Temple complex at Amritsar in Punjab was severely damaged during an attack by the Indian military. The Golden Temple, built by Arjun, is the most sacred site in Sikhdom. The temple, called the *Harimandir*, has four entrances, symbolizing its openness to people from all classes, in contrast to the single entrance of Hindu temples. Not since the Holocaust has a government so deliberately defiled a holy place, and arguably not since the destruction of the Second Jewish Temple has a single structure so central to a religion been so deliberately damaged.

Golden Temple

The Golden Temple, also called the *Harimandir* (or Harmandir; meaning "Temple of God"), is a complex at Amritsar in the Punjab. Built by Guru Arjun, it is the most sacred site in Sikhdom. The temple has four entrances, symbolizing its openness to people from all classes. In addition to the temple itself, the complex includes shrines and memorials. The Golden Temple is open to everyone, regardless of their religion.

Chapter 7

CHINESE RELIGIONS

The Shang dynasty (1600–1046 BCE) is the first documented period of Chinese history. Our two sources for this time are archeology and oracle bones. Oracle bones are tortoise shells or oxen shoulder blades in which a hole was made. The bone was then heated until it cracked. The pattern of cracks foretold the future, provided that interpretation was entrusted to a priest skilled in divination (and perhaps able to exercise some control in the pattern of the cracks). These bones are the earliest writing we have from China. Happily, we also have commentary on some oracle bones regarding what the question was, who did the interpretation, and what the answer was. In some cases we even have commentary as to whether the answer was correct or incorrect.

Oracle bones give us the names of multiple deities in Shang times, and we know that they believed in a supreme Deity called *Shang Ti* (also called *Ti* or *Shang Di*), but we know nothing about these deities. Excavations of Shang tombs have shown that when a ruler died his horses and even his servants were killed and interred with him. Based on this, we assume that there was a belief in an afterlife, at least for these rulers and their servants, but as far as we know, neither Shang Ti nor other gods took an interest in human affairs.

The *Zhou* (or *Chou)* dynasty overthrew the Shang and came to power about 1045 BCE. We have two primary sources of Zhou religious beliefs. These are the *Shih* (the Book of Songs) and the *Shu* (the Book of Documents). The *Shih* contains ritual hymns and legends about dynasties, and is an excellent source for daily life. Two documents in the *Shu,* called *Numerous Officers* and *Numerous Regions,* discuss the Mandate of Heaven, by which the supreme deity gave specific permission to the king to rule, but with the stipulation that the ruler and his advisors be virtuous and pious. The mandate is revoked if he does not comply, and in fact, dynastic changes generally involved a military uprising against a king who was perceived as not fulfilling the conditions of the mandate. We do not know the author or authors of the *Shih* or the *Shu,* but it is likely that at least the portion of the *Shu* dealing with the Mandate of Heaven was written by the Duke of Zhou while he was serving as regent. They were addressed to the incarcerated leaders of the Shang Dynasty to justify the uprising.

The supreme deity referred to in these documents seems to be a composite of Shang Ti and the Zhou supreme deity called *T'ien* (sometimes translated as "Heaven"). In all probability, the Duke of Zhou was attempting to combine deities so that no one would question his mandate. The important points are that the Mandate of Heaven suggests that by Zhou times, the gods took more interest in human affairs, and religion apparently required ethical behavior, which had not been the case in Shang times.

About 800 BCE, social unrest coincided with a severe drought, and the *Shih* gives us a number of songs that describe people's confusion, frustration, and sadness. Times of social unrest and apparently ineffective religious practices are opportunities for skepticism and new thinking, but at the same time, fear and uncertainty often lead to a reinforcement of traditional thought that many feel has not been faithfully followed. In difficult times, some will believe that a new approach is needed, while others feel that greater fidelity to the existing ideas is required. Tumult is indeed fertile ground for new ideas, but only for people who have the capacity to go beyond traditional thinking. Tumult separates those who are committed to tradition from those who have the capacity to escape it.

Let us take a moment to review some of the elements of Chinese philosophy from about 800 BCE, as this was the background for the Chinese religious beliefs we will encounter. Reincarnation was de-emphasized because of the history of ancestor worship. As was the case for all ancient peoples, sacrifices were part of Chinese history and religion. The deity (or, in the case of China, the ancestor spirit) was perceived to consume the essence of the sacrificed animal.

In contrast to other worldviews, the Chinese have accepted change as an integral and vital part of life. They neither fear nor deny change. Chinese philosophers made change their primary focus because they felt that change itself was the only constant. In essence, the universe is made of change. Moreover, they thought that change occurs by means of specific laws and patterns, an idea that did not occur in the West until the seventeenth century. The word "Dao" (or *Tao,* pronounced as if written "Dow") refers to a cosmic guiding force that ensures harmony in the flowing and changing world, and illuminates the pathway of peace and harmony. In the West, the Dao is often simplistically translated as "the way." We will consider the Dao in more detail shortly.

Chinese philosophy focuses on this world, not on some transcendent world to which we might aspire. In addition, Chinese philosophy differs from the West in its conception of the world. Whereas Westerners tend to think there is a single absolute reality, Chinese thinking rejects a fixed reality and holds that the reality as rendered by any given perspective is equally valid. The dragon is a symbol of this varying reality and is an image of a changing cosmos. It is awesome, yet benevolent. It is a composite creature, but it has a basic similarity to a snake, whose coiling movements and shedding of the skin represent constant change.

The *Ch'i* (or *Qi*) is the fundamental energy of the universe. The Chinese conceive of energy as flowing through all things, with the material form that we see being simply a momentary condensation of Ch'i. We are all condensations of the same energy, which flows between and among all of us. This is a fine way to conceive of the interrelatedness of all objects and creatures, and is another philosophical and religious expression of what is now a scientific fact — matter is a condensation of energy. Ch'i conveys life, but it also pervades inanimate objects. Ch'i flows into and through all matter, animate and inanimate, and there is no distinct division between life and non-life. Because there is no mind-matter duality to the Chinese, Ch'i is both material and spiritual. The closer we are to the primordial Ch'i, the more powerful, pure, and animate is our Ch'i. This is *light Ch'i.* The further we are from the primordial Ch'i, the less powerful our Ch'i is. This is *heavy Ch'i.* The Chinese perceive the universe as divided into Heaven, Earth, and Humanity. They believe that primordial or light Ch'i within people can restore the bonds not only among us, but also between Heaven and Earth. For this reason, Chinese folk medicine focuses on Ch'i and attempts to restore primordial Ch'i.

Analogies are important to Chinese thinking and are often employed in their instructive texts. Many of these texts contain seemingly unrelated vignettes. The reader is to interact with the text and to determine how the text, as an analogy, is applicable to him. An example is the *I Ching,* which consists of sixty-four hexagrams, each expressing a particular concept. The text is consulted by casting lots to determine which hexagram is appropriate. The questioner then uses his own judgment, and perhaps textual commentaries, to draw a specific conclusion from the concept illustrated by the chosen hexagram. By engaging the reader's imagination, books like the *I Ching* have a virtually infinite set of possibilities and applications. Another advantage of such books is that they can be consulted in a less dogmatic manner. Because multiple interpretations are possible, there is less chance that the text will become dogma and overwhelm individualism. The text expands, not constricts, the reader's thinking.

This is the context of Confucius and the early Daoists, and it is the background against which indigenous Chinese religions formed. We will now consider those religions in a traditional order, but it is important to note that most Chinese have never identified themselves with any single religion. China's history and geography have made it a giant melting pot for many religions. As we will see, a number of religions melded into a set of beliefs that most Chinese use in their daily lives.

The actual name of Confucius (c. 551–479 BCE) was *K'ung Ch'iu. K'ung Fu-tzu* ("master of the K'ung family") is a not completely accurate rendition of his name, but was Latinized into the name Confucius. Confucius lost his government job when he was about fifty years old. Unable to obtain another government post, he began to teach. Confucius was the first person we know of to have been a professional teacher in China. Prior to him, there were teachers for individual clans, but not for the general public. We do not know how many disciples Confucius actually had. There may have been as many as 3000, but only four are mentioned by name. He probably only had fifteen or twenty, and was undoubtedly quite frustrated at not having a larger following.

No one can understand the thinking of any person of the past without understanding the times in which he or she lived. To attempt to understand someone's thinking without understanding the world they saw is fruitless, yet it is a mistake made with astonishing frequency. Confucius lived in the time of political turmoil, but he knew of times past that had been more tranquil. He sought to bring the wisdom of the past into the present and make it applicable to his time and place, and his teachings should be considered in that light. Whereas Daoism, as we shall see, is concerned with a cosmic guiding force, and the Greek philosophers of Confucius' time pondered the workings of the universe, Confucianism attempted to restore social harmony by addressing immediate concerns: human experience, human relationships, and the social organization that governs them.

Confucius' ideas were not extraordinarily original, but in a less chaotic environment, he might have been more innovative. He had a novel interpretation of existing ideas; for example, Confucius taught that tradition and ritual should be rejuvenated, but this was because of the need to restore social harmony. He felt that nobility resulted from behavior and knowledge, not from birth. Confucius believed that in addition to proper behavior, knowledge of history and the classics was essential to becoming cultivated because these fields provided examples of appropriate behavior. Since proper behavior and knowledge were cultivated skills that could be mastered by anyone, anyone could enter the nobility. Confucius endorsed the prevailing feudal hierarchy, but advocated more equitable treatment of people within that framework, and espoused advancement based on merit, not birth status. As part of the necessary hierarchy, Confucius classified professions (soldiers were at the bottom, with farmers just above them).

Confucius taught along three lines: the conduct of individuals, family relations, and the conduct of rulers. The conduct of individuals should be governed by *Ren* (sometimes spelled *Jen*), which is humanity, or benevolence. According to Confucius' famous version of the Golden Rule, "Do not do unto others what you would not want them to do to you."

Confucius valued *Xiao,* filial piety. Like all of his teachings, filial piety was not a new idea. It was a long-standing and integral part of Chinese culture and popular religion, and China had long imposed severe penalties for failure to show parental respect. But Confucius was the first person to codify filial piety. Confucius' teaching went beyond the nuclear family to the extended family. It also involved obligations of parent to child because the family is where children learn the appropriate and virtuous behavior that they will need as adults.

Confucius spoke directly to leaders and rulers. He believed that they must set an example for moral behavior, after which morality would diffuse to the people. He likened the relationship between a ruler and his subjects to the hierarchy of the family, with reciprocating requirements on both sides. Confucius taught that leaders should rule out of *De* (or *Te*), which is moral force or uprightness. Confucius taught that those who governed with De would find that it actually augmented and maintained their power.

Confucianism is based on five classic works of Chinese literature: the *I Ching;* the *Shu Ching* (the earliest history of China); the *Shi Ching* (also called the *Book of Songs, Book of Odes,* or *The Classic of Poetry,* a collection of 305 ballads and songs); the *Chun Chiu* (a history of the province that Confucius lived in); and the *Li Chi* (or *Book of Rites,* a collection of ceremonies from the Zhou dynasty). A sixth work, the *Analects,* is a compilation of Confucius' sayings written by his followers after his death (many of these sayings were apparently answers to questions that we no longer have).

Confucius continued to believe in sacrifices, but he felt that they were primarily for the benefit of the people who performed them. He felt that proper behavior regarding other people was more important in reducing the strife of his time. Confucius taught that each person has a duty to preserve traditions and rituals because these impart a sense of commonality and strengthen the social order. He recognized that rituals provided a sense of belonging and community in the turbulent times in which he lived, that people can find harmony by adhering to certain time-tested behaviors, and that it was easier to control people through voluntary rituals than by coercion. This does not mean he lacked imagination or innovation. Not only might Confucius have been more innovative under more pacific circumstances, but he was also not as rigid as he is often perceived in the West. He allowed for the possibility that rituals can be changed in some situations and should be made appropriate for the given individual and situation.

Confucius also taught that rituals could benefit a person's personal life as much as his or her relationship with a god. The Chinese concept of *Li* originally referred simply to the proper performance of rituals. By the time of Confucius, Li was also understood to mean the performance of rituals not only in the proper way but also with the proper spirit, because it was realized that the god would not be truly propitiated unless a devoted follower performed the ritual with a glad heart. Confucius further reformulated Li so that it also encompassed making the performer of the ritual a better person. Confucius felt that if rituals were properly performed, the gods would be pleased, and the performer would become a better and more humane person.

Confucius' support of ritual raises the question of the importance of ritual in our own lives. We can develop a greater appreciation for the rituals of other times and places by understanding our own. Everything from putting on make-up in the morning to shaking hands with a stranger is a ritual that might be as foreign to other cultures or other times as theirs are to us. Whenever we see a ritual that seems strange or unnecessary, we must realize that the thought process being employed is surprisingly close to our own. Our differences concern the specifics of the rituals, not their extent, number, or social importance. We must look past the specifics and appreciate the commonalities. In our own time, while rituals may restrict innovation, they help many people find a sense of belonging. The prototypical example is the military, where rituals are central and the damage to individuality is considered an acceptable price for what is perceived to be social coherence, a sense of belonging, and increased collective ability.

Confucianism deals with personal virtue and practical issues of daily life and not at all with deities or life after death. Indeed, Confucius is reported to have denied knowledge of heaven or an afterlife. In a famous passage in the Analects, a man asked how he should serve God. Confucius replied, "You do not yet know how to serve men, how can you ask how to serve God?" Confucius was then asked about death or an afterlife and he replied, "You do not yet understand life or the living, how can you worry about the dead or an afterlife?" On another occasion he is said to have replied to a query about an afterlife: "I know nothing of such things." Confucius apparently believed in a supreme deity, but one that was removed from the affairs of humanity. It is a lesson of history that the first step in loosening the grip of religion is to view the deity or deities as authentic, but to accept that our conduct and our fate are in our own hands. Classical Greece and Enlightenment Deism are additional examples of this.

The absence of deities in Confucianism seems strange to the Westerner, because in the West, religion implies a deity. But if we define a religion, as we have done, as a set of beliefs concerning a higher reality, a greater truth, or an ultimate power that comforts us and helps us cope with the traumas and uncertainties of our lives, then a deity in the literal sense is not required. While this is a major difference from Hinduism and the Western religions that we shall examine subsequently, we have already seen that Theravada Buddhism is not dependent on deities. It is noteworthy that in ancient China, and in Buddhist countries, with no supreme being to dogmatically hold as the essential aspect of life, holy wars have been rare.

Like Buddha and Mahavira, Confucius made a difficult set of beliefs accessible to common people by having the courage and individualism to reinterpret traditional teaching for contemporary times. Confucius codified, preserved, and made it possible to teach the ethics that were an integral part of Chinese culture. He translated ethical thinking into a language that people could appreciate, integrate into their lives, and pass on to their children. Confucianism was much more practical than Daoism and much easier for the uneducated to understand. In a time of unrest, Confucius gave people a foundation and a sense of community. He restricted his message to what was immediately applicable to ordinary people in common situations.

As is always the case with influential thinkers, disciples took Confucius' teaching in different directions. Mencius (also written "Mengzi" or "Meng-tzu," c. 371–289 BCE) was a proponent of what is occasionally called the idealistic interpretation of Confucianism. Whereas Confucius, as far as we know, did not comment on human nature, Mencius taught that people are fundamentally good provided they experience a natural, wholesome development. Mencius embraced Confucianism, with its emphasis on humane behavior and filial respect, as the primary way to ensure this development. He focused on the inner person more than on external practice, and emphasized *Yi* (appropriate behavior in general) more than Li (appropriate behavior in rituals). Mencius' students recorded his teachings in a book called *The Mencius* (or *The Book of Mencius)*, a landmark work of Confucian philosophy that ensured its dominance in China. Today we know that the influences that shape a person's behavior and thinking are more complex than Mencius might have realized, but for all that is wrong in the world today, I believe his fundamental postulate that people are basically good and will behave admirably unless something has derailed their development is absolutely correct and is a pivotal concept in history.

Xunzi (c. 310–238 BCE) is sometimes referred to as a realistic or pessimistic interpreter of Confucianism. It would be wrong to interpret Xunzi as misanthropic, but he did not share Mencius' optimistic view of human nature. He was more sympathetic to rituals than Mencius because he thought that rituals could help people cope with adversity. Xunzi defended social structure, hierarchy, and even coercion as necessary means for the state to survive. Like Confucius, Xunzi thought that some hierarchy was necessary to avoid chaos, but also like Confucius, he thought that the hierarchy should be based on merit and not birth. Unlike Confucius, however, Xunzi favored abolishing hereditary titles as a means of insuring meritocracy. Xunzi had a more pessimistic view of human nature than Mencius did, but they had many similar views. Both believed that anyone could become wise, but both believed that cultivation is a prerequisite.

We have seen that the concept of the Dao, the cosmic guiding force that ensures harmony in the changing world, has a long meaning in Chinese religion and culture, and can roughly be thought of as "the Way," meaning the pathway to tranquillity, because one seeks to live in accord with the harmony of the universe. Every school of philosophy had its own conception of the Dao, but in the specific religion of Daoism (or Taoism), the Dao came to refer to the way of nature, the way that transcends human beliefs and opinions, the path of cosmic harmony to which human life should conform. The Dao flows from the universe and permeates all things, giving life to them and ensuring equanimity in a world that is never fixed. The Dao is not a personally benevolent force that intercedes in the lives of individuals, in the manner of the Judeo-Christian-Muslim God, but rather is an ultimate reality that infuses and enlivens all things, and ensures harmony without attempting to influence the universe or to place any conditions upon its provision of harmony. One does not pray to the Dao as one prays to the Judeo-Christian-Muslim God, nor does one make specific requests of it. By focusing on the Dao, and stressing passive submission to it, Daoism adopts a more global and far-reaching philosophy than Confucianism.

Daoism is traditionally credited to Lao-Tzu, said to have been born in 604 BCE. However, the major text of Daoism, the *Dao De Jing* (*The Way of Virtue;* also spelled *Tao Te Ching,* and sometimes called the *Laozi* or *Lao-tzu),* traditionally credited to Lao-Tzu, appears to have been written in the fourth century BCE. Moreover, there are linguistic differences within the text that suggest multiple authors working over a period perhaps as long as a century. In all probability, Lao-Tzu never lived, lived later than is thought, or was not the author of the principal book of Daoism.

The Dao De Jing is a very small text, consisting of only eighty-one verses. It is an ambiguous text, even without translation. Nowhere in it, for example, is the Dao defined. Indeed, the first words of the work are: "The Dao that can be described is not the universal Dao." Rather, the text is primarily concerned with the description of those who follow the Dao. It is only from the descriptions of its followers, and occasional oblique references, that we are able to learn of the Dao. Later verses tell us: "It preserves and nourishes all things, but it does not claim to be master over them," and "Being looked at, it is imperceptible. Being listened to, it is inaudible. Being utilized, it is inexhaustible." The writer or writers of the Dao De Jing undoubtedly intended to emphasize the mysterious, indefinable nature of the Dao, and sought to make it clear that there was no immediate pathway to understanding. To the extent that the Dao De Jing describes the Dao, it depicts it as undifferentiated, empty, and yet able to give rise to all things. In one verse, the Dao is depicted as analogous to a bellows, which is empty but can give rise to fire. Eventually, in reading the Dao De Jing, we work our way to an understanding that life is governed by an indescribable force that we can partake of by recognizing that the small frustrations in life are not worth either fighting over or being upset about. The Dao De Jing admonishes us not to have specific objectives and goals because these impede the flexibility that is necessary to accept the diversions and delays that nature has in store for us. It asks us to "act with no expectation of reward."

Another important text of Daoism is the *Zhuangzi* (or *Chuang-Tzu),* named for a master teacher of the religion. Whereas the Dao De Jing often very clearly addresses rulers and the ruling class, Zhuang Zi addressed the ordinary individual, and the book that bears his name makes virtually no mention of politics or government. The *Zhuangzi* tells us that the reason we have difficulty accepting disappointments in life is that we have preconceived notions about how things ought to be. These expectations prevent us from accepting change or unforeseen circumstances. To avoid these expectations, Zhuang Zi advocated meditation.

Reflecting Buddhist influence, the three attributes of existence in Daoism are suffering (*dukkha*), impermanence (*anicca*), and no-self (*anatta*). Daoism recommends a moment-to-moment awareness of and response to the world, and holds that a rigid agenda prevents this. Without flexibility and the willingness to give up some unimportant objectives, we will find ourselves in opposition to the world. Reasonable goals are appropriate, but a rigid idea of how things "should" be denies us tranquillity and harmony. We should neither be startled at unexpected events nor use force to try to avoid or change them (in the West, somewhat similar thinking became part of Greco-Roman stoicism). Daoism also recommends shrugging off small problems in order to concentrate on larger ones. Daoism encourages relinquishing control of trivial daily events in order to gain control of one's life, and suggests that we have more power and energy if we avoid small battles. Daoist philosophy enables one to concentrate on the important matters in the present moment. An example would be a person who perseveres in his passion, maintaining an overall vision without getting distracted or angered by small details.

Wu-Wei is the Daoist term for inaction, or to speak more correctly, it is the Daoist term for the very active and difficult action of giving up control and taking no action when we are tempted to act. Daoism recommends Wu-Wei in times of distress, and the concept is implicit in practically every verse of the Dao De Jing. The Daoist assumes a non-aggressive posture, preferring to cede control, knowing that control is a short-term victory that results in long-term failure of harmony. Likewise, Daoism believes that seeking fame and material possessions is a short-term achievement that is detrimental to long-term happiness. Daoists eschew self-aggrandizement and freely allow others to receive credit for accomplishments. Consider these passages from the Dao De Jing:

The best of all rulers is but a shadowy presence to his subjects. When his task is accomplished and his work done, the people all say it happened to us naturally.
It is because a sage never attempts to become great that he succeeds in becoming great.
He who conquers others is physically strong. He who conquers himself is mighty.

One of the great pleasures of any study of the human experience is that unexpected lessons constantly emerge that have great implications for our daily lives. In today's terms of management and business, Daoists were perhaps the first people to realize that if the right people are in the right job, micromanaging and self-promotion are unnecessary.

The wisdom of the Dao is particularly important for the Westerner because we in the West are taught from an early age to compete, to dominate, and to intervene so that we can win and make someone else lose. The Dao teaches us that it is better to be passive, that true victory comes in the long term from less action.

The Dao De Jing teaches that there are three treasures in life — kindness, frugality, and absence of a need to dominate. Daoism teaches that our lives unfold as they should, even when it appears that we have encountered a great obstacle. Every diversion and every apparent setback is an opportunity to increase our knowledge and our experience of life. Setbacks conceal moments of opportunity that will become known to us if we accept the situation. As an analogy, imagine a river following a circuitous course. The direction of the water's flow must change to accommodate the banks of the river, but eventually the water will reach its destination, accomplishing its purpose despite the innumerable obstacles and redirections it encountered throughout its flow.

The modern expressions "blessing in disguise" and "go with the flow" are the Westerner's tangential experience of Daoism. We are part of the world; we blend in with the world and cannot expect to dominate it. Because of this, we cannot expect to get everything that we want. The ebb and flow of the universe — a much more powerful entity than ourselves — forces us to improvise. Daoism asks us not to force issues, even if they seem urgent. Wait for things to fall into place, or at least postpone action until it is completely clear that action cannot be avoided. Likewise, one must minimize one's expectations of others. Beyond a reasonable defense of yourself, recognize that others have their own ideas of behavior and morality. In Daoism, there is a great deal of improvisation, acceptance, and just going along for the ride in life. This acceptance of fate is seen in Daoist art, where people are depicted as a small part of nature.

The Red Cliff

This painting, *The Red Cliff*, painted by Wu YuanZhi in the 12th century CE, is an example of Daoist art. It depicts humans, seen here as a small group in a boat in the foreground, as inconspicuous against the vastness of nature. Nature is shown as peaceful and benign, but its magnitude dwarfs that of the people who pass by the cliff.

Ziran is a term employed by Daoists to indicate naturalness and spontaneity of behavior. Ziran implies that we are at our happiest when we "go with the flow." Ziran holds that life is bigger than any of us and gives all of us a ride that we should sit back and enjoy as much as possible. To Daoists, life is not a taxi ride, where we are the only passenger and get to determine precisely where we go and by what route. Life is a bus ride: someone else often drives, and the route is filled with detours and unscheduled stops for the benefit of other people. An integral part of Daoism is to accept delays and setbacks, large or small, because we are part of a greater whole that is beyond our control. Impatience, domination, and oversimplification are all around us in the West, but if we try to dominate or to force changes at specific times, we do battle with the universe itself.

Tolerating ignorance, both in others and in ourselves, is a major part of accepting setbacks and living in harmony. Our harmony is most sorely tested when we find others who do not agree with our philosophy or beliefs, and it is precisely in these situations that insight into other religions and philosophies is most needed.

Daoists felt that the Confucian emphasis on human relationships and behavior served to alienate humanity from nature and divert attention from living in harmony with nature to hierarchies and interactions among people. Yes, people should behave civilly toward each other, but must at the same time not lose sight of the fact that we are all part of a universe that is unfolding as it should and is taking us on a journey to which we should not object. Daoism did not develop as a modification of Confucianism in the same way that Christianity and Buddhism began as modifications of Judaism and Hinduism respectively. The basic tenets of Daoism were similar to those of Confucianism and preceded its rise, but it is probable that many aspects of Daoism developed as a specific reaction to and refutation of Confucianism. Indeed, the Dao De Jing seems to have been written after Confucian philosophy was formulated, and was probably in large part a specific disagreement with it.

On morality, Daoism disagrees with Confucianism about the importance of rituals and the need for stringent standards of behavior. Of course, common sense and courtesy are expected, but elaborate ethical codes are neither necessary nor desirable for a number of reasons. First, Daoists thought that such standards could not be universally agreed upon. Second, they thought that people who failed to meet such standards would lose self-esteem. Third, standards lead to hypocrisy because people will claim to meet them even when they know they do not. Fourth, standards will cause people to seek to impress others, and many immoral acts stem from self-aggrandizement or a desire to impress others. Likewise, even allowing for the beneficial aspects of rituals, and for the Confucian idea that these should be used appropriately, Daoists regard rituals as artificial constructions that obscure optimal human interaction, emphasize insignificant details, and provide an opportunity for insincere people to appear proper.

While fully agreeing with the primacy of the family and reverence for ancestors, Daoism decreased the Confucian emphasis on filial piety and ancestor worship. Whereas Confucianism sought to reform feudalism, Daoism advocated its abolition, believing that people could never reach their potential in a feudal society.

Confucianism values social harmony, which is one reason why it has been so widely adopted in government circles. The Confucian ideal of having an appropriate person for a given position has also figured heavily in Chinese government. Daoists interpret this situation differently. They believe that a great deal of effort is wasted attempting to attain social positions or government offices. Daoists agree with the need for social order and appropriate positioning of individuals, but they believe that the net effect of the Confucian emphasis on these requirements is artificial behavior, social climbing, and misplaced priorities. Daoists deplore attempts to curry favor, "fit in," or conform, or behave in a manner that is not natural. Daoists believe that our true inner nature should shine forth, that we should blend in with nature — in essence be one with the universe — rather than trying to blend in with other people. They believe that the natural spirit of people, if not obstructed or modified, blends well with the spirit of the cosmos. Daoism believes in spontaneity and that people's impulses can be trusted. The Dao De Jing implies that people are inherently good and can exercise good judgment.

Daoism and Confucianism are clearly opposed in their ideas on rituals, feudalism, ancestor worship, and the importance of social harmony, but they have many similarities. Both reflect the great Chinese desire for harmony rather than dominance (a great contrast to the West). They are therefore best viewed as complementary, and throughout Chinese history many people have tried to be faithful to both doctrines.

When we think of Daoism, we are generally thinking of its philosophical aspects. The Dao De Jing and the *Zhuangzi* are primarily concerned with philosophy. While some people feel that these texts obliquely allude to an afterlife, there is no consensus that they do, and certainly it is not a major part of these works. In practice, many Daoists have removed deities from their religion, but there are religious aspects of Daoism that until recently were relatively neglected in the West. Daoist religion apparently started about 150 CE, well after the philosophical portion, and is not attributed to Lao-Tzu. As was the case with Buddhism, deities came only after the philosophy was well established. There was never any central governing body in Daoist religion, but rather six or seven main sects. One of these is called the Heavenly Master (also called Celestial Master sect or the Five Pecks of Rice sect), founded around 150 CE by Chang Tao-Ling. Another sect was *Mao-shan* (also known as the Supreme

Purity sect or the *Shang-ch'ing* sect), founded in 360 CE by Yang Hsi. The Mao-shan sect, which was important in Tang China (618–907 CE), believes that the Dao is incarnated in the form of three deities called the Three Heavenly Worthies.

These sects have slightly different beliefs, but taken as a whole, they allow for an afterlife, both good and bad, punishment of sinners, anthropomorphic deities, etc. During its development, Daoist religion was clearly influenced by Buddhism. Some later Daoist sects provided for reincarnation, an almost certain Buddhist inspiration. Though Daoist philosophy is ambiguous with regard to immortality, this is clearly a goal of Daoist religion, in which moral behavior, not simply adherence to a set of beliefs, is required for immortality. In Daoist religion, there is a small portion of the Dao in each person. In addition, there are many deities within each person. Meat and wine revolt these deities and are therefore forbidden. Breathing exercises were thought to purify the body, and elixirs consisting of such materials as gold and mercury were taken, on the advice of deities, to assure immortality.

As we have seen, Confucianism and Daoism are not necessarily mutually exclusive in daily life, and many Chinese have been faithful to both religions. In addition, many also subscribe to Buddhist principles, which sit comfortably beside those of Confucianism and Daoism. Superimposed on the formal religions that have blended in Chinese culture — Confucianism, Daoism, and Buddhism — are less formal traditional beliefs concerning ancestors and their spirits, and long-established gods. These traditional beliefs are called Folk (or popular) religion. As Folk religion blended with the formal religions, the result was a set of beliefs that was syncretic or additive. With rare exceptions, such as priests of a particular religion, most Chinese have never identified themselves with a single religion, but rather adhere to a syncretizing set of beliefs. The simultaneous practice of more than one religion in China is difficult for the Westerner to understand because Western religions tend to be mutually exclusive.

Chinese Folk religion, which has no formal name or organization, has three components: gods, ancestors, and ghosts. There are hundreds of deities. Some are Buddhist figures, but many were actual people who have been deified. Many of these deities are local, and not even known to other Chinese, as these revered individuals once inhabited a particular area, and in a culture imbued with ancestor worship, it is only a small step from the veneration of an ancestor by his descendants to his deification throughout the area. Examples are Kuan-kung, a military commander who died about 220 CE, and Ma-tsu, a girl who lived in the tenth century. Ma-tsu is perhaps the most important single deity in Chinese Folk religion. She is called "the Empress" (or "the Empress of Heaven"). Folk deities are worshipped more if the deity grants requests, and practitioners of Folk religion, in contrast to other religions, have no reservations about turning away from a particular deity if their requests are denied.

Reflecting the influence of Confucianism, some deities in Folk religion are thought of as bureaucratic (or administrative) gods that correspond to each level of earthly authority. For example, there is a bureaucratic god for the home, one for the village, one for the province, etc. These gods have a hierarchy and report periodically to their superior gods. This continues all the way up to the supreme god *Shang Ti* (often called *Yu-huang Shang-Ti* or Jade Emperor), the heavenly counterpart of the earthly emperor. Bureaucratic gods can be demoted, and may even be sent back to be people if they have done a poor job. Communication with these many deities is possible, and divination and shamanism are part of Chinese Folk religion.

Ancestors are also an expected component, given the long history of ancestor worship. Whereas ghosts are always vindictive and spiteful, ancestors are usually benevolent and look out for their descendants. If a descendant is particularly lacking in merit, an ancestor may cause some trouble for that person, but not for anyone else.

Biological ancestry does not guarantee cultural ancestry. To be regarded as a proper ancestor, one must have the clan surname and must have made some contribution to the clan, either to its welfare or by having children. This means that deceased minor children are not considered ancestors. The soul tablet verifies that a person was a true ancestor. Traditionally, unmarried women are not considered ancestors and have no soul tablets. In practice, parents may make a soul tablet for a deceased unmarried daughter, but it cannot be displayed in the usual places, such as the ancestor hall or the altar. The rationale is that women contribute to *other* clans by bearing children in those clans, and an unmarried woman has not contributed to *any* clan. It is also possible to arrange a posthumous marriage for this daughter, in which case she can avoid becoming a ghost, and a soul tablet can be made for her; however, it would be made and cared for by the family into which she posthumously married.

To appreciate ghosts, the third aspect of Chinese Folk religion, we must first understand how this religion interprets the soul. Chinese Folk religion believes in two souls. There is a physical soul (*p'o*) that lives with the body in the grave. The p'o has a finite lifetime and will eventually disappear. The spiritual soul (*hun*) will be reborn if conditions are acceptable. This doctrine of two souls, only one of which can be reborn, is a remarkable reconciliation of the otherwise mutually exclusive beliefs in ancestor worship and reincarnation. Practitioners of Folk religion believe that graves must be properly located and positioned. This is the art of geomancy, and is practiced by geomancers. The festival *Ch'ing-ming-chieh* is held in the spring of every year at gravesites and is a time for cleaning ancestors' graves.

Upon death, the hun soul is escorted by the local bureaucratic deity to the local celestial temple, and from there to the Underworld by that deity or his representative. The journey to the Underworld is difficult, and the soul will be lost if it travels alone. Lost souls cannot participate in rebirth and therefore become ghosts. For this reason, there is a ceremony after death in which a priest (Buddhist or Daoist) symbolically conducts the soul to the Underworld. In a parallel with Greek mythology, the last step in reaching the Underworld is the crossing of a river.

With the exception of a few people who will become gods, and another rare group who have lived righteously and will be met by Amitabha and escorted to the Pure Land, all hun souls spend time in the Underworld, a place identical to this world, including perfect replication of individual towns and street plans. People who go to the Underworld retain their identity and usually their profession. The only significant difference is that the Underworld is dark.

Forty-nine days after death, the possessions of the deceased are symbolically sent to the Underworld. Paper models of the possessions, from houses to television sets, are burned — the means of transfer to the Underworld. There is even a specific currency for this purpose, the "Hell Bank Note." Tribute continues in the form of a soul tablet, on which is a picture of the deceased. These tablets are kept in prominent places, and in front of the tablets, food offerings are made to the deceased. Special meals that the deceased enjoyed are put out on the anniversary of the death.

In the Underworld, the hun soul goes through a series of ten courts.

The first of these verifies that the date of death was the intended death date for the person. Courts two through nine then judge worthiness. Each court has an area of specialization and will interrogate a new soul about a specific area of behavior. If the soul passes the second court, it goes to the third, and so on. If any court finds evidence of wrongdoing, the soul is sent to one of the sixteen prisons and does not go on to the next court until it has been sufficiently punished. A soul may remain in these prisons for thousands of years and be subjected to repeated, terrible punishment that is commensurate with its crime. We are reminded of hell as envisioned by Dante in *The Inferno.* But whereas there is no escape from the Christian hell, in Folk religion, hun souls eventually make it through the court system and, after serving their sentences, are reborn, making the process more like the Christian purgatory than hell. The tenth and final court determines what the soul will be in its next life. Bad people may be reborn as animals, but good people have the opportunity to be reborn into a better situation than they had. In Folk religion, twenty-seven months is considered the minimum time that a soul must spend in the Underworld before rebirth. (This minimum period is only forty-nine days in Buddhism, hence the transfer of paper representations after this time).

Most ghosts are hun souls that are not properly cared for and have not settled in the Underworld. It may be that no ritual was performed to ensure their passage there, or perhaps no soul tablet was made for them. Because of this, dying without children is problematic, because children ensure their parents' safe passage into the Underworld. It is preferred that sons, not daughters, make the soul tablet, though daughters are not prohibited from doing so. One solution for childless people is to adopt the son of a relative.

A smaller category of ghosts results from those who suffer untimely and unnatural deaths. The feeling is that the souls of murder or accident victims are eligible for rebirth, but are too angry to pursue this. People who have committed suicide are ineligible for rebirth because by ending their own lives they have usurped authority. These souls are consigned to a special city across the river from the Underworld. Another problematic group is people who die away from home, where proper rituals and burials cannot be performed. Many of the people who are considered likely to become ghosts are outcasts. This is somewhat similar to people who were suspected of being witches in the Middle Ages. It is a tragic lesson of history that society's fears and paranoia, both in regard to the here and now and to the afterlife, will always be centered around those who are stigmatized.

Ghosts wander aimlessly, hungry and angry. They may work individually or in groups, but always cause trouble, ranging from a minor nuisance to possession (requiring exorcism), and perhaps even the death of the targeted person. Ghosts can often be appeased by leaving food for them. There is even an annual festival in which villages put out large quantities of food. A posthumous soul tablet made for a neglected soul may also be effective.

Most aspects of Folk religion — certainly anything pertaining to ghosts or ancestors — are officially banned in China because authorities want to discourage any form of superstition. But Folk religious beliefs persist, and some form of Folk religion has always been the backbone of religious belief in China.

Though Chinese Folk religion uses Buddhist and Daoist priests, it has its own informal "clergy." Certain individuals, called ritual masters or redheaded priests, are skilled in the performance of certain rituals. Shamans and spirit mediums are able to communicate with the dead. Unlike ritual masters, spirit mediums go into trances.

We close our discussion of Chinese religious thought with a brief consideration of *Yin* and *Yang,* a concept that few Westerners fully comprehend. The concept was developed between about 250 BCE and 200 BCE, after the advent of Daoism. Yin and Yang are part of the Dao, but they do not figure as prominently in Daoism as many Westerners believe. Indeed, Yin and Yang are equally important in Confucianism and Folk religion.

Yin and Yang represent the changing nature of reality and the merging of apparent opposites. Yang is energetic, active, hot, and masculine; Yin is cool, inert, passive, and feminine. Yang is associated with life and Yin with death. The two are conceived of as forces that waft and wane, and in so doing affect all living things. In another remarkable parallel with contemporary science, the Chinese believe that opposites are artifacts of perception. Moreover, opposites are constantly *becoming* each other as reality changes. The major features of our lives at any given moment are likely to be inconspicuous features later, and vice versa. What we perceive to be beneficial may become deleterious, and vice versa..

Yin and Yang

Yin and Yang are important in all Chinese religions. Yang is energetic and active, associated with life, while Yin is cool and passive, associated with death. This familiar Yin and Yang diagram is called the *Taijitu*. The *Taijitu* merges black and white areas into each other, with each area containing a dot of the other. Its curved outline illustrates that Yin and Yang are not the opposites they might at first appear to be, but actually give rise to each other. The small dots within each element reinforce the concept that there are no pure opposites. Beyond Yin and Yang, per se, the larger point of the Taijitu is that there are no opposites in nature and that change and constancy coexist.

The familiar Yin and Yang diagram (the *Taijitu*) shows black and white areas appearing to merge into each other. Each contains a dot of the other color. The curved nature of the two elements indicates that each constantly gives rise to the other. Yin gives rise to Yang which gives rise to Yin. The small dots within each element illustrate that there are no pure opposites. The Taijitu perfectly symbolizes the Chinese belief that change and constancy coexist and that there are no absolute opposites. It is a wonderful example of how images can express philosophical ideasYin and Yang also have associations with numbers, time, elements, seasons, and direction. All even numbers are Yin; important Yin numbers are two and six. All odd numbers are Yang; important Yang numbers are three and nine. The Yang part of the day is the morning, the time of greatest freshness and productivity, after which Yin begins to take over. There is still some Yang influence in the afternoon and early evening, but the night belongs to Yin. Yang begins to coexist with Yin as dawn approaches. Notice the gradual transitions between Yang and Yin during the twenty-four-hour day. Likewise, Yin and Yang gradually turn into each other during the progression of the seasons. Yang begins to exert its influence in the springtime and reaches a maximum at the summer solstice, when the world is full of life. It then begins to wane and Yin begins to take over. Yin reaches its peak at the winter solstice, bringing with it the loss of life, at which time Yang begins to rise.

The five elements are wood, fire, earth, metal, and water. Each of these is associated with a direction (the center is a fifth direction). The elements also have seasonal associations. Wood is associated with spring, and yields to the fire of summer. Earth becomes discernible in late summer and is a bridge to autumn, which is associated with metal. Water is associated with winter. Each of the elements also has its own color. Putting all of these associations together gives us a sense of Chinese religious cosmology (i.e., the philosophical and religious explanation of the universe). The north, winter, water, and black are associated with each other at the peak of Yin. As Yang rises, we move into the east, which is associated with spring, wood, and green. At the peak of Yang, we have the south, summer, fire, and red, after which Yin begins to rise. Metal and the continued ascent of Yin characterize autumn.

Religious cosmology figures prominently in Chinese architecture, particularly in the design and construction of the imperial palace (the

Forbidden City). When Beijing was designed during the Ming Dynasty, the Forbidden City was placed in the center because this is the locus of power. It is from the center that Earth communicates with Heaven and with the Underworld. Control and harmony come much more easily from the center. Buildings in the Forbidden City are red and yellow because red is associated with Yang, indicating the gender and vitality of the emperor, while yellow is associated with the central direction, which is the direction of power. The old walls of Beijing (now destroyed) had three gates on all sides except the north, which had only two, so that it would be more difficult for Yin to enter.

The emperor entered and left the Forbidden City through the south gate (Yang) while the empress entered and left through the north gate (Yin). Beijing's one hill was constructed north of the Forbidden City to protect it from Yin. Every building in the Forbidden City faces south — as do many other buildings in China — so as to receive energy and life, and away from the death and coldness of Yin. Also, the Jade Emperor lives in the pole star and therefore faces south.

In the Forbidden City, there are two sets of three buildings each, forming a southern and a northern complex. The southern complex consists of the buildings of government (the southernmost of which was the Hall of Supreme Harmony, the Imperial throne room). The buildings of the northern complex were residences, less important structures where no vital decisions were made. The emperor worshipped at a second complex called the Temple of Heaven, located in the southern part of contemporary Beijing (in ancient times, the Temple of Heaven would have been outside the city's southern wall).

India and China have given us astonishing cultural, philosophical, and religious diversity. We now turn to the Western heritage.

Chapter 8

JUDAISM

With Judaism, we move into Western religions, which reflect the dichotomous, black-and-white thought processes that we see in such areas as domination of nature, linearity of time, absolute reality, and the separation of the material and the spiritual. Exploring the religions of the West, we notice how much more simplistic doctrines tend to be. Even complex concepts, such as the Christian Trinity, are intricate elaborations of what is fundamentally a simple notion. This thinking is also found in the Western concept of right and wrong and our approach to social problems. I believe it is a lesson of history that dichotomous thinking is comfortable because it is simple, easy to understand, and perceived as effective. People want to believe that they understand, and they want to reach this belief as soon as possible. Western thinking has been a triumph and a tragedy. It has permitted wondrous technological advances, but it has also deprived us of much of the tranquillity of the East and of traditional societies. We are beginning to learn that the comfort of absolute reality and absolute right and wrong may be illusory.

Let us begin our discussion of Western religions with Judaism, the religion of about 17 million people, and is the foundational belief system for Christianity and Islam. Understanding Judaism must begin with recognizing that unlike other religions Judaism centers on a unique and historically identifiable people, and is both a culture and a religion. For this reason, one can be a Jew without believing in a deity. This is impossible in Islam or Christianity. At the same time, however, Judaism is the only major religion that throughout most of its history has not had a country or political unit specifically or primarily devoted to its practice. Judaism has been a religion *in* every place, but *of* no place. The Jewish history is one of being a minority struggling to maintain cultural identity in the face of opposition and oppression.

The first Jews are more properly called Hebrews. It is often said that the Hebrews are perhaps the most politically insignificant, and most culturally significant, nation in all of history. The legacy of Judaism is frequently summarized as *ethical monotheism.* Judaism simultaneously developed new ways of thinking about both our relationship to each other and to a deity, and both of these legacies came slowly and painfully. All religions — including Judaism — began as a belief in multiple deities, often with a chief or principal god. The Egyptian Pharaoh Akhenaton (or Ikhnaton) is said to have experimented with monotheism, but the Western formulation of this concept was a Jewish contribution. Likewise, all religions have a code of conduct, but the Hebrew code became the basis for Western civilization.

No other cultural unit has left us such a complete and influential record of their history as the Hebrews. To understand Judaism, we must begin with an understanding of what Christian society calls the Old Testament (reflecting the fact that they also recognize a New Testament). Because Jews do not recognize a New Testament, the Old Testament is the entirety of their Bible, which they call the *Tanakh* (or *Tanach*). The Tanakh is a remarkable chronicle of the Hebrews and their adoption of both monotheism and the code of ethics that we still live by today. The record of history, in all its forms — — visual, auditory, and literary — gives people a view of the past that guides them in the present. This is truer of the Tanakh than of any other Western literary work, making it the most important guide for the past and present lives of Westerners, and the most influential book in the Western world.

The Tanakh is similar to the Catholic and Orthodox versions of the Old Testament, and nearly identical to the Protestant Old Testament, but is arranged differently. Part of the oral tradition of the Tanakh dates to the Bronze Age, perhaps about 1200 BCE, but the earliest written portions date to perhaps 900 BCE (some would say 750 BCE). Chapter and verse headings were added in the Middle Ages. Almost all of the Tanakh is written in Hebrew, with a small portion in Aramaic. No one knows where, when, or by whom the canon of the Tanakh was assembled, but it consists of three divisions, called the Torah (or Pentateuch), *Nevi'im* (or *Neviim*), and *Ketuvim* (the word "Tanakh" is an acronym of these three divisions). The Torah consists of the books of Genesis, Exodus, Leviticus, Numbers, and Deuteronomy. Traditionally, the Torah is held to be the direct word of God, as transmitted through Moses, and therefore divine. The remainder of the Tanakh is divinely inspired, but the work of people. The Nevi'im portion of the Tanakh follows the Torah and is virtually identical to the Christian prophets, except that the Christian version of Daniel has some text not accepted by Jews (Daniel is a prophet to Christians, but not to Jews). The books of the prophets attempt to communicate divine will to people. The Ketuvim (also called *Writings*) is the third part of the Hebrew Bible and consists of what is commonly called wisdom literature, meaning practical advice on living a righteous life. The books of the Ketuvim are Psalms, Proverbs, Job, Song of Songs, Ruth, Lamentations, Ecclesiastes, Esther, Daniel, Ezra, Nehemiah, and Chronicles. The Tanakh ends with Second Chronicles (in which Cyrus frees the Jews), whereas the Christian Old Testament ends with the minor prophet Malachi.

The Tanakh is among the oldest works of prose literature in the West and is also among the first writings to depict everyday life. Indeed, the Tanakh is a masterpiece of literature precisely because its characters are ordinary people whose attempt to deal with their frailties forms the very basis of the work. The translations of the Tanakh have lost some of the nuances and subtleties and have presented us with a more formal work, but many of the original passages actually used much more common language.

Much of the writing in the Tanakh is simple narrative or uncomplicated wisdom literature. Much of the remainder is in the form of literary conventions that were in use at the time of its writing. One of these is the folk tale, a literary form employed by almost all cultures. It usually involves a hero, who, with his acolytes, is separated from his homeland, usually on an expedition of great importance. There is an enemy or obstacle that is overcome by courage, strength, and adherence to the values of the culture that created the folk tale. It is similar to the epic, a longer literary form that also centers on the exploits of a hero.

There are other literary conventions in the Tanakh, called type scenes, which deal with common themes and plots of the day, just as modern sitcoms, "whodunit" mysteries, and horror movies employ common motifs and techniques. These are more difficult for us to recognize today, however, just as people of the future will have difficulty recognizing the predictable settings and plot for many of our literary works and television shows. These types of scenes may be parodies on literary conventions that are no longer in use, and might even have been humorous to the people of the time. Because of the modifications of previous religious and literary works, the application of folklore, and the use of type scenes, the Tanakh is a rich and original adaptation of existing material and motifs, modified by and for the early Jews.

As intriguing as it would be if a single person named Moses really did write the Torah, he probably did not. Differences in writing style, differing names for God, varying context, and numerous repetitions (and contradictions) strongly suggest that no single person wrote it. There were probably four Torah authors. The hypothesis of four sources, called "J," "E," "D," and "P," is called the Documentary Hypothesis, or the Graf-Wellhausen Hypothesis. According to this hypothesis, the earliest portion of Genesis (chapters 2 and 3), in which God is called *YHWH* (the Tetragrammaton, written as *Yahweh)* was written by an author named "J" (after the German sound for "Y"), perhaps in the tenth century BCE. "J" probably wrote most of Genesis. "E" is close to "J" in time and content, but refers to God as *Elohim* (hence his designation as the "E" author). "E" probably lived in the ninth or early eighth century BCE, and wrote part of Genesis as well as portions of Exodus and Numbers. "D" wrote the book of Deuteronomy (accounting for his designation), and probably also wrote Joshua, Judges, Samuel, and Kings. "D" probably lived in the seventh century BCE. "P" (for priestly writer) lived after the other three, probably during the Babylonian captivity, and also used the name "Elohim." The "P" writer apparently prefaced and organized the Torah and wrote much or all of Leviticus.

Genesis 1, attributed to "P," was actually written several centuries after Genesis 2 and 3. It probably dates to about 600 BCE, whereas Genesis 2 and 3, attributed to "J," are several hundred years older. This means that Genesis 1 was written to provide a background for the preexisting chapters 2 and 3, which relate the story of the creation of Adam and Eve. However, Genesis 1 also discusses the creation of humanity, and this later account is slightly different from the original account in Genesis 2–3. The account of the creation of people in Genesis 1 uses the phrase "in his own image," which is not found in Genesis 2–3. Genesis 1 was probably written when Jews were exiled in Babylon, and was likely influenced by the principal Babylonian creation myth, called the *Enumah Elish* (or *When on High,* from its first three words). There are a number of parallels between the Enumah Elish and the first chapter of Genesis, suggesting that the writer of this chapter adapted the Babylonian story for monotheism. In the Babylonian story, the God *Marduk* created humanity to serve the gods. The exiled Jews, compelled to serve another culture's gods, may have modified those passages to indicate that God created man in his own image and took a personal interest in humanity. Genesis 1 further affirms that we should be fruitful and have dominion over the Earth. "P," the Jewish adaptor of the Enumah Elish in Genesis 1, not only changed the Babylonian epic to reflect monotheism, but also changed the nature of humanity to accommodate the Hebrew view that Jews were not servants of God, but rather were His beloved children, endowed with power and transformed into a Chosen People. This is the first example in the Tanakh in which we see a basic change in humanity's self-concept. Whoever "P" was, he exerted an enormous influence on humanity by changing the way we believe God perceives us.

Some language in the Torah is almost certainly symbolic. For example, by stating that God created the sun and moon on the fourth day (i.e., using the word "day" before the creation of the sun), the Torah is implying that the word does not have our usual meaning. The Garden of Eden can also be understood as a symbol. For a people who were accustomed to farming the difficult terrain of the Middle East, paradise would be a garden whose abundance flowed without effort. Indeed, the word "Adam" is probably derived from the Hebrew word *adamah,* which means "arable soil."

The creation of Eve, from the side of a man, has parallels in earlier mythology. There are several examples in mythology of men giving birth, and they do so by the abrupt creation of a fully formed person from their bodies (e.g., Athena sprang from the forehead of Zeus). Eve is not called by her name until after the expulsion. Nowhere in Genesis is she told that she is not to eat from the Tree of Knowledge. God has not specifically instructed her in this regard, nor has Adam. Only the serpent has spoken to her about the Tree and its fruits. We do not know why Eve was the first to eat, and it may be that it was written this way as a warning to men in and around the royal court to be careful of women with power. The passage about Eve's punishment being "pain in childbirth" is probably better translated as the pain of work *and* pregnancy rather than work and pain *in* childbirth.

The remainder of Genesis tells the story of Cain and Abel, the Flood, and other stories familiar to Westerners. In approaching the Torah, it is important to note that it is an adaptation of many preexisting stories and that much symbolic writing is lost to us. There are references to mythological characters that would have been familiar to contemporaries, but are foreign to us. Works of art are indeed timeless, but they cannot speak to us precisely as they did at the time of their creation.

Mesopotamian cultures, from the Sumerians to the Assyrians, had stories of a great flood, complete with a hero who escaped because of a divine warning. Indeed, Genesis is part of a long Mesopotamian tradition of flood stories that were shared among ancient Middle Eastern cultures. *The Epic of Gilgamesh* was the Mesopotamian flood story that was closest in time to Genesis. Similarities to Genesis are striking, including the sending out of a bird after the flood to find dry land, and it seems certain that the writer of this portion of Genesis knew the story of Gilgamesh.

Some areas in Genesis indicate that Noah took two of every animal on the Ark, but other areas say seven (the larger number presumably allowed for food and sacrifices). The Torah states that after the flood, humanity is permitted to eat meat for the first time. God did not actually send a rainbow to signal there would be no further flood; rather, he took a war bow and put it in the sky as a signal of peace. Genesis says that after the Flood, Noah became a vintner, in effect repeating Adam's beginnings in agriculture, but like Adam, Noah succumbed to temptation, getting drunk and abandoning clothing. Noah's sons, Ham, Shem, and Japhet, covered their father, but when Noah awoke, he cursed Canaan, a son of Ham. Apparently, this story is based on or influenced by a previous story that is now lost to us.

After Noah, Genesis 11 gives us the story of the Tower of Babel, the destruction of which was followed by the proliferation of languages, so that humanity could never again work together to rival God. This story is probably inspired by the Mesopotamian *Ziqqurats,* but whereas the

Ziqqurats were a testament to man's power as he reached toward heaven, the adaptation in Genesis becomes a story of God's power as he destroyed the tower because of the arrogance with which people were attempting to reach his domain.

The aftermath of the destruction of the Tower of Babel finds humanity yet again in sad shape. The ouster from the Garden of Eden, the Flood, and the destruction of the tower all fail to correct humanity. At this point, a frustrated God changed his strategy and turned to a subset of humanity — the Hebrews — and formed a special relationship with them. To do this, God entered into a special relationship with Abraham, the forefather of the Hebrews. This relationship, called the Covenant, obliges Jews to obey God's commands and set an example for the rest of humanity. Circumcision (bris) was the proof that the male child had entered into the Covenant.

In return for obeying God's commandments, Jews would receive his special protection. This is what is meant when the Jews call themselves the chosen people. It does not mean that Jews consider themselves superior, simply that they have been chosen by God to facilitate harmony in the world by acting, in effect, as examples of righteous conduct. A covenant can be thought of as a contract, but with two important differences: First, the Covenant encompasses the entire being of the person, not just one aspect of his life. Second, there is no fixed time period for the Covenant; it lasts the lifetime of the person. As envisioned by Jews, the Covenant binds the whole being of each Jew to God throughout his or her lifetime. The Covenant also binds posterity.

The Judaic Covenant is based on a format that was common in Middle Eastern treaties between a dominant and a subordinate party. This was called the suzerain-vassal model, and its basic theme was the absolute authority of the dominant party. The Judaic Covenant is the one of many examples in which the foundations of Judaism can be found in their historical context, emerging from existing cultural traditions.

To understand the full significance of the dual heritage of ethical monotheism, as established by the Covenant, we begin with a study of the Hebrew God. Early Judaism was polytheistic, but whereas most cultures of the time practiced syncretism — the addition of gods of other cultures to the pantheon. The early parts of the Tanakh show that the Hebrews refused to incorporate other deities into their pantheon — Judaism then seems to have entered a phase of henotheism, wherein multiple gods are recognized, but one is predominant.

Absolute monotheism was fully developed by about 750 BCE, but Judaism believes in monotheism with four defining and novel characteristics that allowed it to have an enormous effect not only on Hebrew culture, but also on Western culture. First, the Jewish God, unlike previous deities, is compassionate. Second, he is intimately concerned with the affairs of people. Judaism conceived of a god who did not create people for his own pleasure, or to relieve his toil, but rather seeks to relieve their suffering. In Judaism, human events matter. Third — and this is often overlooked — the Hebrew God, unlike other deities, is infallible. He cannot die, be injured, or make a mistake of any kind. Prior to the Jewish God, deities, though superhuman, made mistakes and could be harmed. For example, the *Iliad* tells us that the God Aries was kidnapped by two men and would have been killed had Hermes not rescued him. The Jewish God was still anthropomorphic, but in a much more powerful way. Judaism demonstrates that there are different kinds of anthropomorphic deities, some less like people than others.

It is probably not a coincidence that infallibility was ascribed to the Hebrew God at about the time that monotheism prevailed in that culture. In polytheistic religions, the gods must have weaknesses and foibles because if all of them were omniscient and omnipotent, how could they get along? Who is in control? If there is one infallible god, what is the purpose of other, imperfect, deities? It is only with monotheism that it becomes possible for a deity to be omnipotent and infallible because he has no other deity with which to share power.

By introducing an infallible God, the Jews placed into Western history a deity that could survive people's increasing sophistication. I cannot imagine that the Greco-Roman or Scandinavian gods, with all of their weaknesses, jealousy, and other human foibles, would have lasted long in a developing technological age. I believe that these much weaker, fallible deities would likely have been easier to dislodge in an increasingly sophisticated society than a single omniscient God, and I suspect that the Western world would be more secular today if it were not for Jewish monotheism and the nature of its single God.

The fourth characteristic of Jewish monotheism — also often overlooked — is that it introduced linear thinking into Western religion and philosophy. A linear concept of time is a major difference between East and West, and this comes in substantial part from Judaism. In Judaism, human affairs and the events of the physical world do not repeat in an ever-cycling universe, as they do in Eastern religions, but rather progress together in linear time. What people do therefore makes a real and permanent difference because actions are not lost in the recycling of the universe. A linear conception of time makes a cause-and-effect view of the world easier to establish and sustain. Religion, philosophy, and science are intertwined, and perhaps it is not a great leap to postulate that the linearity that has made Western scientific thinking so effective emanates from Jewish monotheism.

Because of these characteristics, Jewish monotheism furnished a single value system throughout its community and those of many Western communities today, but it also heightened the difficulty of acceptance of evil. Prior to the Jewish God, reconciling the existence of evil with the existence of deities was not difficult because no one expected the many fallible, disinterested gods to be able to remove evil, or even to desire to do so. Indeed, the gods appeared to be the cause of some of the evil. But far more could reasonably be expected of the compassionate, omnipotent, and infallible Jewish God. Monotheism — in its unique and penetrating form — is, for better or worse, one of Judaism's great gifts to the world.

The Hebrews received the power, compassion, and personal interest of God from the Covenant. Now we ponder the other half of the contract — what the Hebrews were obligated to give. Foremost among the commands the Hebrews were required to keep as part of the Covenant are the Ten Commandments. Jews prefer the term "Decalogue" because "Ten Commandments" implies that these are the entirety of their obligation, and the Jewish canon actually specifies 613 commandments. The Decalogue is enumerated three times in the Torah — twice in Exodus and once in Deuteronomy. Pursuant to the dual heritage of ethical monotheism, the Decalogue enumerates requirements vis-à-vis both God and other people. The Decalogue was later adopted by Christianity and Islam, and underpins the legal and moral tradition of the Western world, as well as the systems of jurisprudence in most countries. No other work of literature has been as influential in our history as these seventy words (more or less, depending upon the translation).

The essence of being Jewish is acceptance of the Covenant, an important component of which is that it is entered into voluntarily. Judaism demanded much from its followers, but it gave something unprecedented in return — the assurance that they possessed value and would receive the personal concern and attention of God. Affirming the goodness and power of God and the basic goodness of people led to another tenet: people, through God, have power over the world, and, like God, can be just and powerful. The idea that people could dominate nature was revolutionary. Christianity and Islam inherited this idea, and it has remained part of the Western tradition.

In Abraham we have, for the first time in the Tanakh, a figure who may have actually lived. The story of Abraham suggests that it took place about 1800 BCE, but references to people and practices of a later period (for example, the Philistines and domesticated camels) indicate that it was written much later, probably between 900 and 750 BCE. In fact, there may have been some modifications to the story of Abraham as late as the Hellenistic period ("Hellenistic" refers to the Western World in the time of Alexander the Great and his successors, in contrast to "Hellenic," which refers to the earlier period of classical Greece).

Abraham, his son, Isaac, his grandson, Jacob, and their wives are the patriarchs and matriarchs of Judaism. With the suspense of the finest novels, the Torah shows us how these founding figures are righteous, but imperfect, like ourselves, and how they overcome adversity through their faith. The story of the near sacrifice of Isaac — only nineteen verses in Genesis 22 — is one of the most familiar passages in religious literature, and one of literature's finest accounts of the conflict between love and duty.

When Sarah was unable to get pregnant, she put her servant, Hagar, in bed with Abraham. Hagar became pregnant, but then Sarah abused her, forcing her to flee. In a moment of true literary genius, the writer of this portion of Genesis has an angel appear to Hagar and counsel her to return to Abraham. After she gives birth to their son, Ishmael, mother and child are both expelled from the home. Ponder for a moment the significance of this passage. Here is a writer of Hebrew scripture, well before the Common Era, who has God appear to a woman who is a slave, an Egyptian, and about to become an unwed mother. The concern of the Hebrew God for Hagar tells us something about his compassion, and also how the Hebrews viewed humanity. As is the case with many other passages in the Tanakh, we see that early literature can be humanistic and depict the unchanging nature of humanity.

The traditional early history of the Hebrews is that, in fulfillment of their destiny, Abraham led them into present-day Israel, though realistically, they probably were evicted from their homeland by superior military power. No one knows how, or even if, the Hebrews came to Egypt. It is possible that some were carried into Egypt as prisoners in the wake of the Egyptian-Hittite Wars. It is also possible that many voluntarily migrated to Egypt because of the greater prosperity and ease of agriculture there. Assuming the Hebrews did go to Egypt, we cannot trace how they were treated there, and it is not established that they were captive, but it is probable that in the New Kingdom, which exhibited a greater interest in nationalism and conquest, the Hebrews had a subordinate status.

Likewise, there is no archeological documentation of the Exodus from Egypt. During the Exodus, Moses is said to have parted the Red Sea, but this is now known to be a mistranslation. The actual text says that he parted the "Reed Sea," simply referring to wetland in which reeds grew. After the Exodus, the Hebrews supposedly wandered in the desert for forty years, then made their way back into the land of Canaan (now called Israel), a land that Moses was permitted to see, but not to enter. The Torah ends at this point, and because it is the sole source of divine revelation in Judaism, this ends as well. But the account of the Hebrews is continued by the Nevi'im (prophets).

The Nevi'im covers the period from settlement in the land of Canaan to the destruction of the First Temple by the Neo-Babylonians and the exile of the Hebrews to Babylonia, though the lives of several of the minor prophets overlap with the Second Temple period, and there are literary indications that some of the books were written during Hellenistic times. Because the third portion of the Tanakh, the Ketuvim, is not a narrative history, the chronology of the Hebrew Bible essentially ends with the destruction of the First Temple and exile to Babylonia.

The absorption of the Hebrews back into Israel probably involved both cultural assimilation and some military campaigns (among them Joshua's conquest of Jericho). Upon the return to Israel, the Hebrews existed as small groups of people ruled by local leaders called judges. They subsequently adopted a monarchy about 1000 BCE, perhaps in emulation of other cultures, and perhaps to unite them against external threats such as the Philistines. The unification was incomplete, and the Hebrews were still left with two states: a northern state, Israel, with a capital at Samaria, and a southern state, Judah, with a capital at Jerusalem.

The prophets began as advisors to the king in the monarchical period. These prophets attempted to communicate the will of God to their people. They also held that the private life of a king had great ramifications for the Jewish nation, and were among the first to suggest that kings should behave in a manner similar to other people. The prophets then moved from this role to crusaders for social justice and monotheism (which was not fully adopted until perhaps two centuries after the advent of a monarchy). But at no time did the Hebrews see their prophets as foretellers of the future. Christians changed the primary role of prophets to that of foretellers so that they could be seen to predict the coming of Jesus, thereby ensuring the understanding of Christianity as the continuation of the Tanakh.

The prophets clearly had a marvelous combination of writing ability and social conscience, and in the process of championing monotheism and social justice, they left us the record of the Hebrews. Their writing is a model of how to communicate in a way that people will understand and be willing to listen to. In every generation, a few individuals are able to give voice to humanity's continuing struggle for justice, peace, equality, freedom, and peace. Anyone who questions the ability of writers, philosophers, and creative artists to exert a long-term influence equal to that of political leaders need only realize that the prophets are among the most influential people who ever lived, while the kings they worked for are largely forgotten.

Some of the prophets, such as Amos and Hosea, the first two, preached in the northern state, Israel, which fell to Assyria in 722 BCE. Contrary to popular belief, the Assyrians did not destroy Israel and everyone in it. As was the custom at the time, the Assyrians relocated the upper class of Israel and replaced them with their own people in order to gain control over the society. Hosea witnessed the fall of Israel and recorded his grief by addressing Israel as a lost child or lover:

> *I will... speak tenderly to her. There she shall respond as in the days of her youth.*

The alleged destruction of Israel by the Assyrians gave rise to the story of the ten lost tribes, but the fate of these people is no mystery; they merged with Assyrians. This amalgamation of the Hebrews who remained in Israel and the new people brought in by the Assyrians gave rise to a people known as the Samaritans. Ironically and tragically, these Samaritans, many of whom were of Hebrew descent, became the enemies of Judah.

After the fall of Israel, refugees took the words of its prophets south to Judah, where they were edited and written. It is possible that Judah also fell under Assyrian control. The Hebrew account is that Judah held off the Assyrians, but the Assyrian account is that they conquered both Israel and Judah, but did not relocate any citizens of Judah because Judaeans paid tribute. In either case, the Neo-Babylonians conquered the Assyrians in 612 BCE and captured Judah.

The first prophet from the south, and the first of the major prophets, was Isaiah. It is now thought that the writings of Isaiah encompass at least three different people, the first of whom lived between 750 and 700 BCE. The first Isaiah was an advisor to king Hezekiah. Under Hezekiah, Judah suspended its tributes to Assyria, but these were reinstituted under his successor, who also reinstituted the worship of other gods, a practice that Isaiah protested.

It was only after a revolt by Jehoiakim that the Neo-Babylonians began to deport upper-class Judaeans, following the custom of the time. A year after a second revolt by Zedekiah in 587, the Neo-Babylonian king, Nebuchadnezzar, destroyed the Temple built by Solomon and instituted another wave of deportations, the Babylonian captivity. Were it not for these two revolts, the Babylonian captivity and the destruction of the First Temple may not have occurred. Jeremiah witnessed of all of this, and concluded that the old Covenant was obsolete, but he envisioned a new one centered on Jerusalem. During a third wave of deportations in 582, Jeremiah was whisked away to the safety of Egypt, and it was here that his works were assembled into the book that bears his name.

The Deuteronomic history considers the books of Deuteronomy, Joshua, Judges, First and Second Samuel, and First and Second Kings to reflect the same viewpoint (Deuteronomy is part of the Torah; the other books are part of the Nevi'im, or prophets). Some regard Deuteronomy as an introduction to the next four books, perhaps even that these are all the work of a single author or editor. The Deuteronomic theology expounds upon the Covenant and gives details of reward and punishment that God might inflict. These books were written after the fall of the Hebrew monarchy and the beginning of the Babylonian captivity, and probably discuss the question of what the Hebrews could have done that broke the Covenant and resulted in their punishment. The story of David's transgression with Bathsheba, for example, is likely an attempt to explain what appeared to be divine punishment. Another probable example is idolatry — a sin that was easy to commit in the time of the monarchs because the Hebrews were not yet completely converted to monotheism.

Ezekiel and Second Isaiah were prophets in exile. Second Isaiah (also called Deutero Isaiah) cautioned that the exile would not end quickly. Ezekiel's writing is of a different style from that of other prophets, and there are places in which he compares the Hebrews to adulterous women in sexually explicit language.

The Babylonian exile had multiple consequences. First, it diminished the power of the kings because the Neo-Babylonians held power. Second, it weakened the power of prophets, because they were advisors to weakened kings. Third, it undermined the power of priests because there was no longer a Temple. Fourth, it increased the Jews' sense of isolation. It is presumed, but not proven, that it was during the period of exile that worship in synagogues became widespread due to the loss of the Temple. It was also during this period that the Torah was organized, though it was not yet written. This is why one of the overriding themes of the Torah is the preservation of Jewish identity. To preserve their heritage during this period, Jews adopted a stricter observance of dietary laws and the Sabbath. The Sabbath was a unique contribution of Judaism. Genesis suggests that its purpose was to celebrate the creation by resting when God rested. The book of Deuteronomy indicates that another reason for the Sabbath might be to give Jews, who had been slaves, the first time for themselves they had known in a very long time. These strict observances reflected Judaism's new emphasis on the individual and individual practice.

In one of the great success stories of history, the early Jews preserved their culture in exile in the face of overwhelming odds. They did this by working within the system and by paying attention to themselves and to their relationship with each other, rather than their relationship to the greater power. The Hebrews knew that by maintaining their culture and looking inward they would eventually prevail against the transient external power. Using this philosophy, the early Jews were not only able to withstand persecution, but also the loss of their homeland. Nowhere in history is there a better example of cultural preservation providing a sense of belonging and resiliency than in Judaism.

Perhaps the greatest contribution of the Jews is to teach us that oppressed people need to look inward before they look outward. Perhaps their greatest gift is to demonstrate that an oppressed people who make internal affairs, cultural maintenance, and the maximal development of individuals the priority will eventually triumph more certainly than a people who concentrate on fighting an external enemy, however legitimate that enemy may be. It is easy to focus on an enemy that is obvious and immediate, but history teaches that the more important battle is always within. This is not only true of groups but also of individuals, and it is a tragedy of history that so many individuals and groups have failed to recognize this.

Looking inward also means that the individual is not dependent upon the appearance of a messiah. Unlike Christianity, the Jewish canon makes only passing reference to a messiah, and gives no details. Individual Jews have a variety of beliefs regarding the eventual coming of a messiah, but neither their individual lives nor their cultural identity is dependent on a savior.

During the Babylonian captivity, Jewish and Babylonian culture blended in ways that we will never fully understand. Another possible consequence of the exile may have been the acquisition of a dualist religion, having good and evil deities, from Persian Zoroastrianism. Early Judaism, even after it became fully monotheistic, was not dualist. With the notable exception of the book of Job, Satan is rarely mentioned in the Tanakh and not mentioned at all in Genesis. Even in Job, he is not depicted as evil, but as a friendly adversary of God. Jews may have borrowed the concept of dualism from Zoroastrianism, but this is not proven, and they may have developed dualism independently, as a reflection of the general Western belief in sharply defined dichotomies, or to explain the coexistence of a benevolent Creator and worldly evil.

The influence of Zoroastrianism on Judaism is unclear, largely because very little is known about Zoroaster (Zarathustra). Teaching attributed to him is clearly dichotomous, describing absolute good and absolute evil, charging people to make a choice between these extremes, and postulating that this choice would determine their fate in the afterlife. Zoroaster may also have been among the first to envision a final Apocalypse. To the extent that he is an identifiable historical figure who was indeed the driving force behind these conceptions, he and the religion named for him may have influenced the thinking of some Jews. It is tempting to speculate that Judaism drew from Zoroastrianism because definitive monotheism, a good-evil dichotomy, and the idea of an Apocalypse came into Judaism about the time of the Babylonian captivity, when they were held in a land that practiced Zoroastrianism. But coincidence of time is far from evidence of influence, and it is best to conclude that the precise influence of Zoroastrianism on Judaism is unclear.

The Ketuvim (or writings) is a fascinating collection of literature of different styles. It does not provide a narrative history as do the Torah and the Nevi'im. Rather, the Ketuvim advises people on how to get through life, in a manner analogous to contemporary self-help books. The Ketuvim consists of the Psalms, Proverbs, Job, the Song of Solomon (also called Song of Songs, or Canticles), Ruth, Lamentations, Ecclesiastes, Esther, Daniel, Ezra, Nehemiah, Chronicles I, and Chronicles II, which concludes the Tanakh. The wisdom literature of the Ketuvim often relies on traditional motifs, such as rhetorical questions. For example, repeating passages in a psalm probably represented a response to a chorus. Many psalms were meant to be sung. The Song of Solomon, attributed to the famous king, is love poetry that takes the form of a passionate dialogue between a woman and a man. It is extremely sensual, nearly erotic in some passages. Proverbs and Ecclesiastes are also attributed to Solomon. Proverbs is wisdom literature adapted for monotheism by imparting to the reader the certain knowledge that there can be no wisdom without God. The book of Ruth tells the story of how a gentile woman became the ancestor of King David, but it was probably written during the post-exile period.

The Book of Job is a particularly interesting portion of the Ketuvim. Most scholars believe it was written by multiple authors, probably between 1100 and 300 BCE. It may have originally been written in Hebrew, Arabic, or Aramaic. Job deals with theodicy, the question of reconciling a just and omnipotent god — the legacy of Judaism — with evil. Why is there evil if God is omniscient, omnipotent, and benevolent?

Job questions the idea set forth in Deuteronomy that God will quickly reward good behavior and punish bad behavior (this questioning can also be found elsewhere in the Ketuvim).

The book of Job is in prose with a poem in the center. The dialogue is between God and Hasatan (the origin of the word "Satan"). God lets Satan inflict great misfortune on Job, who remains loyal to God but questions what is happening to him and insists that he does not deserve his punishment. He rejects responsibility, and says that his problems are signs of God's capriciousness. Job has four friends, or comforters (the fourth may have been added by a later writer). The first tells him he must have done something wrong and simply doesn't remember. The second asks rhetorical questions about God, the purpose of which is to prove that God cannot act arbitrarily or unjustly. The third tells Job that there must be a divine plan, though he may not understand it. The fourth criticizes Job for questioning God. All four adhere to the strict Deuteronomic theodicy that either Job or his children must have sinned. God appears at the end and restores Job to his former prosperity, but never explains his rationale, and tells Job that he must not question divine judgment.

There are differences in style within the text, suggesting several authors at different times, probably the result of superimposing a philosophical discussion upon an older folk tale. We really do not know Job's response to his misfortune because the acceptance for which he is so famous could equally well have been translated from the original text as hopelessness or defiance (indeed, the story illustrates how dependent we are on the translation). Despite this ambiguity, the lesson is clear — we cannot know anything about God, and we cannot attribute evil to his caprice or malice. The book of Job teaches that the whole question of theodicy is unanswerable and unapproachable, and counsels us to submit to God completely and unquestioningly.

One could argue that this is a very reasonable conclusion, and one could also argue that Job has lessons for atheists — to be careful of self-justification and to accept fate. As is the case in much religious literature, the message of Job transcends religious beliefs and speaks to all of us. At the same time, one could also maintain that accepting the omniscience and the benevolence of God in the face of evil, based on the arguments in Job, is a thought process inappropriate for the modern world. In either case, Job is a wonderful meditation on the acceptance of evil. Indeed, if we substitute Job's tribulations for those of the modern world, such as disease, war, or poverty, we can read Job as an entirely modern text.

There is controversy about the book of Esther, the basis for the Jewish holiday of Purim. It describes a Persian King who goes by a name not recognized by archeology, but who was possibly Xerxes. There is no archeological evidence for Haman, a major character in the story, or for the events of the story. The Hebrew version does not even mention God, though other versions do (it is possible that the original version was in Greek). Though the story ends with great violence as the Jews rise up and slay thousands of Persians, much of the text of Esther appears to be a farce, and may have been written for humor.

The book of Daniel is very difficult to date. It probably arises from the late Persian or early Hellenistic time, about 170 BCE. Parts of the book are written in Aramaic. Daniel is considered a prophet in Christianity, but not in Judaism, which is why his book is in the Ketuvim, not the Nevi'im.

Apocalyptic literature combines prophetic and wisdom literature with Persian and Greek thought, and is not intended for the general public, but for those already deeply committed to the faith. The last chapters of Daniel in the Tanakh are apocalyptic, as are parts, but not all, of the New Testament book of Revelation. Apocalyptic literature is based on the assumption that only an act of God can effect righteousness; people are powerless and superfluous. Apocalyptic literature is intensely dualistic, with a fully developed Satan. Apocalyptic writers often wrote, or were edited, to show that they lived a few centuries before they actually did, probably to enhance their believability as foretellers of the future.

A small portion of the Nevi'im may have been written after the return of the Hebrews to the land of Israel, but for all practical purposes, no part of the Tanakh is a good source for the history of the Hebrews after their capture by the Neo-Babylonians, and this portion of Jewish history has been assembled from other sources. The northern kingdom had already been lost, but the southern kingdom, taken into captivity by the Neo-Babylonians, retained its identity and survived. No one can say with certainty why one survived and the other did not, but part of the answer may be the retention of a viable priesthood and a canon in the south. Also, the Neo-Babylonians did not splinter the southern kingdom as brutally as the Assyrians had done in the north. In addition, the Neo-Babylonian captivity was slightly less than fifty years, while the Assyrian occupation lasted twice as long. This means that the Neo-Babylonian captivity was less than one lifetime, so there were always people who remembered and taught about pre-captive times.

After the Persians conquered the Neo-Babylonians, their king, Cyrus, permitted the Jews to return in 538 BCE, an action recorded on the Cyrus cylinder, now in the British Museum. But this was not a magnanimous gesture. Cyrus knew that by permitting the Jews to return he would enjoy their loyalty in their native land, while maintaining his power as the occupier. Though Cyrus permitted the Jews to return, many had scattered before the Persian victory and did not return to Judah. This diffusion of Jews after the Neo-Babylonian conquest was the beginning of the Diaspora, the worldwide dispersal of Jews (later augmented by failed revolts against Roman rule in the first and second centuries CE).

When the Jews returned, they found Jerusalem in ruins. Colonists from Syria and Mesopotamia, called "People of the Land," were living on what had been Jewish land. Some had taken the Jewish religion and become, in effect, a second group of Jews vying for legitimacy in the eyes of the Persians. But the returning Jews did not accept these people as true comrades. Moreover, there was hostility with the Jews who had not been exiled. Writers of the period record that the people seemed to have lost faith. Indeed, Malachi protested that even the priesthood was corrupt.

The Second Temple was built only by the returnees and was largely completed by 515 BCE, but this did not restore the people's confidence in the Covenant. Even in their homeland, Jews were still under Persian domination. During this time, priests held the community together. The monarchy was either gone or was a puppet of the Persians. There were a few prophets, such as Third Isaiah, but for all intents and purposes, the period of exile to Babylonia marked the end of the prophets.

Amidst the Persian occupation and the essential loss of their institutions, the returnees came together as a single cultural unit and formed Levitical Judaism, which laid the basis for the future version of the religion. Levitical religion was centered on the Temple because God lived there, specifically in a room called the Holy of Holies. The book of Leviticus enumerates three ways of interacting with God — sacrifices, ethical behavior, and rituals. Sacrifices repaired the broken relationship with God (thereby rendering a messiah unnecessary in Judaism), and were performed at an altar in front of the Holy of Holies. Ethical interactions with other people were perceived as, in effect, interactions with God. In the observance of rituals, the priests regained much of their former status, and derived power in large part because of the great importance of ritual in Levitical Judaism. Both before and after the exile, priests were a caste, so the only means of entry was hereditary.

Originally, people were to eat only plants, so Jewish dietary laws mandated that if this was no longer possible, people must eat only animals that eat plants, in an attempt to keep this link to the earth intact. The consumption of carnivorous animals was forbidden. Specifically, the connection to the Earth was thought to be strongest if only animals that *both* chewed a cud and had cloven hooves were eaten. Camels, rabbits, and pigs were specifically prohibited because they appear to fulfill both of these requirements but in actuality do not. For example, a camel's hoof is partially cloven. The constant mouth movements of a rabbit resemble the chewing of cud, but it is not. Pigs have truly cloven hooves, and it would be easy to assume that they chew cud, but they do not.

The body of Jewish dietary laws is called *kashrut*, and food that conforms to those laws is said to be kosher. A blessing is often said before the slaughter, but this is not essential. In kosher dietary practice, all blood must be drained from the animal because a passage in Leviticus prohibits the eating of blood since blood is life itself (this is the same passage that prohibits Jehovah's Witnesses from accepting blood transfusions). Kosher meat refers first to the acceptability of the animal, second to an immediate and painless death by severing the major vessels of the neck and the trachea in a single blow, and third to separation of blood and meat. Because there is a passage in Exodus that says, "You shall not boil a kid in its mother's milk," meat and dairy products are separated in kosher practice.

When Alexander the Great conquered the Persians, Judah became part of his territory. Upon his death, the empire fragmented into three major regions. The Ptolemies controlled Egypt, the Seleucids held Syria, Babylon, and parts of what is now Turkey, and the Antigonids controlled Macedon. Judah was originally under the Ptolemies, but was subsequently passed to the Seleucid Empire. The Jewish community in Judah was reasonably well treated by the Seleucid Empire and enjoyed considerable autonomy, but the Seleucid ruler Antiochus IV, defeated by the Romans and facing the threat of a united Rome and Ptolemaic Egypt, plundered Jewish treasure to replenish his coffers. The final straw was his erroneous belief that Judah intended to revolt. Antiochus dispatched an army to Judah and slaughtered many Jews. Beginning in 166 BCE, the Maccabees (also referred to as the Hasmonean family) led a revolt and recaptured the Temple in 164 BCE.

Jewish society under the Maccabees adhered to strict Levitical practice. It would be wrong, however, to believe that there was the only type of Judaism at this time. Unlike Christianity, Judaism has no specific creed, and the Jewish canon does not definitively answer some of the questions that Christians regard as settled. The second century BCE saw the rise of sectarianism in Judaism. These sects disagreed, but only within the framework of Levitical Judaism. The sects accounted for only a minority of Jews — most Jews were "mainstream" — and we have limited sources and incomplete knowledge of these sects and their beliefs. The three most important were the Pharisees, Sadducees, and Essenes. Before examining these sects, let us consider the concepts of an afterlife and resurrection of the body, as these are key points of difference between the Pharisees and the Sadducees.

Many Christians assume that Jews have always held to eternal life and bodily resurrection and that those concepts transferred smoothly into Christianity, but this is not true. The Tanakh has little to say about an afterlife, and mentions only a shadowy place that all people, good or evil, go after they die. There is no reference at all to a paradise that worthy people will enjoy forever. To the extent that there was any focus on a subsequent reward for a righteous life, many Jews thought that it would take the form of their children being permitted to continue to live in peace in Israel. This seems strange to us today, but we must remember that an afterlife was not a prominent part of most ancient religions. In Egypt, it was restricted, at least in the Old Kingdom, to the pharaoh and a few noblemen who were close to him. In Greece, the afterlife for most people was a gloomy and unenviable existence. The writers of the Tanakh would not have had a model for a generalized paradise into which all worthy people go upon death. Another reason that the Tanakh is largely silent on an afterlife is that much of it was written in happier times, before the Babylonian captivity and the destruction of the Temples. An afterlife acquires greater significance when earthly life is unhappy. Most Christians would be even more surprised to learn that bodily resurrection is not mentioned at all in the Tanakh. Sometime in the fifth or fourth century BCE, after the Babylonian captivity, some Jews began to better develop concepts of heaven, hell, the immortality of the soul, and bodily resurrection.

The Pharisees supported both immortality of the soul and bodily resurrection, but they appear to have received these ideas from Hellenistic thinking, not from the Tanakh. These Hellenistic notions were attractive to the Pharisees not only because they provided hope for eventual reward, but also because they provided a sense of justice and allowed for the punishment of the wicked. During the Levitical period, the Pharisees were among the minority of Jews who held to these doctrines, and they passed them to the subsequent Rabbinic period of Judaism. As we will see, early Christians, seeking to formulate their new religion, appropriated these ideas from the Pharisees. Thus, neither of the critical Christian ideas of immortality of the soul nor resurrection of the body came from mainstream Judaism, but from a Jewish sect that itself derived these concepts from other sources, not from common Jewish belief or the Tanakh.

The Pharisees were predominantly laypeople, and many were what we would now call blue collar. They believed in an oral tradition that was equivalent to the Torah, provided that it did not change, and from this they derived their belief in resurrection of the body and in an afterlife. Pharisees accepted divine providence and thought that all events stemmed from the will of God. They believed in a degree of free will, but felt that God's plan superseded it. They further believed that Judaism could be purified if all Jews followed the same strict laws that priests observed.

The Sadducees were primarily members of the aristocratic or priestly class and were generally more educated than the Pharisees. The Sadducees thought that God was removed from the affairs of daily life. They did not support a strong oral tradition and thought that the Torah was complete. Accordingly, they did not accept an afterlife or bodily resurrection of the dead, since neither is clearly specified in the Torah. They believed in free will, and for this reason they did not believe that God was omniscient. How could people have free will if God predetermined all decisions?

The Essenes were even more fatalistic than the Pharisees and held that God ordained *all* actions. Nothing was voluntary. The Essenes were strongly apocalyptic and believed in an imminent struggle between good and evil, with good prevailing. Their belief in an afterlife is not completely clear, but they apparently recognized some form of spiritual survival. They left the main community in Jerusalem (largely to protest the Maccabees) and founded a community near the Dead Sea. The Essenes are associated with the Dead Sea Scrolls, but it is not known how much these scrolls reflect general Jewish opinion of the time as opposed to beliefs that were unique to the Essenes. The Dead Sea Scrolls are the earliest manuscripts that we have of any of the books of the Tanakh. Some of them furnish a fascinating dissenting voice to what would become the oral Torah and Jewish law.

Rome conquered all of the Hellenistic kingdoms and took control of Judah, naming it Judaea (or Judea). Once again, Jews were at the mercy of the region's powerhouse. Like other Roman subjects, Jews were reasonably well tolerated as long as they paid their taxes and did not cause trouble. But the hallmark of Judaism — and its great heritage — has always been its insistence on preserving and practicing its own culture at all times. History can never know how much of the conflict between Rome and the Jews stemmed from Roman mistreatment and how much from Jewish intransigence. We must try to be fair to both parties. No criticism is offered of any group that wishes to preserve its cultural tradition, and the contemporary world owes a great debt to the Jews for having done so. Likewise, no defense is offered of any empire that uses excessive force to suppress a people who wish only to preserve their culture, but Rome did not fundamentally threaten Jewish heritage and culture. Might open challenge to Roman authority have represented a poor choice of battles for Jews, just as it was a poor choice of battles at about the same time for early Christians, another group that was persecuted much less than many people believe?

The Jewish-Roman war of 66–73 CE culminated in the Roman destruction of the 600-year-old Second Temple in 70 CE, an act that threatened Judaism more than any other in its history. The Second Temple had stood for nearly 600 years. The seventy-year interval between the First and Second Temples had long passed from memory, so Jews had an essentially unbroken tradition of centering their religion in one building in one place. This building was the focal point for Jews all over the world. Without the Temple, there was no place for the Jews to go to repent (this was not a problem for the fledgling Christianity because the death of Jesus made possible anybody's repentance from any location). Moreover, several of the Jewish holidays required a pilgrimage to the Temple. Its destruction was not only a crushing blow to Jewish culture, but also raised questions about the power of God. Why would God not defend his own house?

It is difficult for us to understand the implications of the destruction of the Second Temple because our common religious practices are not so intimately connected to a single structure. Today, the destruction of the local synagogue, church, or mosque, as tragic as that would be, would not threaten the existence of the religion. Perhaps the closest we can come to understanding the significance of the loss of the Second Temple would be to ponder what Islam would be like if Mecca were destroyed.

Because seventy years passed between the destruction of the First Temple and the construction of the second, some Jews began to believe, in 132 CE, sixty-two years after the destruction of the Second Temple, that the time was right for God to send a messiah and make a Third Temple possible. This was the background for a second rebellion of 132–135 CE, led by Simon Bar Kokhba (also spelled Bar Kochva, originally named Simon Bar Koziba). After crushing the rebellion, the Romans banished the Jews from Jerusalem, a more sweeping and brutal exile than those inflicted by either the Assyrians or the Neo-Babylonians.

During this catastrophic period, Rabbinic Judaism (also called classical Judaism or Talmudic Judaism) arose. The Pharisees were very influential in the development of this new formulation of Judaism. Though they were a minority, they were the most numerous of the Jewish sects, and the only one to survive the destruction of the Second Temple. The Sadducees had been intimately connected with that temple and therefore had no legitimacy after its destruction. The Romans simply obliterated the Essenes. Most Jews remained mainstream — not affiliated with any sect — but as fate would have it, the Pharisees contributed disproportionately to Rabbinic Judaism after the destruction of the Second Temple.

Rabbinic Judaism was a redirection of Judaism, very much as the *Upanishads* redirected Hinduism. Prior to the Rabbinic period, the primary means of public worship was sacrifice at the Temple, but in its absence, sacrifices were replaced by observance of religious laws, good deeds, and study of the Torah. Rabbinic Judaism places the site of God within people, not within a building. Likewise, priests had been based

Wailing Wall .

It is commonly believed that the Wailing Wall is the Western Wall of the Second Temple, but the complete truth is a bit more complicated. The Second Temple was completed in 515 BCE. In 20 or 19 BCE, Herod expanded the Temple Mount (the plateau area on which the Temple was built). Herod's expansion, along with the original Second Temple, was destroyed by the Romans in 70 CE, after the first Jewish-Roman War. Today's Wailing Wall was part of the extended retaining wall of Herod's expansion. About half of the Wall is a remnant of Herod's expansion. The remainder of the Wall is from additions dating to the 7th century CE and later. As much as we would like for some part of the Second Temple of 515 BCE to still be with us, very little, if any, of the Wall is from the original Second Temple. However, it is still true that the Wall has been part of Judaism for centuries and Jews of the time between 19 BCE and 70 CE would have accepted Herod's addition — much of today's Wailing Wall — as part of the Temple Mount.

in the Temple, so their role was diminished in Rabbinic Judaism. The hereditary priest was replaced with the sage, or rabbi, whose position was based on erudition, not heredity (hence the term Rabbinic Judaism).

The origin of synagogues is not clear. They existed during the Second Temple period, and are documented in Egypt as early as the third century BCE. Perhaps they began during the Babylonian exile, in a response to the loss of the First Temple. Wise men, the precursors of rabbis, were also found in early Judaism, and rabbis predated the destruction of the Second Temple. Indeed, there is speculation that Jesus, who lived before the Second Temple's destruction, was a rabbi. But synagogues grew in number and importance after the destruction of the Second Temple. Moreover, while it is not clear that early synagogues were necessarily sites of prayer, those established after the destruction of the Second Temple certainly were. Rabbis rose in influence with the new synagogues because they were greatly needed at the local level. In addition, synagogues and rabbis became linked. Early rabbis probably did not have the relationship with individual synagogues that they do now.

In the synagogue, the reading of scripture replaced sacrifice, and a reading desk stood in place of an altar. The Torah became the focus of worship, and the ark — the resting place of the Torah — replaced the Holy of Holies. The synagogue faces Jerusalem, giving the worshipper the sense of being in that city.

Rabbinic Judaism elevated scripture to a sacred status. As an illustration, the Sabbath could be violated only to save a human life or to save a scroll of scripture. As with people who have died, worn-out scripture scrolls must be buried; they cannot be burned. Moreover, Rabbinic Judaism holds that God revealed the Torah to Moses in a written and an oral form, equally authoritative. Both forms go back to Mount Sinai and both are discoveries of what God told Moses. We have seen that the Pharisees believed in an oral Torah, and its the acceptance in Rabbinic Judaism is evidence of their influence.

The loss of Judaism's place of worship, the threat to its very existence, and the belief that the written Torah could be supplemented, gave rise to a new literature. This was when the *Mishna* (or *Mishnah)* matured and the Jewish canon expanded. The Mishna was completed about 200 CE. It is the work of the *Tannaim* (or *Tana'im)*, a group of scholars spanning seven generations from the time of Hillel (fl. c. 30 BCE–10 CE) to about

200 CE. Perhaps 150 rabbis over the course of some seven generations completed the Mishna, but the bulk of the work, so far as we can tell, seems to have been done by about twenty individuals over about three generations. Much of the early work seems to have been done at Yavneh (also written Javneh or Jabneh; near modern Rehovot), and Johanan (or Yochanan) ben Zakkai is remembered as a primary early contributor to the Mishna.

Because the oral Torah is as authoritative as the written Torah, and the Mishna is the cornerstone of the oral Torah, its contribution to Judaism is enormous. Given that the Mishna and the commentaries based on it furnish the foundation of Jewish daily life, these twenty individuals, whose names we know, are among history's most influential people. They transformed two disasters into a work of literature that became the underpinning for Judaism and Western civilization.

Despite having been written over the course of several generations, the stylistic uniformity suggests one or a few editors working in the early third century CE. One of these editors is said to be Rabbi Yehudah HaNasi (Judah the Prince or Judah the Patriarch).

There is a widespread misconception that the documents of Rabbinic Judaism are derived from the scripture, but they are based more on the oral Torah, whose equality with the written Torah is a characteristic of Rabbinic Judaism. The eventual recording of oral law probably stemmed from fears that a shortage of scholars after the suppression of the two uprisings against Rome would endanger its survival and transmission.

The Mishna was the basis of additional texts in Rabbinic Judaism. The Mishna does not frequently cite scripture and is not arranged according to the biblical verses that it addresses or uses to support its assertions. Rather, it contains sixty-three sections, or tractates, organized into six orders: *Zera'im* ("seeds," laws regarding agriculture or blessings); *Mo'ed* ("appointed times," writings concerning festivals and the Sabbath); *Nashim* (women, marriages, divorce, etc.); *Nezikim* (damages, torts); *Qodashim* (holy things, temple procedures); and *Tohorot* ("purity," rules for rituals). The Mishna is primarily a legal text. Because Judaism did not distinguish between secular and religious codes of conduct, the six sections of the Mishna each contain both secular and religious rulings. Instead of a litany of commandments, it also includes dissenting and minority opinions so that scholars of the future might come to different conclusions as circumstances change. This is in sharp contrast with Christian literature, which typically presents a single viewpoint.

The *Gemara* is a commentary on the Mishna, and is much longer than the Mishna. There are actually two Gemaras. One originated in Israel in the fourth century CE, called the *Jerusalem* (or *Palestinian) Gemara,* and the later one, completed in the sixth century, is the *Babylonian Gemara,* which is considered the more authoritative of the two, because the Roman devastation after the Bar Kokhba revolt in 135 CE led to the exile of many Jews to Babylonia, making it the center of Jewish scholarship. In fact, the unqualified term "Gemara" refers to the *Babylonian Gemara.* The Mishna and Gemara together are called the *Talmud.* Because there are two Gemaras, there are two Talmuds (the Mishna is invariant). The *Jerusalem Talmud* (also *Talmud Yerushalmi,* or *Palestinian Talmud)* is the Mishna plus the earlier Gemara from the land of Israel. The *Babylonian Talmud* (or *Talmud Bavli)* is the Mishna plus the later Gemara from Babylonia. Because of the greater authority of the Babylonian Gemara, the unqualified term "Talmud" refers to the Babylonian Talmud, which is in both Hebrew and Aramaic. There are minor semantic differences, and the term "Gemara" is sometimes used as another term for Talmud, and if unqualified, for the Babylonian Talmud. Most, however, use the word "Gemara" to refer to the actual commentaries on the Mishna, and reserve the word "Talmud" for the combined Mishna and Gemara. Reading the Gemara is like surfing the web; one topic segues into another seamlessly, over and over again, until you are reading on a subject that has little to do with the original question.

The Palestinian Gemara is concerned with finding scriptural support for the Mishna, probably because it predates the Babylonian Gemara, and the oral Torah was not yet seen as equal to the written Torah. The later Babylonian Gemara treats the Mishna and the written Torah as equivalent. In fact, the Babylonian Gemara merges the Mishna — the great compilation of the oral Torah — with the written Torah into a unified whole. Thus the great importance of the Babylonian Talmud is that the written Torah and the oral Torah are combined into a unified whole that breathes life into Judaism.

The Mishna was the first major compilation of Jewish law, the *Halakhah* (also *Halakha, Halacha, or Halakah)*, and the Babylonian Talmud became the settled foundation of Halakhah. The Babylonian Talmud is also the basis of the other major code of Rabbinic Jewish tradition, the Aggada. Whereas the Halakhah concerns Jewish jurisprudence, the Aggada includes ethics and folklore. Like the Mishna, the *Tosefta* is a compilation of oral law, and is also a product of the Tannaim. It has the same structure as the Mishna. Most of the Tosefta was written fifty or one hundred years after the Mishna, and is a commentary on it, with specific references to the Mishna, though it may contain some material that predates the Mishnah.

The *Midrash* is commentary on the Tanakh (not on the Mishna) by rabbis between 300 and 1200 CE. The Midrash uses allegory and commentary to clarify the Torah. There are two categories of Midrash: the *Midrash Halakhah,* relating to the law, and the *Midrash Aggada,* which concerns non-legal matters and is the more generally important. The Midrash contains many types of literature and is an attempt to extend the Tanakh into what were then contemporary times. In its organization, the Midrash follows the Tanakh.

The sanctification of the oral and written Torahs contributed to the ability of the Jewish community to function without their Temple. In addition, though some rabbis maintained that only they could fully understand the Torah, the sanctification of the Torah also permitted common Jews to function with less dependence on intermediary figures.

The enormous volume of Jewish literature is not only the underpinning of the religion, but also a key component of Jewish culture and, I believe, a driving force of its scholarship. Jews have long had such reverence for books that if one is dropped it is kissed when it is picked up. It is not the content of the books that is important. What matters is that reverence for books is reverence for learning, and Jews have passed this reverence for learning on to their children as part of a parenting style that is more intensive than is found in other groups. If the content of the books or the immediate lessons is incorrect, then inevitably a reverence for learning will set them right. In Judaism, as in Greek philosophy, the correctness or incorrectness of the beliefs is irrelevant. Reverence for religious learning positions one well for secular learning — if the religious ideals are not stifling — because the love of knowledge and the desire for more of it are in place. What matters is that people were thinking, they were trying to understand, they were not satisfied with the knowledge necessary to get through daily life, but rather demanded more. A demand for knowledge over and above what is immediately necessary to cope with daily life is a prerequisite for enlightenment.

A Judaic academy established at Yavneh became a center of Judaism and supplanted Jerusalem as the seat of the *Sanhedrin,* the system of courts and religious assemblies (the Great Sanhedrin, the supreme religious body — roughly equivalent to our Supreme Court — was weakened and eventually dissolved after the Second Temple's destruction). After the fall of the Second Temple, Judaism became less dependent on a particular city and temple, and learned that it could survive without a specific point source. Jews saw that Judaism could exist in the form of devoted individuals, wherever they might be, studying the Jewish canon. Jews saw that righteous living could replace sacrifices. The preservation of Judaism after the destruction of the Second Temple represents extraordinary resilience. Reclaiming the religion from disaster was only possible because Judaism changed very significantly. An idea of how sharply it changed can be obtained by realizing that the word "rabbi" does not appear in the Hebrew Tanakh. The form of Judaism practiced today, even by orthodox Jews, would be barely recognizable, if at all, by Jews of antiquity. A great part of Judaism's survival has been its ability to change its expression without compromising its beliefs. After the destruction of the Second Temple, Jews returned to first principles and reformulated their religion, focusing on ethical living and faithfulness to their convictions. This would be the final wedge between them and Christians, whose messianic thinking, based on the then recent Jesus, was the focal point of their religion.

Synagogues, books, and practice replaced the Temple. Study and introspection became more important during the Rabbinic period, and arguably, Jewish scholarship began here. It was also probable that daily prayer became standard. One of the advantages of Rabbinic Judaism was that Jews everywhere were included. Gone were the days when Jews who lived away from Jerusalem believed themselves too far from the Temple to be true participants in their religion.

Rabbinic Judaism also elevated the status of women. In pre-Rabbinic Judaism, a man essentially purchased the wife by paying her father what was called the bride's price. Her consent was not necessary, and she paid a dowry. A man could have as many wives as he wanted, and only the man could initiate divorce, called a *gett* (also *ghet* or *get),* though a divorced woman did get her dowry back. In the Rabbinic period, the marriage contract originated, and a man's obligation to support his wife was stipulated. The effect was greater security for married women and a reduction in the number of arbitrary divorces. Even in the Rabbinic period, however, a man could have multiple wives and therefore needed no gett upon a divorce, but a woman, restricted to a single husband, required a gett to remarry. Though technically only a man could initiate a divorce, and could deny one to his wife, in practice the Jewish community would heavily pressure a man to grant a divorce, and there are instances of the rabbi's annulling the marriage if the husband would not do so. It remains true even today that the Halakhah states that only a man can initiate a divorce, but this is rarely an issue in daily life.

Rabbinic Judaism also re-examined the concepts of resurrection, afterlife, and the coming of a messiah. We have seen that despite what many Christians believe, the concepts of resurrection of the body and an afterlife were not integral to Judaism and came to the religion largely from Hellenistic thinking, by way of the Pharisees. Likewise, many Christians believe that a messiah is an integral part of Judaism and that Jesus smoothly and seamlessly fulfills that role, but this is not true either. It surprises Christians that the Tanakh, which is essentially their Old Testament, mentions a messiah only in passing. Rabbinic Judaism, with its very large canon, discusses a messiah much more thoroughly, but is ambivalent on the matter. Some Jews did long for and anticipate a savior or leader in those terrible times, but many others had given up on the idea, believing that if a messiah were coming, he would not have permitted two crushing Roman victories and the destruction of two Temples. The messiah, if expected at all, was not considered the initiator or the sole means of atonement. Messianism was de-emphasized in the Mishna because most of it was edited after the Bar Kokhba disaster, which had been caused by a belief that a messiah would assist in the building of a Third Temple.

Jews have typically been more interested in "laying the groundwork" for the coming of the messiah than in actually awaiting or identifying one. There are a variety of opinions in the Talmud regarding when he will come and what form he will take. One opinion is that the messiah has already come and gone. His presence resulted in the Kingdom of Israel that was lost and cannot be reclaimed. Some Jews believe that the messiah will come when all Jews behave in an exemplary manner, and indeed, one opinion in the Talmud is that the messiah will not come until conditions on earth are improved, but others believe that the Jewish community has no influence on when or whether a messiah will come.

There is also no consensus as to what the messiah will do when he does come. While some envisioned the messiah as bringing utopia, others envisioned him as a descendant of the House of David who would restore Jewish autonomy and the grandeur of the Jewish state and gather all of the Diaspora back into the Holy Land. The former view is more global, extending to nations beyond Israel and to Gentiles, whereas the latter view held that the primary beneficiaries of the messiah would be Jews. The former opinion envisions a world beyond this one, whereas the latter vision could take place here on Earth.

While Rabbinic Judaism dealt more openly with a possible messiah, the concept did not become central to Judaism and continues to this day to be peripheral to Jewish thought. Many Jews do believe in resurrection and an afterlife. In particular, heaven is described in Rabbinic Judaism and is accepted by many Jews. But only a minority of Jewish thinkers believe in a hell for those who have sinned. In contrast to Christians, most Jews either believe in a form of temporary punishment or an absence of paradise for sinners. While this general acceptance of an afterlife represents a major shift in the religion and is another indication of its adaptability, Jews have never agreed on a single belief regarding resurrection and an afterlife, and these doctrines have never been as central to Judaism as they are to Christianity or Islam.

Cultural identity, which bestows a sense of belonging and community, the nurturing of children, reverence for learning, ethical behavior, and a focus on the present — not the Christian concepts of a messiah, a resurrection, and an afterlife — are the great legacies and lessons of Judaism, which has always placed a much greater emphasis on the present life than Christianity has. Moreover, it is not one's beliefs, but one's actions in the here and now, that determine one's fate in the afterlife, if there is one. At no point was mainstream Judaism ever more concerned with an afterlife than with the current life.

Judaism did present the idea of a savior, but Christianity enormously expanded the concept, almost entirely reformulating it from the few passages in the Tanakh that do address a messiah, to make Jesus appear to be the culmination of a Jewish tradition that in fact was never well developed in the religion. For all practical purposes, the three central Christian doctrines of the messiah, bodily resurrection, and the eternal life of the soul were either derived by Christians from Hellenistic sources through the Pharisees, or were developed nearly de novo, based on only a rudimentary foundation in the Tanakh.

As we shall see, Christianity employed a more human embodiment of the messiah, whose subtle workings would nevertheless lead to sweeping global changes and eternal salvation. Christianity recast the prophets as foretellers of future events, including the coming of Jesus as the messiah. I believe early Christianity used disagreements and confusion about the nature of the messiah to make Jesus appear a reasonable candidate. If Judaism had held an unbroken, unopposed belief that the messiah could only be a great and powerful king whose actions would immediately transform the entire world in a glorious and obvious way, Christians would have had a more difficult time gaining acceptance for Jesus. Jews have never argued that the messiah would suffer for humanity or would be one with God. These characteristics were Christian modifications of the messianic tradition.

Nor has Judaism ever held that only Jews can be saved. Whereas Christianity and Islam are just now accepting that believers of other religions may achieve salvation through their own pathways, Judaism has always held that practitioners of other faiths have an equal opportunity for salvation. For this reason, active proselytizing has rarely been a major part of Judaism; however, converts have always been accepted without regard for their ethnicity, national origin, or previous beliefs.

In the Rabbinic period, Judaism changed into a form that would have been scarcely recognizable to a Jew of Moses' time, but even under the harshest of circumstances, it held fast to and preserved the essential ideals of Judaism — the concept of the Covenant, ethical monotheism, and the Jewish way of life. Leaders of the Rabbinic period had the wisdom to know that not every detail of their religion could be perfectly preserved and followed, and they knew what could be and must be changed to preserve the integrity of Judaism. As we are individually and culturally traumatized by life, we must change the details of how we think and behave in order to preserve the essence of who we are. Knowing what to keep and what to relinquish is a lesson we can all learn from Jewish history.

Philo, living in the first century CE in Alexandria, was the first great Jewish philosopher. He interpreted many of the stories and lessons of the Tanakh in an allegorical manner. This was resisted by Jewish leaders, but justified the belief of early Christians that the Jewish Bible was "forecasting" Jesus. For this reason, the Christian church preserved his writings, but the Jewish community did not.

From 658 to about 1000 CE, roughly corresponding to the Abbasid dynasty of Islam, there were large numbers of Jewish academies in what is now Iraq. These were called *yeshivot* (singular, *yeshiva,* meaning a place of learning of the Torah). The yeshivot were led by people called *geonim* (singular, *gaon,* someone with an excellent knowledge of the Torah). The reputation of these scholars was such that this period is called the Geonic (Gaonic) period. This was when the Talmud was finalized and disseminated, thanks in large measure to the roads and trade routes established by the Muslims. Many prominent Jewish scholars sought to preserve the Rabbinic legal tradition, and the Jewish canon expanded greatly in the Middle Ages.

Jews, Muslims, and Christians lived in peace for much of the Middle Ages; ironically and tragically, however, persecutions of European Jews increased in the High Middle Ages, a time of prosperity and the beginning of the Renaissance. Some reasons have been suggested, but in a time and place of overwhelming Christian primacy, it was inevitable that Jews would face persecution, and many of the apparent reasons were probably excuses to persecute non-Christians. One of these reasons involved money lending. Because Christians were forbidden to lend money at interest, the concept of interest was not well developed in the Middle Ages. Consequently, Jews, who were permitted to lend at interest, were prominent in the early days of banking and lending, but were considered exploitative by those to whom they lent money. Moreover, because Jews were not permitted to own property, they had no collateral when they themselves needed a loan. This forced them to charge higher interest rates than they normally would have, making their supposed exploitation of other people more acutely perceived.

The Crusades did not officially target Jews, but they facilitated anti-Semitism because some believed that non-Christians at home should be removed concurrently with those in the Middle East. Conflating Jews and Muslims as equally wicked, many Crusaders massacred Jews on their way to the Holy Land.

A particularly vicious form of anti-Semitism was blood libel, accusations that Jews had killed, kidnapped, or even crucified Christian children. Though neither civil nor Christian authorities sanctioned it, this bizarre charge was often leveled against Jews after a child went missing or was found dead.

During the High Middle Ages, Jews in England, France, Spain, and Portugal were compelled to convert to Christianity, or were expelled and forced to move into central and eastern Europe. In their new locations, Jews were forced into large, semiautonomous communities called ghettos.

Scholarship was a way for Jews to maintain their identity in times of crisis. The earliest prayer books appeared in the eighth and ninth centuries. Another type of Jewish literature is *Responsa,* the answers of individual rabbis to specific questions. Responsa have not been collected into a single work, but supplement the Jewish canon and are a rich resource for social historians. Many responses and interpretations are from identified individuals, many of whom have "Gaon" in their name.

Another philosopher was Sa'adya Gaon, who lived in tenth-century Iraq. One of the issues that Sa'adya dealt with was *Karaism,* an offshoot of Judaism that denied the validity of the oral Torah. He also discussed *kalam,* the discovery of Greek works by Arab thinkers, a development that led to scholasticism — the integration of contemporary and Greek knowledge — in Europe. Islam had been the custodian of Greek knowledge, and when it came to Europe, both Judaism and Christianity incorporated the new knowledge. Sa'adya's book, *Beliefs and Opinions,* is a discourse on kalam. This is the first systematic Jewish theology and the first philosophical defense of Judaism. In this work, Sa'adya Gaon visited two themes that would occupy many subsequent Western philosophers — epistemology (the theory of knowledge) and the relationship between faith and reason. He differentiated between understanding derived from reason and that derived from revelation. Though these two pathways are very different, they are complementary and may exist together. Indeed, he argued that an understanding of theology is augmented by the use of philosophical reasoning.

Rabbi Rashi (acronym for Rabbi Shlomo ben Yitzchak or Solomon Isaac) was born in Troyes, France, about 1040. He taught and commented on all aspects of Jewish literature, and is often regarded as the most important biblical commentator of the Middle Ages. He is remembered for his line-by-line commentary on the Talmud. Rashi also left a number of Responsas. Another Jewish scholar and poet of the Middle Ages, from a different tradition and approach from that of Rashi, was Judah ha-Levi (or Halevi; b. c. 1080), who wrote a defense of Judaism called the *Khuzari* (or *Kuzari*), and a poem called *Ode to Zion.*

Moses Maimonides (1135–1204; Rabbi Moshe ben Maimon, often referred to in Hebrew by the acronym "Rambam") was born in Spain, but was forced to flee to Cairo (notice that a Jew fled Christian persecution and found refuge in a Muslim country). Maimonides was a physician and theologian who accepted the new philosophy that would become scholasticism. He accepted Aristotelian thought as compatible with and a supplement to traditional beliefs, and integrated it with Judaism. His respect for Aristotelian thought led Maimonides to interpret much of the Jewish canon metaphorically and to believe that God and his laws are best understood by the intellect. Maimonides also argued that some passages in the Tanakh were incorrect, but written with the best of intentions because such writing was the most effective way to prevent people from going astray.

Maimonides enumerated thirteen core beliefs of Judaism. These initially appeared as a commentary to the Mishna, called *Kitab al-Siraj,* but stood independently by the sixteenth century. The *Kitab al-Siraj* interpreted the Mishna in light of then-new information arriving from the Muslim world. Another great work is *Dalat al-has'irin* (*The Guide of the Perplexed*), a philosophical treatise discussing the relationship between Judaism and the new knowledge. "The Perplexed" were Jews who, like Maimonides, had to reconcile religious beliefs with the new Greek philosophy. Maimonides was willing to modify religious opinions in the face of compelling scientific evidence, but he pointed out — correctly — that Aristotle had not proven his assertions that the universe was eternal or that natural processes do not need a deity. Maimonides's successful synthesis of old and new knowledge influenced Albert Magnus (the Great) and Thomas Aquinas. The West rightly associates Aquinas with scholasticism, but does not always understand the pivotal role of Maimonides. The *Cairo Genizah* is a large body of Jewish documents from the Middle Ages that was discovered in 1896 ("genizah" is Hebrew for "hiding place"). This work contains insight into the daily life of Jews of the Middle Ages, as well as papers and poems of Maimonides.

Summaries of the Talmud were written from 600 to 1800, as people sought a more accessible guide to laws. At first, these followed the order and categories of the Talmud, but later they developed an organization of their own and introduced categories not necessarily found in the Talmud. The most famous of these is the *Mishna Torah* (also *Mishnah Torah* or *Mishneh Torah,* meaning "second Torah"), a code of Jewish law by Maimonides. The Mishnah Torah makes no direct reference to the Talmud.

The *Tur* (also called *Arba-ah Turim,* or "Four Rows") was produced by Rabbi Jacob ben Asher in the fourteenth century CE. He divided all the legal components of the Halakhah into four categories: prayer and festivals, dietary, family law, and civil law. Because the Mishna Torah was generally used as a textbook, the Tur served as a practical legal guide until the work of Joseph Karo (or Caro, 1488–1575). Karo wrote *Bet Yosef* ("House of Joseph"), based on the *Tur.* His subsequent digest of the Bet Yosef, called the *Shulkan Arukh,* became a major statement of the Halakhah. Karo's *Kesef Mishneh* is one of the standard commentaries on the Mishnah Torah.

This was also the period in which Jewish mysticism, called *Kabbalah,* took form. Mysticism is a seeking of a direct experience of an ultimate reality, usually through meditation, prayer, or ritual. This is always done on an individual basis because the goal is a one-on-one, unmediated experience with God. Whereas mainstream Jewish scholarship centers on Talmudic study, Kabbalah speculates on metaphysical topics, particularly on the beginning of the world, the reasons that God created the world, and the relationship between God and the world.

The major work of Jewish mysticism, the *Zohar,* was probably compiled by Rabbi Moses de Leon in the thirteenth century. The Zohar introduces the idea that God, the Torah, and Israel are linked into a single unit. It is set in the second century and is reputed to be a treasury of ancient knowledge. Kabbalah held that the true nature of God was completely unknowable, but he manifests himself to humanity in the form of a series of powers referred to as *sefirot,* each of which is a specific attribute of God and has its own name. For example, two are called wisdom and understanding. The Zohar discusses ten sefirot.

Lurianic Kabbalah is a form of mysticism created by Isaac Luria in the sixteenth century. Luria believed that God drew into himself to make room for creation, after which he emitted light that created primordial man. Primordial man then emitted light that was transported in vessels. When these vessels shattered, sparks of light were trapped in the shards. These shards, called *kelippot,* emanated evil powers that were the source of the material world. Restoration was to come from newly created cosmic structures called *partzufim.* Adam was supposed to be the culmination of this restoration, but his sin corrupted the relationship between humanity and *partzufim.* Instead of being restored, human souls were trapped within the *kelippot.* However, if Jews are pious and righteous, they can release the trapped souls and complete the restoration. The point of this obscure thinking is that people can restore good with righteous conduct. Lurianic Kabbalah places responsibility for the restoration of creation upon people, not upon God. It also believes in reincarnation.

Hasidism (or *Chasidism)* is a form of Judaism that adopted a greatly simplified form of Kabbalah. It arose in Poland in the eighteenth century. The founder of Hasidism is considered to be Israel Ba'al Shem Tov (1700–1760; also known as Israel Ben Eliezer). Hasidism placed emphasis on the love of God and ecstasy through prayer (Hasid means "pious"). There are several forms of Hasidism, but each Hasidic community possesses an individual, the *Tsaddiq* (also *Tzadik* or *Zaddik),* who is very close to God and who is an intermediary between the rest of the community and God. The concept of the Tsaddiq is based on Lurianic Kabbalah and on Shabbetai Zevi (a seventeenth-century Jew who claimed to be the Messiah, but actually converted to Islam under threat of death). Each Tsaddiq has great influence on his community. He can even change evil thoughts into good ones. Devotion to the Tsaddiq represents a new way of interacting with God, and directly challenged traditional order. For this reason, it was strongly opposed by rabbis. Today, Hasidism is often considered to be part of the Orthodox movement, but it is perhaps better regarded as a separate expression of Judaism.

Most Jews today in the United States and Western Europe are *Ashkenazim,* meaning their origin is from France, Germany, and Eastern Europe. Historically, most Ashkenazic Jews spoke a Slavic language or Yiddish, which is an amalgam of Middle German with several other languages, including Hebrew. By contrast, the ancestors of *Sephardic* Jews lived in Spain and Portugal, which were under Muslim control until 1492. Just as Yiddish was an amalgam based primarily on German, the local language of many Ashkenazic Jews, so Sephardic Jews had their own language, which was a mixture of medieval Spanish and other languages, primarily Hebrew. This language is called by several names, including Judeo-Spanish, Spanioli, Judezmo, or Ladino, and like Yiddish, is rarely spoken today. Because Muslims of the Middle Ages were more tolerant of Jews than Christians were, Sephardic Jews were generally accepted into mainstream Spanish society until 1492, when Christians obtained control of all of Spain and forced the conversion or expulsion of both Muslims and Jews. After this expulsion, Jews settled primarily in North Africa and the Middle East — again with general acceptance by Muslims — with smaller communities in a few places in Europe. These new Sephardic communities retained much of the culture and language of their Spanish homeland. While the fundamental beliefs of Sephardic Jews correspond to those of their Ashkenazic counterparts, Sephardic Jews tend to be Orthodox, and there are minor differences in customs and in the interpretation of the Halakhah. Today, about 80 percent of the World's Jews are Ashkenazic and 20 percent are Sephardic, with a very small number that do not fit well into either category.

Jews have adapted to modernity with flexibility and scholarship. Moses Mendelssohn (1729–1786) brought secular reasoning into Judaism. Mendelssohn thought that God had revealed legislation and ceremonial details to Israel, but not unique religious truths. He believed that the real truths of religion are comprehensible by the intellect. It is people, not God, who make an understanding of religion possible. Mendelssohn vigorously defended Judaism while maintaining a respect for other religions. Because God did not reveal religion to any particular people or group, all people could unite and use reason to work through their differences of opinion.

The Enlightenment of the eighteenth century and the first half of the nineteenth century constituted a period of emancipation of the Jews, beginning in Germany. Previously, Jews were able to live in a given area (ghetto) largely because their labor was desired. This ghettoization was the legal basis for the expulsion of Jews. They were ordered to leave a community under the pretense that their labor was no longer needed, very much like a temporary worker today might find that his or her contract has been terminated or not renewed. Emancipation began with the Edict of Tolerance issued by the Habsburgs in 1782. A provision of the edict was the explicit desire to "Gentilize" Jews by giving them an educational and professional experience that was much closer to that of the Gentile community. Emancipation also carried with it the stipulation that Jews would cease to think of themselves as a single community transcending national boundaries and instead began to think of themselves as citizens of a particular country.

As emancipation unfolded, it provided Jews with new educational and professional opportunities, making possible their own Enlightenment, the *Haskalah.* Jews who supported the Haskalah were called the *Maskilim.* The Jewish Enlightenment began in the early nineteenth century in Germany and France, and extended throughout the century to the rest of Europe. The Maskilim wanted to take advantage of the new opportunities for non-religious education that were available in the gentile world. Like Gentile leaders, these Jewish leaders believed that Jews should diversify in their professions. Unprecedented opportunities were opened to Jews, who were uniquely prepared to take advantage of them because of their history of learning. This was the beginning of modern Jewish scholarship and the beginning of the enormous contributions that Jews would make in every area of secular scholarship. Thousands of hours of Talmudic study might not have immediate application to the modern world, but it prepared Jews for new secular learning.

The Haskalah rejected the idea that the Diaspora was in exile, and thought instead that the Jews had been dispersed throughout the world to serve as examples of righteousness. To them, the word "exile" implied punishment. This new interpretation of the Diaspora redefined Judaism because, traditionally, Judaism was intimately tied to the land of Israel, but now the Haskalah accepted and even championed Judaism without a homeland. Some synagogues dropped the traditional benediction for a return to Israel and began calling themselves temples. To them, the concept of a Third Temple no longer had immediacy, and the word "temple" need no longer be restricted to one of the two destroyed temples, or the supposedly imminent third. Emulating Protestantism, they wanted something like a sermon in their services, and wanted it to be practical and to be delivered in the vernacular. Also, they wanted shorter services and the introduction of music.

The eighteenth-century emancipation was also a time of introspection and internal change for Jews, who were brought into contact with the ideas of the Enlightenment and a secular world for the first time. Jews were thus confronted with a dichotomy as sharp as that caused centuries earlier by the influx of Greek knowledge. The Jewish Enlightenment presented Jews with a quandary. What role, if any, do current environment and recent history play in a religion that has always defined itself as much by history and culture as by beliefs? As is always the case with new knowledge, there is both gain and loss. New opportunities brought Jews a sense of belonging that was unprecedented in their history. They stepped out of their ghettos and into a new world with confidence and a belief in their place in the world. The Science of Judaism movement in the early nineteenth century believed that a thorough study of Jewish history would establish their legitimate place in Europe. The downside of emancipation was that Jewish tradition and philosophy, including the Halakhah, no longer necessarily carried the day. Some Jews worried that their numbers would dwindle because of the now-available attractions of the Gentile world, and that it was therefore imperative that some of the more onerous aspects of Judaism be loosened.

The Maskilim wanted to integrate ideas of the Enlightenment into Judaism, "updating" and making it more appealing. Reformers also thought that Judaism must change if Jews were to fulfill the Covenant requirement of being an exemplary people. At about this time, Biblical scholarship questioned the divine nature of the Torah, upon which all of Jewish religious thought, including the Halakhah, was based. This was profoundly troubling to traditional Jews. Some of the proposed changes were difficult to accept, but a portion of the Jewish community adopted other changes. Abraham Geiger pointed out that Judaism had always undergone very significant changes, and that what was proposed now was actually no more radical than what the Jewish community had already experienced. The idea that caused the most angst among Jews was the proposed human nature of the Torah. The Maskilim extrapolated from this that Jews need not be bound by traditional commandments because these came from people, not from God. The result was the birth of the Reform movement in Western Europe.

Reform Judaism represents an acceptance of modernity. In 1818, the first Reform temple was established in Hamburg. Because the messiah was de-emphasized in Reform Judaism, the belief that there would not be another Temple until his return was also de-emphasized, and it became permissible in Reform Judaism to use the term "temple" interchangeably with "synagogue." Nineteenth-century biblical scholarship satisfied Reform Jews that the Tanakh was the work of people, not of God. The teachings of the prophets were given relatively equal weight to the Torah. Reform Jews revere the Halakhah, but do not accept it as binding, and instead focus on ethical behavior and social justice.

Reform Judaism simplified services and introduced prayers in vernacular. It rejected literal revelation in favor of a progressive revelation that was linked to knowledge; that is, people could participate in revelations through learning and self-improvement. Reform Judaism argued that individual Jews had choices and need not necessarily agree on every aspect of practice and belief. Reform Judaism dispensed with a belief in bodily resurrection, but not in the immortality of the soul. Whereas Judaism since its inception was considered to run only through the mother, Reform Judaism in the 1980s accepted patrilineal heritage. Also, in the 1980s, it accepted mixed marriages between Jews and Gentiles, and is the only form of Judaism to do so.

Reform Jews have also struggled with the issue of Zionism, the belief and political movement asserting that Jews should once again have a sovereign homeland in the ancient land of Israel. After the establishment of the modern state of Israel, Zionism has focused on the maintenance and prosperity of the new Jewish state. Reform Jews have not reached consensus on Zionism. The Pittsburgh Platform of 1885, which was the first of three major platforms of American Reform Judaism, stated that Jews were a religious community, not a nation, and gave scant weight to Zionism. A second platform, in Columbus in 1937, adopted Zionism as a goal. In 1976, the third platform recognized both the state of Israel and the legitimacy of the Diaspora. Because of bias in immigration policy, the United States initially had a higher percentage of Reform Jews among its Jewish population than did other countries, but after 1880, most Jewish immigrants were from Eastern Europe, and it was no longer true that they were predominantly reformed.

Positive historical Judaism was founded by Zacharias Frankel (1801–1875), who sought a middle ground by accepting some aspects of modernity, while adhering to some aspects of historical Judaism and accepting more of Rabbinic Judaism than the reformers. Positive historical Judaism maintained that the behavior and thinking of previous generations should provide the blueprint for the present and the future.

Frankel's followers merged scholarship with the existing Rabbinic outline of Judaism. They accepted the human origin of the Jewish canon, but in contrast to reformed Jews, maintained that it was nevertheless inviolate in its mandates and wisdom.

The Conservative movement, based on the ideas of Frankel, was founded in the United States in the nineteenth century. Like Reformed Judaism, Conservative Judaism accepts that the Torah was written by people, but maintains its primacy. Conservative Jews believe that God did not directly issue the Torah, but guided people in its creation. Likewise, Conservative Judaism respects the binding nature of the Halakhah, and holds that it is essentially unchanging as a whole, but allows for occasional changes in a portion of the Halakhah as new wisdom and experience accumulate. Unlike Reform Judaism, the concept of a homeland is integral to most expressions of Conservative Judaism. The American Conservative movement was founded about the time that more Jewish immigrants began arriving from Eastern Europe, and was more appealing to most of these immigrants than Reform Judaism.

Intuitively, we might expect Orthodox Judaism to have preceded Reform Judaism, but the reverse is true. Orthodox Judaism is a response to Reform Judaism. One of the founders of Orthodox Judaism was Moses Sofer (1763–1839). Sofer taught that the Torah was indeed the direct word of God and that it expressly forbids everything that is new. Sofer had little use for secular learning unless it was immediately applicable to a specific situation. In contrast, Rabbi Samson Raphael Hirsch (1808–1888) taught that traditional Judaism, with a divine Torah and a binding Halakhah, could be combined with secular life. Hirsch was a founder of Neo-Orthodoxy, which does not compromise on the divine nature of the Torah, in contrast to Conservative and Reform Judaism, but accepts some aspects of modernity. Today, Orthodox Jews are diverse, with variation among many of their specific beliefs, and with some overlap with the beliefs of Conservative Jews. We must be careful not to assume that we understand an individual Jew's beliefs from the movement he or she is affiliated with, but generally speaking, Orthodox Jews are united in their commitment to an unchanging Halakhah and the divine nature of the Torah. Orthodox Judaism might have a sermon in a vernacular language, but its prayers are in Hebrew. Many Orthodox congregations practice separate seating for men and women. Some

Orthodox Jews are vehemently Zionist while others are non-Zionist. Though there are many exceptions, in general, Orthodox Jews regard Reform rabbis as lay Jews, Reform lay Jews as Jews who have strayed, and Reform converts as non-Jews.

Reconstructionist Judaism is often considered a fourth movement, though it is very similar to Reform Judaism. God is de-emphasized in favor of humanism, social change, and individual self-improvement. Reconstructionist Jews see Judaism more as an evolving civilization than as a religion. As is the case in Reform Judaism, paternal lineage is accepted. In contrast with all other movements of Judaism, including Reform Judaism, Reconstructionist Jews do not believe that God chose them.

Jews without God, also called the Society for Humanistic Judaism, was organized in 1969. This is another expression of the continuing coexistence of the autonomous religious and cultural aspects of Judaism, and the integral role of humanism in Judaism.

We can use divorce and ordination as examples of how the different forms of Judaism deal with daily life. Because Halakhah does not allow for a woman to initiate a divorce, Orthodox and Conservative groups still hold to this traditional doctrine, though there are a variety of methods of extricating women from a bad marriage. Among Reform Jews, who do not see themselves bound by the Halakhah, a wife can initiate a divorce and receive a gett over her husband's objections. The Conservative movement began ordaining women as rabbis in 1985, after considerable and very scholarly soul searching. They recognize that women in the past were not given the necessary experiences to make the judgments that rabbis are called on to make, but that this is no longer true. Increasing opportunities for women have removed a legitimate objection to their ordination, satisfying most Conservative Jews that ordination of women is now acceptable. Orthodox Jews have still not formally ordained any women, but one has been privately ordained and several are currently studying for ordination.

The heterogeneity of Jewish thought is reflected in educational institutions at all levels. The Hebrew Union College in Cincinnati, New York, and Los Angeles is a reform seminary. The Jewish Theological Seminary in New York is Conservative. Yeshiva University is Orthodox.

During emancipation, Jews were granted citizenship in their respective European states and were free to leave their ghettos. At the same time, however, this caused most Europeans to encounter Jews for the first time. Jews were no longer "out of sight and out of mind." Emancipation was far from integration, and when confronted with the prospect of integration, Europeans either took an integrationist approach, which held that Jews should be admitted as individuals, or they took a segregationist approach, which held that Jews should be admitted collectively as a distinct and separate nation. Unlike the integrationist model, the segregationist model would have required Jews to continue to live together.

But even with emancipation, Jews often remained a separate ethnic group within their home country, with customs and behavior that were not shared or understood by their countrymen. Without a pathway to integration and acceptance, the significance of emancipation was greatly diluted. It is difficult for outsiders to understand the need for a group of people with a common heritage to behave in a different way in order to preserve that heritage and a sense of community. We may be put off that they are not identical to us in their customs and behaviors, but we must realize that these differences are an integral part of their religion. For this reason we must be exquisitely tolerant and understanding, not just of cultural and religious differences, but also of the different behaviors and thought processes that underlie and reinforce those cultural and religious differences. It is a lesson of history that we are not truly tolerant of religious differences, and have not truly emancipated a group of people, until we are tolerant of the different customs and behaviors that emanate from these differences. We owe this to others, and we must ask it from them, because we are all outsiders, in one way or another, more often than we are insiders.

The situation facing Jews after emancipation was somewhat similar to that facing African Americans today in that laws were changed to theoretically allow equal participation in society, but there was no pathway by which to achieve this. The inevitable persistence of hostility and sense of otherness requires that the target group have a clearly defined and reasonable pathway into full participation in society. Changing laws does not change minds, erase prejudices, or create opportunities, and unless specific steps are taken to give the target group full and immediate access to all aspects of society, these prejudices will carry the day despite the changes in laws. One of the pleasures of studying history is that it offers lessons in unexpected places, and here we have one: anyone who doubts the continuing need for affirmative action need only study the fate of the Jews after their "emancipation."

Despite emancipation, the persistence of hostility toward Jews, combined with the reality that they had no clear pathway toward integration, made it only a matter of time before anti-Semitism again emerged. Nationalism, sweeping through Europe, accentuated the differences between Jewish culture and language and those of the dominant culture, and augmented the sense of otherness that was associated with Jews. Adding fuel to the fire was the conception, beginning in the nineteenth century, of Jews as a separate and inferior race. These factors, augmented by paranoia and the Great Depression of the 1930s, and magnified by the Nazi agenda, led to the Holocaust. Attempts at genocide are not inescapable or predetermined in the human experience, but for them to be avoided, we must address the factors that make them more likely.

Catastrophes of history arise from a cascade of events, not from one incident, and the Holocaust was no exception. It came from a series of events, none worse or more alarming than the one just before it, but the inexorable, unrestrained cumulative effect resulted in the extermination of 6 million Jews. We know why the Holocaust occurred. First, the different customs, beliefs, and often language of German Jews distinguished them from other Germans. They were "other." This otherness was reinforced by the new view of Jews as a distinct and inferior race. It has been our curse that we have distrusted anyone or any group perceived as not being "one of us" in every way. Second, the economic conditions of Germany in the 1920s and 1930s benighted people and brought out the desperation, ignorance, irrationality, and anger that can lie below the surface in better times. Once these terrible aspects of humanity came to the fore, the inevitable target was "the other." Third, other nations were unwilling to move against Germany in the early stages of the Reich. To prevent future holocausts, we must rectify all of these causes. Only when the prerequisites are removed can we prevent future genocides. We must recognize the right of all people to follow their customs and traditions, and we must realize that we are all far more alike than different. We must work for the economic improvement of all societies, so as to ensure a reasonable and stable security for all, and we must be willing to intervene in the early stages of any systematic attempt to eliminate an ethnic or cultural group.

With the same remarkable resilience that has always characterized Judaism, it survived the Holocaust and remains vibrant in large measure because of its continued reverence for its great literature. The Torah scroll, also called the *Safer Torah,* is indispensable to a Jewish community, and is, in fact, the only item that is irreplaceable in the formation of a Jewish community. A Torah scroll is written without vowels or punctuation, and must be written on a special type of parchment in a particular style of script, so that every scroll is identical. The scroll is not to be touched, and people should stand when it is opened. Many Jews will place a portion of the scripture in a cylinder and attach it to a doorpost. This is called a *mezuzah* (or *mezzuzah*). A phylactery (or *tefillin*) is a portion of the scripture that is worn by some Jews during the morning prayer service.

Torah Scroll

The Torah scroll, also called the *Safer Torah,* is the only item that is indispensable and irreplaceable in the formation of a Jewish community. A Torah scroll is written on a special type of parchment in a particular style of script, so that every scroll is identical in style and content.

The Jewish prayer book, the *Siddur,* contains prayers from many times and places, and could theoretically be added to. There are three times to pray — morning, evening, and night. These times are called *Shachrit,* Minchah, and Ma'ariv, respectively. The *Shma* (also *Sh'ma* or *Shema*) is a central prayer in Jewish life and is a major part of both the morning and evening prayers. If possible, Jews try to recite the *Shma* upon someone's death. The first paragraph of the *Shma* is as follows:

> *Hear O Israel, the Lord is our God, the Lord is One.*
> *Blessed is His name, whose glorious kingdom is forever and ever. Love the Lord your God with all your heart, and all your soul, and all your might. These words that I command you today shall be upon your heart. Repeat them to your children, and talk about them when you sit in your home, and when you walk in the street; when you lie down, and when you rise up. Hold fast to them as a sign upon your hand, and let them be as reminders before your eyes. Write them on the doorposts of your home and at your gates.*

The *Amidah* (or *Shmona Esrey)* is another central Jewish prayer. It contains nineteen benedictions. It begins with three benedictions of praise for God, followed by thirteen benedictions of petition, and closes with three benedictions of thanksgiving to God. On *Shabbat* (the Sabbath), the middle benedictions (those of petition) are not performed. The *Amidah* is always recited silently and while standing, and is sometimes called the Standing Devotion. In the morning and evening prayers, the *Amidah* is preceded by recitation of three chapters from the Torah.

The *Hallel* is a collection of six psalms — 113 through 118 — that are recited at festivals. A *minyan,* consisting of ten adults (in Orthodox Judaism, ten men) is required to initiate a communal religious ceremony. A minyan represents the entire community of Israel.

In Judaism, the day begins in the evening because Genesis describes the first day as being evening and morning and the second day as being the next evening and morning, etc. The Jewish calendar counts the year by the sun, but uses the moon to calculate months. In the Jewish calendar, months begin with each new moon, making them either twenty-nine or thirty days in duration. Twelve such months total 354 days, but unlike the Muslim calendar, the Jewish calendar periodically inserts a thirteenth month to ensure correspondence of the lunar months and the solar year. This leap month allows holidays to occur in the same season every year. The names of the Jewish months come from the Jews' time in Babylonia. In the Diaspora, Jewish holidays tend to last for two days instead of one because of historical uncertainty in the transmission of the calendar to these communities.

More than other religions, Judaism measures time and records events in relation to its holidays. Jews often do not say that something happened "last month" or on such and such a date. They often say instead that something happened before, during, or after a particular holiday. The awareness of and practicing of the Jewish calendar is not the definition of a Jew, but it is a very important part of being Jewish. The Jewish scholar and theologian Abraham Joshua Heschel (1907–1972) said that Jews have created "cathedrals in time" to compensate for their loss of the Temples in space.

Pesach (Passover) commemorates the mercy of God in sparing Jews from the slaughter of the firstborn ordered by the Egyptian pharaoh. During this time, Jews eat no leavening because they had no time for their bread to rise during their flight from Egypt. Many Jews will use different dinner plates and utensils at Passover to ensure that there is no trace of leavening. A special meal, called a *Seder,* is eaten during Pesach.

The *Omer* is the forty-nine-day period between Passover and *Shavuot.* Marriages are generally not performed during this period. Other modern holidays have been inserted in this period, such as Holocaust Remembrance Day (*Yom Hashoah*), which is one week after Passover, on the anniversary of the 1943 Warsaw Ghetto uprising. But the somber tone is interrupted by levity on the birthday of modern Israel, on May 14.

Shavuot (also called Pentecost) occurs fifty days after Pesach (Passover). It originally celebrated the spring barley harvest, though tradition has attached historical significance to the holiday (the revelation of the Torah).

The Days of Awe (also called the High Holy Days) fall between *Rosh Hashanah* (the New Year) and *Yom Kippur* (the Day of Atonement). This is a time of introspection in which Jews often will apologize to people whom they have wronged or offended. Many Jews believe that even God cannot forgive a sin against another person; only the offended person can. At the beginning of the Days of Awe, traditional Jews believe that their names are written in the *Book of Life* or the *Book of Death,* but that those books stay open until the end of Yom Kippur and their names can be moved from the *Book of Death* to the *Book of Life* if they atone sincerely. Yom Kippur is a full-day fast — actually twenty-five hours, since it lasts from one half-hour before sunset of one day to nightfall of the next — during which time traditional Jews will not eat, drink, work, engage in sexual relations, apply lotions or cosmetics, wash, or wear leather shoes. The reason for the latter prohibition is that leather shoes were removed in holy places in ancient times, and it is thought that the comfort they provide should be forgone during this time, as is the case with other comforts.

Shofar

The Shofar is a horn, traditionally from a ram, that has long been used to announce holidays and special occasions in Judaism. It is mentioned in the Tanakh. Today, the Shofar is primarily sounded during *Rosh Hashanah* (the New Year) and *Yom Kippur* (the Day of Atonement), marking the beginning and end of the Days of Awe.

Five days after Yom Kippur, *Sukkot* (or *Sukkoth)* celebrates the autumn harvest and commemorates the wandering in the desert. This simultaneous celebration of natural and historic events is a frequent occurrence in Judaism. During Sukkot, Jews construct a hut called a *Sukkah* to commemorate the makeshift shelters necessary during their wanderings.

Hanukkah (also *Hanukah* or *Chanukah)* commemorates the miraculous burning of oil in the Temple for eight days as it was re-dedicated after the successful Maccabee revolt (this kind of miracle, where supplies last far longer than thought possible, is a common biblical theme, and we see it a number of places in the Bible, most notably the story of Jesus feeding the 5,000). Hanukkah uses a nine-branched candelabrum called a *Hanukiyah* (*Chanukiah)*, which has a central candle and four candles on each side. The standard *menorah* is an ancient symbol that predates the Hanukiyah and has only seven candles, three on each side of a central candle. For Hanukkah, a special menorah was needed because the oil had burned for eight days, and a traditional seven-branched candelabrum was insufficient. Hanukkah is a minor holiday and is not even referenced in the Jewish canon, but is widely known because it occurs near Christmas.

Menorah

The standard *menorah* is an ancient symbol that has seven candles, three on each side of a central candle. The menorah is one of Judaism's oldest symbols (the Six-Pointed Star, though of ancient origin, was not routinely used by Jews as a symbol of their religion until the 15th century CE). The standard menorah is a seven-branched candelabrum that is distinct from and older than the nine-branched candelabrum used during Hanukkah. It is said to symbolize the burning bush through which God spoke to Moses.

The Sabbath, which seems to be a unique Jewish contribution, has great significance, and any Sabbath is more holy than any holiday. Many of the rituals associated with holidays are not performed if that holiday falls on the Sabbath.

Like Islam, Judaism forbids the direct depiction of God because this may facilitate idolatry, and Judaism does not have the well-developed artistic tradition that Christianity does. Until the early synagogues, there was no pictorial art at all. Most art that is specific to Judaism is in the form of manuscript illuminations. Music is also very important in Jewish practice and worship.

There are four life-cycle events: birth, puberty, marriage, and death. Some would add conversion, which essentially confers newborn status on the convert. Circumcision (*Brit Milah*) occurs on the eighth day. It brings the child into the Covenant and serves as a permanent symbol of his inclusion therein. It usually takes place at home in the presence of a minyan. At one time, this was performed by the father, but now is performed by a *Mohel,* with the baby typically being held by a grandfather. After the circumcision there is a responsive reading, after which the baby is named. The reading of verses from the Tanakh then completes the ceremony.

Jewish girls come of age at twelve and boys at thirteen, at which time they undergo the *Bat Mitzvah* and *Bar Mitzvah,* respectively, representing entry into adulthood.

The first stage of marriage is betrothal (*Kiddushin*) during which time the groom gives the bride an object to symbolize their attachment. The second stage is the marriage contract, the *Ketuvah* (or *Ketubah*), which enumerates the obligations of each party according to scripture, Jewish tradition, and ethical behavior. A central obligation is that the man will pay the woman in the event of a divorce. This was designed both to prevent impulsive divorce and to guarantee the rights of wives. A marriage ceremony, called a *Nisuin,* is then performed under a canopy called a *Huppah,* which symbolizes a prayer shawl. Until modern times, a rabbi was not required as long as there were two acceptable witnesses. In antiquity, the different stages of marriage took place at different times, but they are all done concurrently today. The bride circles the groom because of a passage in the Tanakh stating that a woman should court a man. Then the Ketuvah is read. Seven blessings are then pronounced, usually by the couple, but occasionally by their relatives.

In Orthodox and Conservative Judaism, only a man can initiate a divorce. This is part of the reason why the Ketuvah requires the man to pay the woman in the event of a divorce. If a woman wishes a divorce, she can petition the court. The court cannot require the man to grant divorce, but it can issue sanctions. In Reform Judaism, a woman can initiate a divorce over her husband's objections because the binding nature of the Halakhah is not recognized.

The *Chevra Kadisha* (or *Hevrah Kadisha)* is a group of people who prepare a corpse for burial. The deceased is dressed in white, as is the case with Muslims, and often also with a prayer shawl. Burial is the only permissible disposition after death. Caskets are optional, but if used, should be simple. Between death and burial, a period called *Aninut,* the mourner is released from his or her normal religious obligations. Burial takes place within twenty-four hours of death. There is no wake, no embalming, and no viewing, because nothing should interfere with returning the body to dust. In antiquity, bodies were sometimes left to decay, after which the bones were retrieved and placed in an ossuary.

Shiva (or *Shivah)* is observed for the deaths of parents, children, spouses, and siblings. The period of Shiva begins after burial and lasts for seven days (Shiva means "seven" in Hebrew), during which time a memorial candle burns continuously. Typically, the grieving person will spend much of this time sitting, as proximity to the ground represents a grieving state. No cosmetics are worn, and simple meals, prepared by family and close friends, are eaten. During Shiva, prayers are said in the presence of a minyan three times a day. The Shiva is not carried out on the Sabbath or on Festival days, and these days can even terminate a Shiva with full fulfillment of the obligation.

The second stage after burial (called *shloshim)* lasts for thirty days, during which time there is no gaiety. Only the immediate family enters a third, yearlong, stage of grief, and some Jews participate in this stage only for a parent. During this year, the immediate family member recites the *Kaddish,* a memorial prayer. It is recited every day for the first eleven months, in the presence of a minyan, and then on every anniversary of the death. A memorial candle is also lit on every anniversary. Festivals are avoided for one year.

In conversion, the convert first studies and receives instruction, after which there may be an examination by a *Bet din* (Rabbinical court).

After his approval, a male convert is circumcised; he is then immersed three times in a ritual bath called a *Miqveh,* as are female converts, for the purpose of removing impurities. The *Miqveh* is the origin of Christian Baptism, though Christians have shifted the purpose of the water toward washing away sin — an indication of evil — and not simply impurities. The official policy of Judaism is the complete equality of Jews by birth and Jews by choice (conversion).

The rise of nationalism and the creation of new nation-states in the nineteenth century fueled the desire of many Jews to see a reestablishment of a homeland, a movement called Zionism. Theodore Herzl (1860–1904) was the driving force in the early Zionist movement. Eastern European Jews, who were neither assimilated nor as well treated as their Western counterparts, were more attracted to Zionism. At one point, the British offered a Jewish state in Uganda, an option that was rejected by the seventh Zionist Conference in Basle in 1905. Russian and Eastern European Jews blended nineteenth-century nationalism with religious fervor and their own experiences to insist on a homeland in Palestine. Three million Jews left Russia between 1882 and 1918. Whereas Herzl and the first Zionists had worked for international recognition of a Jewish state, many were now more interested in settlement in Palestine and a de facto Jewish state by "squatters' rights."

Contemporary with Zionism was Jewish Autonomism, prevalent in Eastern Europe and Russia. One of its major proponents was historian and activist Simon Dubnow, who held that Jews could continue to live in their present location and form, in effect a nation within a nation, maintaining self-rule and rejecting assimilation. Whereas Zionists envisioned a Jewish state based on Hebrew, Autonomism was to be based primarily on Yiddish culture. Individual Jews might or might not be Zionists, but one need not be Jewish to be a Zionist. There are two types of Christian Zionists, neither of which has adopted Zionism in the best interest of Jews. One group of Christian Zionists want Jews to settle the land of Israel in order to prepare for the second coming of Jesus, after which all Christian good wishes would evaporate. Historically, another type of European Christian Zionist was anti-Semitic and simply wanted the Jews living elsewhere.

The current conflict in the Middle East initially appears to be a struggle between religions or cultures, but is actually a clash over how to deal with the feeling of being threatened. Religious differences are a veneer underneath which lies the real quarrel. The Middle East conflict in very great measure is a legacy of WW I. During the war, the Ottoman Empire allied with the Central powers, Germany and Austria-Hungary. Arab territories under the Ottoman Empire were promised independence if they would revolt against the Ottomans and join the Allies, but the British were also negotiating with Jews for the same land. The Balfour Declaration, passed in Britain in 1917, promised a homeland to Jews (its hidden agenda was to provide an incentive for Russian Jews to resist the Bolsheviks and for American Jews to pressure their government to enter the war). After the war, the colonies of the defeated Central Powers were taken away, made protectorates of the victorious powers, and promised independence. These lands included Palestine. The allies did not honor their pledge of postwar independence, and instead kept the Arab territories. In 1922, Arabs persuaded Britain to carve off a major portion of the land that the Balfour Declaration had earmarked for Israel, creating Transjordan. The League of Nations then approved the Balfour Declaration and gave a mandate to Britain to establish a home for Jews in Palestine.

Between 1919 and 1939, about 350,000 Jews settled in Palestine. They purchased land from Arabs, but the legitimacy of those purchases did not relieve the hard feelings of Jewish settlement. The British ignored these problems until 1939, when they issued a white paper that retracted the Balfour Declaration and curtailed further Jewish immigration. Concurrent with Nazi persecution, this white paper closed off one of the few remaining avenues of escape for Eastern European Jews. In 1947, the United Nations partitioned the western part of Palestine into Arab and Jewish areas. Jews accepted this, though it was a smaller piece of land than they had hoped for, but Arabs rejected it. The creation of Israel simultaneously recognized Arab nationalist claims in the region, but because only the Zionists accepted the UN declaration, a Palestinian state never came to be. After the May 1948 invasion of the new Israel by a coalition of Arab countries, the victorious Jewish state acquired much of the land that had initially been offered to the Arabs. Declining the UN proposal, followed by their military defeat, cost the Arabs the Palestinian state that they could otherwise have had.

I believe Israel is entitled to feel a measure of exoneration that it accepted a United Nations proposal and then defended the land that had been offered it. The difficulty is the legitimacy of the proposal, given that the land the UN offered to Jews had long been home to many Arabs, who have the right to question the power of the UN to divide their land. To Arabs, Zionism became another manifestation of Western imperialism and European colonialism. While sympathy for Jews in the aftermath of the Holocaust was among its driving forces, the establishment of Israel can also be viewed as an extension of European colonization, with the apparent blessing of the UN. European intervention and insistence on control of a region or a people interrupts the normal course of history, makes the indigenous people feel powerless, and sets up confrontations that would not otherwise have occurred.

Twice in its history, Judaism has shown us that it is better to look inward than outward, and that the strength of a people is its culture, not in its geographic location. Is this lesson applicable today? If a student and admirer of Judaism could ask his teachers for one more gift, I would plead with Israel to have a greater understanding of the Palestinian situation, and to recognize that no group can fully control the few extremists in its midst.

With the hope for peace in the Middle East, we end our study of a small group of people who began as nomads and laid the foundations of the Western world. We now turn our attention to Judaism's religious offspring.

Chapter 9

CHRISTIANITY

There are 2 billion Christians in the world, making it the world's predominant religion, both in numbers and in the military and economic power of its adherents. Jesus is the most enigmatic of all religious figures. We can have no direct knowledge of him or those around him because no primary sources mention him. The closest we have to a primary source is a reference written in the year 93 CE by the historian Josephus, who simply repeats what he had heard. Historians cannot experiment in the way that natural scientists can, and therefore never can achieve complete certainty. In general, to accept something as true, historians require three criteria: attestation by multiple, independent sources, attestation without an incentive for gain by the source, and contextual consistency (meaning the alleged action or event must make sense for that time and place). Using these techniques, historians have used intelligent speculation and contextual understanding to form a plausible reconstruction of the life of Jesus and the development of Christianity.

In the fifth century CE, the date of the commencement of Jesus' teaching was assumed to be what we now call the year 30, and he was assumed to be about thirty years old, though there is no documentation for either of these beliefs. This is the origin of the idea that he was born at what we would call the year zero. It is impossible to match all of the biblical record of Jesus' birth to what is historically known; however, all parts of the biblical account did occur in some form in at least some part of the eastern Mediterranean at some time close to the supposed year of Jesus' birth. There is no date at which all of these occurred, but his birth seems to have been between 8 and 4 BCE.

Nazareth was near a large city called Sepphoris, but there is no indication that Jesus ever went there. He seems to have spent most of his time in the town of Capernaum. It is unclear how much Jesus traveled, and the only evidence we have of his going to any large city was his trip to Jerusalem at the end of his life.

Though it is widely assumed and probable that Jesus spoke Aramaic, this has never been proven, and there is a growing belief that he also read and spoke Greek, which had penetrated even to the remote areas of the Holy Land by the time that Jesus lived. There is a high probability that any educated person — and Jesus seems to have had some education and may have been a rabbi — spoke Greek.

Jesus restricted his teachings to Jews, and as far as we can tell, had no opinion about Gentiles. Most scholars agree that Jesus believed in an imminent apocalypse. He was a follower of John the Baptist, who believed that the end of the world was near, and most (but not all) scholars believe Jesus adopted an apocalyptic view from his mentor. Many of his teachings that are considered revolutionary (if in fact they occurred), such as gender egalitarianism, nonviolence, and association with outcasts, tax collectors, and prostitutes, make more sense in an apocalyptic context because egalitarianism was to be the rule after the apocalypse. Perhaps his ideas might have been different had he known that no apocalypse was soon to come.

We cannot know how much of Jesus' teachings and beliefs originated with him, but based on contextual reconstruction, it is doubtful that his message was unique or that he was a particularly radical thinker. His major teachings were already in the air at the time. In historical terms, there is nothing unique about Jesus. He was one of many people at the time who believed in an imminent apocalypse and who practiced Judaism while holding that Jewish authorities were often corrupt and could be questioned. At no time and over no issue was it ever a matter of Jesus against everyone else. He clashed with mainstream Judaism, and particularly with Jewish sects, but so had many earlier people, and many

Jews agreed with him. Precise details will forever be unclear, but Jesus apparently taught that the letter of religious law could be kept without really pleasing God, and that truly religious people transcend the letter of the law and are inwardly transformed.

Jesus asked for adherence to the spirit and not just the letter of the law. This was the essence of his teachings concerning morality and behavior, and this was his criticism of the Pharisees. Likewise, the Sadducees put a great deal of emphasis on sacrifice. Jesus did not oppose this, as far as we know, but thought that sacrifice alone was insufficient. In contrast to the Essenes, Jesus did not think that God demanded physical separation from, and near zealous contempt for, other Jews. In all probability, because of his belief in an apocalypse, Jesus asked for engagement and for actions that made an immediate difference, rather than rituals performed in isolation. But he undoubtedly asked for these things in addition to, not in lieu of, traditional observance of the Torah. Jesus did not teach the sacredness of the family, but rather taught that it would be necessary for families to split up and experience strife because not everyone in the family would be able to understand what must be done. This dissolution of families is another teaching that makes sense in light of an impending apocalypse.

Jesus disagreed with the Pharisees on a number of issues, but it would be wrong to consider all Pharisees his enemies. One area of disagreement was divorce, which could only be initiated by men. Jesus seems not to have supported divorce, probably because it usually left women destitute (we do not want to read too much into this, but it may have been an example of Jesus' egalitarian treatment of women). A second disagreement was taxes, which Jesus accepted, possibly because his apocalyptic views suggested that it was soon to be a moot point. A third divergence concerned observance of the Sabbath. In contrast to the Essenes and some Pharisees, he thought that humanitarian work could be performed on the Sabbath. The common denominator of these opinions is that within the framework of Judaism, Jesus supported people over a rigid interpretation of Jewish law. Jesus did support Jewish law and was by no means an insurgent, but he thought that the details of the law often obscured the larger message of helping others.

Jesus preached that even those who followed traditional Jewish law would not survive the coming apocalypse unless they followed his teachings and immediately surrendered their positions of superiority. Even the high priest and the institutions themselves would not survive because of their arrogance. Jesus is said to have prophesied that the Temple itself — the very symbol of Judaism — would be destroyed because of corruption. While we cannot know if this prophecy was actually made, it is contextually consistent. His prediction of the Temple's destruction, in conjunction with the expectation that the imminent apocalypse would destroy everything evil, was tantamount to saying that the priests who ran the Temple were evil. With this prediction, he offended both Jewish authorities and the Roman authorities with whom they colluded.

Jesus probably also had a reputation as a mystic and exorcist, as did others of his time. Some — probably not many — believed him capable of miracles and miraculous healing of the sick, abilities often ascribed to mystics and exorcists. Others of his time were also associated with these abilities, and people we would now call faith healers were known at the time of and before Jesus. In Jewish tradition, the prophet Elijah was reputed to have raised someone from the dead.

It appears that Jesus' ministry lasted only a short time, from less than a year (according to Mark) to between two and three years (according to John). As far as we can ascertain, Jesus had few followers, and endured much rejection. He did gather around him a small group — said to be twelve — called apostles (the terms "disciple" and "apostle" are often used interchangeably, but "disciple" refers to any past or present follower of Jesus, while the "apostles" were the twelve immediate followers; Paul, though not among them, is also often called an apostle). But his hometown and most of the people to whom he preached rejected him.

But Jesus lived in a profoundly fortuitous time and place. We forget that a belief in magic was pervasive in the underdeveloped regions of the world in ancient times. In Jesus' time and place, any number of actions by a charismatic figure could be construed as miracles and legitimatize his status as a special individual. Jesus' life, filtered through apocalyptic beliefs, the belief that he was a very different kind of person, and the hope that he gave to outcasts could have magnified his supposed powers. But even so, his following was small, and it was only after his death and supposed resurrection that he was regarded as a messiah.

Jesus' prediction that he would be killed probably reflects his true words. Rome was more tolerant than is generally realized, but it certainly was feared. It is known that Jesus saw two failed revolts against the Roman Empire before he reached adulthood. All Jews, and especially those who attracted attention, would have had the power of Rome foremost in their minds. Jesus certainly would have known the fate of earlier Jews who had dared to oppose Rome. It was a long-established Jewish custom to teach in parables, and those that Jesus told, such as the parable of the prodigal son, continued this tradition, and may have been told to avoid inciting Roman anger.

There is no historical evidence at all that Jesus ever thought of himself as a messiah or claimed to be the Messiah or the Son of God. In his time, a number of people either claimed to be the Messiah, or were at some time believed by others to be a messiah. Nowhere in the Gospels does he claim to be the Messiah until he is arrested. His references to God as "my father," if they occurred, were meant in a general sense, as Jews held God to be the father of all. After the death of Jesus, early Christians might have added that he had claimed to be the Messiah in order to promote the new religion.

Jesus spoke of the Kingdom of God, but it is not clear what he meant by that term. It is possible that he thought he would preside over the Earth after the apocalypse. There clearly were a handful of people who thought that he would be some sort of future ruler. Jesus claimed that only people who accepted his message would participate in this Kingdom of God, suggesting that he foresaw a leadership role for himself in it. This is not the same as claiming to be the Messiah, but it might have been close enough to convince a few of his followers that he was, and if this private teaching became public knowledge, Jewish authorities might have understood it as blasphemy. Moreover, because only the Romans could appoint government officials, the claim to be king of the Jews was also open defiance of Rome.

Tensions came to an abrupt head when Jesus went to Jerusalem. He was killed within a week. He arrived during Passover (the Last Supper was undoubtedly a seder) and went into the Temple. The Temple was the only place in which sacrifices could be made, and Jews were commanded to sacrifice there, but it was impractical for them to bring the animal with them, so it had to be purchased locally. Because Jews came from many lands, moneychangers were present in the Temple for the necessary currency conversion, just as airports and large cities today have currency converters. Scholars agree that Jesus created some sort of disturbance in the Temple, but the details are probably exaggerated. It is not clear why Jesus would have found the Temple or the moneychangers offensive. Perhaps he thought the Temple had become corrupt, perhaps he made only a few symbolic gestures, or perhaps he thought that with the coming apocalypse the Temple was no longer necessary. Recalling that everything that Jesus did and preached was in accord with the apocalypse, the last hypothesis makes sense, and perhaps he sought to remind people that a Temple would not be needed much longer rather than to protest conduct within it. He might have symbolically acted out the destruction of the Temple by overturning tables. In any event, his actions brought him into conflict with the Sadducees, the aristocratic Jews who administered the Temple. Now there was a dangerous rabble-rouser in the most important Jewish city, at the most important Jewish site, at the most important Jewish time, behaving in a way that might draw a large crowd and fill it with a resolve.

We do not know what happened after the incident in the Temple, but Jesus came to the attention of Roman authorities in one of two ways. In one scenario, Jesus angered Jewish leaders, who, under Roman occupation, lacked the authority to take definitive action themselves. Because Jews had a certain amount of autonomy, Jewish authorities may have arrested Jesus and held a preliminary hearing before the Sanhedrin, a Jewish court. We do not know much about this preliminary hearing, if it took place, but it would have been presided over by the high priest, Caiaphas. The Romans then accepted the charges initiated by Jewish leaders and took Jesus into the custody of the Roman governor, Pontius Pilate, for a criminal trial. In support of this scenario, the Romans had granted appreciable autonomy to the province of Judaea, and even permitted the circulation of a coin that did not have a portrait of Caesar. Vicious oppression makes great press, but the fact is that the Romans were very tolerant of the people they ruled, including the Jews, and Jewish leaders almost certainly would have had the authority to try Jesus. In addition to the offense that they took at Jesus' actions, Jewish leaders would have wanted to apprehend and try Jesus because Rome collaborated with local leaders in conquered lands, and probably had an agreement with Jewish leaders that they would be more lenient with Jews if Jewish leaders controlled and informed Roman authorities about potential troublemakers.

For example, there seems to have been collusion between Pilate and Caiaphas, both of whom were removed by Roman authorities in 36 CE. We must, however, be careful with this scenario because Christians may have added the idea that Jews initiated charges, to implicate the Jews in Jesus' death.

In the second scenario, Jesus came directly to Roman attention, particularly since the Romans were on high alert at the time of Passover. In this scenario, he was taken straight to Pilate. In support of this theory is that the Romans had a history of executing anyone in an occupied land, including Judaea, who might foment rebellion, as a way of immediately seizing control and sending a message. These two possibilities are not mutually exclusive; Jewish leaders may have tried Jesus in the Sanhedrin, but more from fear of Roman backlash than from Jesus' criticism of them. They may also have brought Jesus to Roman authorities, but not tried him themselves. In either case, the Romans, already paranoid about any Jew who might make trouble or incite an uprising, took the final actions that changed our world. The tradition is that an apostle (historically assumed, but not proven, to be Judas) betrayed Jesus by identifying him to Roman authorities. However Jesus came into the Roman judicial system, the primary accusation against him appears to have been that he considered himself the king of the Jews in this world, not that he was the Messiah.

This raises an intriguing question: what did the Romans possibly have to fear from a Jewish reformer? If anything, such a person would more likely have fragmented any Jewish opposition that might have been present. Moreover, arresting or killing Jesus did little to quell Jewish unrest. A government cannot change or permanently suppress what people think by repressing particular behaviors or silencing individuals — nor do they need to. As intellectually challenged as most people are, governments do not need to protect them from truly bad ideas. If the welfare of the people is the issue, and the ideas are bad enough to warrant suppression, they will die from their own inadequacy. Great ideas cannot be permanently buried by persecution. Such an attempt is likely to legitimatize a controversial idea and lead to its greater long-term survival. Whatever offers both belonging and hope will always be embraced and will always survive any persecution. It is said that power corrupts, and absolute power corrupts absolutely. Aung San Suu Kyi, the contemporary crusader for human rights in Myanmar (formerly Burma), would refine this lesson two millennia later: it is really the fear of losing power that drives the use of power, and it is the use of power that drives the fear of the powerless. The common maxim can be transformed into "Power becomes paranoid, and absolute power becomes absolutely paranoid." Many of the most tragic acts of history arise from the unfortunate corruption of power by paranoia, causing governments to take unnecessary action to protect themselves. This was what drove the Roman reaction to Jesus.

Contrary to the Biblical account, there would not have been many people at the Roman trial, and the few who were present would not have had input into Jesus' fate or the release of any other prisoners. Christians who were eager to blame the Jews probably added this account later. In Luke and Matthew, for example, it takes even greater input from the Jewish crowd to achieve the crucifixion than it does in the earlier Gospel of Mark. In Matthew, we have the famous hand washing of Pilate, the effect of which is to place all the blame on Jews. Matthew also has a Jewish crowd accepting responsibility on behalf of themselves and their children, clearly an effort to implicate Jews eternally in the death of Jesus. It becomes even more ridiculous in the Gospel of John, which says the crowd threatens to go over Pilate's head to the emperor if he does not crucify Jesus. John also says that Pilate handed Jesus over to the Jews to carry out the actual crucifixion.

The crucifixion and the events immediately before and after it are closed to us, but it was traditional for people to be flogged before being crucified, so this may well have been done to Jesus. It was also traditional for the condemned to carry the crossbeam of the cross (the uprights were left in place and reused). Despite the enormous number of paintings to the contrary, people were not crucified through the hands, but rather through the wrists. It is questionable whether or not the feet or ankles were involved. There may have been a ledge to stand on, and the arms may have been tied. None of Jesus' apostles would have been permitted to witness this event. The accounts of his women followers watching it may be true, but they would have been kept at a distance and could not possibly have heard his last words. Occasionally, family or friends buried the body in a private grave, but it was much more usual for the Romans either to leave the body for scavengers or to bury it in a common grave.

Jesus' life served as the centerpiece and collecting point for the set of beliefs that became Christianity. He sought to begin a reform movement within Judaism, not to start a new religion. That reform movement came to an end with his death, apparently marking Jesus as a failure, but re-emerged as a new religion shortly thereafter. The key to this was the perception that Jesus was resurrected. The belief in his Resurrection was the foundation for the perception that he was the Messiah, and the defining and initiating moment for Christianity. When a subset of Jews, and some Gentiles, came to believe that Jesus had been resurrected, a new religion was born. Were it not for the perceived Resurrection, the crucifixion of Jesus would have appeared to his followers as the end of the very short and ill-fated mission of one man. But with the supposed Resurrection, Jesus' followers saw his life and message in a profoundly different way: it was now possible to see Jesus as the Messiah who could recover the purity of Jewish culture and provide hope. The perceived Resurrection transformed Jesus from a reformer into a savior.

Since Rabbinic Judaism held that bodily resurrection would not occur until the end of the age and the coming of the Messiah, Jesus' apparent resurrection made sense to people who thought the Apocalypse had already begun. By this thinking, Jesus was chosen by God to begin the end of days because he was the first person to undergo bodily resurrection. Whereas the Gospels — especially Matthew, Luke, and Mark — overlap significantly in most areas, reflecting a common source yet to be discovered, there are important differences in their discussions of the resurrection, suggesting that this portion was written independently. It is interesting that all accounts state that women found the tomb empty. The testimony of women had minimal credibility in that time and place, and writers fabricating a story would hardly choose women for its central characters. I believe that people accepted bodily resurrection because it was consistent with the idea of an imminent apocalypse, and it verified Jesus' messianic status at a time when a savior was desperately sought.

How does an ordinary person become divine, especially when he never made a public claim of divinity? Convincing other Jews that Jesus was the Messiah was very difficult for several reasons. First, as we have seen, the concept of a messiah was never well developed in Judaism, and, in general, Jews have never awaited a messiah with the eagerness that is so characteristic of Christians. The Tanakh, the Jewish Bible, makes little mention of a messiah, and the remainder of the Jewish canon provides a variety of opinions as to when or if a messiah is coming, and if so, what form he might take. Second, there was a general feeling that the Messiah, if and when he did come, would be a figure of grandeur and power. Third, Jews have never anticipated that the eventual messiah would suffer, and the Tanakh makes no mention of a messiah suffering or dying to save humanity, nor was there anything in Jewish tradition about a messiah being resurrected. Early Christians added these concepts to support their preconceived idea that Jesus was the Messiah.

We can never fully understand the thinking that elevated Jesus to a messiah, but there are three relevant considerations. First, the new religion would have been influenced not just by Judaism but by several religions in the region at the time. Early Christians would also have adopted characteristics that were common in Greco-Roman religion. These included the capacity for miracles and the occasional assumption of human form by deities. While Judaism provided only a vague possibility that an anthropomorphic form of God would someday come, Greco-Roman religion provided many examples of clearly mortal humans who were the children of gods. A great leader sired by a god was a popular theme. We encounter this as early as the *Iliad,* and it persisted well into Roman times. Greco-Roman religion also provided for intermediary figures — lesser gods, or titans — to plead the case of humanity to a supreme being. Many of the lesser gods frequently interceded to the supreme god Zeus on behalf of people, and the titan Prometheus defied Zeus to give humanity many benefits, including fire. It should also be noted that numerous other religions had deified people. The Egyptian pharaohs were thought to be sons of the sun god Ra. The Egyptian intellectual Imhotep was deified after his death. Today, the concept of a corporeal figure who is divine and who intercedes directly with God is familiar to most people only in the Christian context, suggesting to them that this was a unique, truthful occurrence, but in fact, these ideas were well established and in the air at the time of the formation of Christianity. Early Christians would surely have incorporated them and applied them to the man they needed to see as the Messiah.

Some theologians believe that the cult of the god Mithra (or Mithras) contributed to early Christianity. Mithra was an Indo-Iranian sun god who was worshipped in Europe after the time of Alexander the Great, and was prominent in the Roman Empire until about the third century CE. Documented details of the deity are sketchy, but in some accounts, he came as a savior, was born of a virgin on December 25, had twelve disciples, and was resurrected after death. While we cannot say that early Christians fashioned their model of a messiah from Mithra, details concerning the older deity would surely have come to mind, and would have been available as a model for people attempting to construct a new religion based on a recent messiah.

The second consideration in the elevation of Jesus to a messiah was that the conception of the Messiah was reformulated. To the extent that they thought of a messiah, many Jews believed he would use obvious divine power to bring about a literal paradise, but only for them. Christians, thinking specifically of Jesus, conceived the messiah not as a great king, but as an ordinary person. Moreover, again thinking of Jesus, they believed that the miracles of the Messiah would be found within the heart, not in the use of obvious divine power and an immediate and massive correction of all wrong. The Christian Messiah, therefore, worked in subtle ways, but was capable of being the savior of all, not just of Jews. Jesus' eventual return at the time of final judgment would complete the unfolding Apocalypse, at which time the obvious power and grand triumph of the Messiah, as anticipated by Jews, would be realized, but until then his manifestation was restrained. Though Jesus cannot possibly be regarded as a messiah in the strict and literal sense of bringing about an immediate paradise and ending the suffering of the Jewish people, Christians see him as the Messiah because belief in him makes possible an inner transformation that prepares one for the final judgment, at which time his full grandeur will be apparent. He was the first to undergo what all righteous people can aspire to — a new beginning. Christians transformed the conventional thinking that the Messiah would be a returning king into a belief in a humble, suffering individual who worked in subtler ways. It was essential to early Christianity that the definition of a messiah was changed. Indeed, if Jesus had been successful in the expected sense as a messiah, only Jews would have so recognized him, but by this new way of thinking, the door was open to people of all faiths to accept him.

The third consideration in the elevation of Jesus to a messiah was that his followers re-interpreted some passages from the Tanakh and some of Jesus' words. For example, his supposed reference to God as "my father" and the phrase "Son of God" acquired very different meanings after the supposed Resurrection. Jesus' followers had heard him refer to God as "my father" in a sense that might be employed by anyone believing in a single god, but after the apparent Resurrection, the phrase acquired new significance. To Jews, the phrase "Son of God" simply meant a righteous man, but when applied to Jesus, the term acquired the literal meaning that it still retains. The phrase "My God, My God, why have you forsaken me?" is attributed to Jesus in his last moments. In actuality, none of his followers would have been close enough to the cross to hear these words. They are from Psalm 22, the plea of a righteous man whom God has apparently forsaken, and would have been the logical choice for early Christians to assign to Jesus.

Early Christians, including Paul, labored to present Christianity as the continuation and fulfillment of the Tanakh. The gospels depicted Jesus as a descendant of David because it was understood that the Jewish monarchy had been hereditary and that any proposed king of the Jews would have to be from the House of David. The Tanakh was reinterpreted so that it could foretell the coming of Jesus as the Messiah. The prophets, who were regarded in Judaism not as foretellers of the future, but as the voices of heroes denouncing corruption, were now seen as primarily pointing to the coming of Jesus. Whereas Judaism understood the Tanakh as instruction, Paul preached to the early Christians that for them it was a work of predictions. Genuinely and sincerely believing what they wanted to believe, early Christians re-interpreted events, quotations, and the Tanakh to fit their new ideas, and early Christians remade Jesus into the Messiah. This new understanding of Jesus permitted a shift of thinking from an imminent apocalypse to Jesus as Messiah.

It may appear that Christianity was a most unlikely accident, and in its specifics, it probably was; however, the eventual triumph of some belief system that offered this combination of belonging and hope was by no means unlikely. Indeed, it was inevitable. History teaches us that, just as surely as water flows into cracks, beliefs offering belonging and hope will be distorted as needed to appear believable.

There has always been a curious belief in religion that there must be suffering to make people more worthy or to rectify their standing with a deity. I believe this is an outgrowth of the common belief that people should suffer for their unworthiness. If everyone should suffer for his or her sins, as a means of individual atonement, then it is only a short step to postulate that there should be a supreme suffering as a general atonement. It would then follow that the individual who made this supreme sacrifice would be a savior, and that a required behavior of such a savior would be his sacrifice. Many religions, including Judaism, allowed for death — the sacrifice of an animal — to restore the relationship between people and their god or gods, but whereas Judaism made no allowance for the suffering of a messiah, or any benefit this suffering might bestow on humanity, early Christianity incorporated suffering and death as integral characteristics of the Messiah. In this matter, it appears that Christians were influenced by a passage in Isaiah, concerning a mistreated servant, which indicates that suffering of the innocent will correct the relationship of people and God. To Jews, this passage simply meant that Israel would eventually prevail, but Christians turned it into a prophecy about the suffering of Jesus.

Many misconceptions and differences of opinion exist about the precise content and meaning of portions of the Bible, caused largely by mistranslation and a failure to appreciate the cultural differences between the original writers and the translators. The most important of these concerns the virgin birth of Jesus. To contemporary Christians, the fact that Jesus was born to a virgin is central, but early Christians never claimed this. Later Christians were probably influenced by another passage in Isaiah, which mentions a young woman who is pregnant. The word "unmarried" was added in the Greek translation from the Hebrew because any young woman was assumed to be unmarried and a virgin. This is not so much an overt mistranslation as a cultural misperception. In our time, the terms "young girl," "unmarried," and "virgin" are by no means synonymous, but at the time of translation into Greek they were. Those who used the word "unmarried" in the Greek translation did not make an actual mistake; they were functioning within the appropriate scholarly bounds of their time and place. The mistake came later, when it was not realized that the word "unmarried" came from cultural bias and not from the actual text.

Later Christians, thinking of the unmarried pregnant woman in Isaiah, continued to conflate the terms "young girl," "unmarried," and "virgin," then transferred the concept of birth to an unmarried woman from the passage in Isaiah to the virgin birth of Jesus. The word "virgin" thus became embedded in Christian writing — it was even incorporated into the account of Jesus in the *Koran* — and has come down to us today. Most Christians have no idea that the virgin birth was not claimed by early Christians and is derived from a misunderstanding during translation.

Christianity has made plausible an enormous disparity between the historical facts of a founding figure and subsequent beliefs about him. I believe Christianity succeeded because it offered an immediate path to salvation, without having to be reborn or to wait for the eventual (and questionable) appearance of the Jewish Messiah. This immediacy was underscored by the presence of an intermediary figure who lived as a person and experienced the life that we experience. His presence indicated that God was immediate, loving, and available to humanity. By accepting a slightly different version of the Messiah — one in which the savior worked more subtly and individually than had been anticipated — Christians could have the comfort of believing that a great and wonderful promise had been fulfilled. The ecstasy among the early Christians must have been electrifying. After more than a millennium of persecution of Jews, here was a way to bring it to a close and receive their reward for the fulfillment of their obligations under the Covenant.

Christianity illustrates how a set of beliefs can be compelling for many in the modern world, despite being based on assumptions and beliefs that arose in a different time and place. The persistence of Christianity in its traditional form is an illustration of the fantastic power of social inertia. Each generation in each culture is taught a collection of beliefs that are historically sacrosanct to most of its members and are passed on without question. Many will slightly modify what they are taught, or reduce the overall impact of religion in their lives, but only a few people in each generation can completely reexamine and reassess basic ideas. Most Westerners are taught as children that Jesus was the Son of God, and most of us in the West live our entire lives without questioning this idea. There is enough sophistication today that if Jesus were alive now, he would not be thought of or remembered as divine, and Christianity as we know it could not form today, but there is not enough sophistication to undo centuries of inertia and blind acceptance. Like all religions, Christianity is brilliant and beautiful, and has added much to civilization, but it can still be a great force for good without adhering to an increasingly untenable belief that the corporeal man Jesus was the literal Son of God, with a unique divinity not shared by other people.

The success of Christianity shows that it is possible to strike a common chord with humanity. Unlike Islam, Christianity spread rapidly without economic, political, or military power. In a short time, Christianity jumped from rural areas of Palestine to urban areas all over the world, overcoming significant linguistic and economic differences. It moved from the Jewish community to the community of Gentiles, and from the Jewish world into the Greco-Roman world. The spread of Christianity was initially facilitated by a superb organization, modeled in large part on that of the Roman Empire. The excellent roads and postal service of the Roman Empire made communication among early Christian communities easier.

Today, the terms "Jewish" and "Christian" are essentially mutually exclusive — one cannot be a Jew and a Christian at the same time, but it is important to remember that in the early days of Christianity, this was not true. Indeed, the early Christians *were* Jews, equally committed both to traditional Judaism and to the idea that Jesus was the Messiah. Not only was there no conflict between these ideas, they fit together seamlessly — Jesus was the Messiah who had long been foreseen by some Jews. Some early Jewish Christians remained tied to their Judaism while others did not. These latter Christians broke away completely to form an entirely new religion, just as some early Buddhists had broken away completely from the Hinduism that was their parent religion. Likewise, some early Christians who had been Gentiles wanted to first convert to Judaism en route to becoming Christian, but others did not. Paul, a Jewish convert to Christianity, universalized the new religion by making it attractive to Gentiles and accepting converts who were not Jewish. Paul allowed the fledgling religion to separate from its parent. When criticized for allowing people to become Christians without rigorously adhering to Jewish practices, Paul claimed that his ideas came from a divine revelation. On a more practical level, Paul traveled widely and was comfortable with the many faces of Judaism, including the less rigorous forms outside of the Holy Land. Because he was familiar with less severe forms of Judaism, he was willing to bypass Judaism altogether. Paul's extension of Christianity to Gentiles was critical to its survival because all Jews, including the early Jewish Christians, sustained a devastating setback after the Jewish-Roman war of 66–73 CE and the destruction of the Second Temple, after which Paul's Gentile-based Christian Church became the dominant expression of the new religion.

The life of Jesus was the inspiration for Christianity, but Paul was its sculptor and essential creator. Paul's work seems to have been written between 49 CE and his death in 62 CE. His writings predate the Gospels, which date from the late sixties to eighties CE, or possibly the early nineties. All of Paul's writing is in the form of letters, or epistles. Paul's letters fulfilled two critical functions at a critical time — they explained the essentials of the new religion in simple terms, and they gave much-needed practical advice. Paul's *Letter to the Romans,* written between 55 and 60 CE, is perhaps the most important of his writings because it was the foundation for much of Christian thought. In this letter, Paul argued that people must first be made righteous before they can be saved, and that making people righteous required an act of God. This thinking follows directly from Judaism, but the new part was that Jesus was the Messiah and provided the necessary divine pathway to righteousness. It was faith in Jesus that provided righteousness. It is only through belief in and following the example of Jesus that we can attain this righteousness. This is justification by faith alone (justification refers to the correction of a person's relationship to God). Most scholars think that Paul intended a broader meaning of faith that included charitable deeds, and not just belief in the messianic status of Jesus, though his exact thinking is not clear. Interestingly, though Paul is unequivocal that Jesus is the Messiah, he seems to equivocate on the actual divinity of Jesus during his life on Earth. In some places, Paul hints that Jesus was divine on Earth, while in others, there is the suggestion that he is not truly divine until his return.

Another of Paul's contributions to the new religion was to bring the concept of immortality to the fore. Prior to this time, religions either had no fixed position on an afterlife, or had only a vague perception of one (often not as a utopia and not necessarily even as a pleasant experience). Even Rabbinic Judaism, as we have seen, while believing philosophically in an afterlife, accorded it little weight in daily thought and practice. But Paul taught that all Christians could achieve immortality after death — including bodily resurrection — if they believed in Jesus as the savior, and the hope for eternal salvation, with preservation of the individual identity, has always been central to Christianity.

The first three Gospels, those of Matthew, Mark, and Luke, are called the synoptic Gospels because they are very similar to each other, and different from the Gospel of John. These Gospels were written after the failed Jewish revolt of 66–73 CE. The writers of the synoptic Gospels wanted to convey an image of Jesus that established his messianic status and was favorable to potential converts, while simultaneously convincing Roman authorities that followers of the new religion were not rebellious. Consequently, their approach was to portray Jesus as a teacher, ethical role model, and prophet in the Jewish tradition.

The prevailing hypothesis is that Mark was the first Gospel to be written and was the primary, but not exclusive, source for Matthew and Luke. A second source, referred to as "Q," has never been found, but is safely postulated from literary analysis of the Gospels. "Q" apparently contains only the sayings of Jesus and nothing about his life, death, or resurrection. Most of the quotes attributed to Jesus in the Gospels are considered to be from "Q." "Q" presents Jesus as an apocalyptic figure. Like Paul's writings, "Q" predates the Gospels, the Roman war of 66–73 CE, and the destruction of the Second Temple.

There is no record of a man named Mark. It is currently thought that he lived after Jesus and had no contact with him, but he might have had contact with the Apostle Peter. For some time, Mark's Gospel was considered the most definitive source of the life of Jesus. More recent scholarship, however, has established that Mark wrote with a specific thesis in mind. He had to depict Jesus as more than a miracle worker because "miracle workers" were relatively common in his time. Mark has Jesus opposing Temple authorities and predicting its destruction, but his Gospel was probably written between 70 and 90 CE, after the destruction of the Second Temple. Mark not only believed that Jesus was the Messiah, but he also thought that Jesus was the Messiah during his lifetime, and not just on his return, having achieved messianic status during his baptism. Moreover, Mark thought that Jesus kept his messianic mission a secret. His book so clearly advances this message that it is no longer considered a historically accurate account of Jesus.

In contrast to Mark, Matthew and Luke write that Jesus was divine from his birth, not from his baptism. Matthew and Luke were clearly written after the Temple fell, when Judaism was in the Rabbinic phase and the Pharisees were prominent. Matthew portrays Jesus as devoutly Jewish, a proponent of the Torah, whose practices and beliefs were similar to those of the Pharisees (though he does cite occasional disagreements between Jesus and the Pharisees). The Doctrine of the Trinity is most completely referenced in Matthew, which became the most important of the Gospels in the early Church.

Luke was likely a Gentile, writing for Gentiles. He clearly wanted to show that Christians could be good Romans, and was somewhat antagonistic to Jews, indicating that his writing coincided with the separation of Christianity and Judaism. He may have been a physician and may have been a follower of Paul. Luke also wrote the book of Acts, and his contributions are often collectively referred to as Luke/Acts. Only Matthew and Luke tell the story of Jesus as an infant, and none of the Gospels tells us about his childhood. We see him again briefly at age twelve, then there is no record until he begins his preaching. The Gospels also differ in their discussion of the Resurrection. Mark ends with women discovering an empty tomb, but then fleeing without telling anyone. But in Matthew, Jesus meets the women and tells them to inform others of his Resurrection.

John's Gospel is different from the earlier synoptic Gospels, and discourses more on doctrines than on biography. As is the case of the writers of the other Gospels, we do not know who John was, and he may have been more than one person, but it is thought that the writing attributed to him was written in Western Turkey or on the islands off the coast of Greece. His writing is characterized by an exceptional elevation of Jesus to divine status. Whereas the synoptic Gospels portray Jesus as relatively human, Jesus is more revelatory and more spiritual in John. As an example, in the synoptic Gospels, Jesus eats a Passover meal, and in Mark, Jesus is tormented before the crucifixion. But in John, there is no Passover meal (in fact, Jesus dies on the day that lambs are slaughtered for the Passover meal), and Jesus is strong and bold throughout his trial and death. John's Gospel is later than the synoptic Gospels, and reflects the fact that in the early Christian Church, Jesus was increasingly seen as divine, necessitating scripture that elevated his status. Concurrent with this new view of Jesus, Christianity increasingly used such terms as "savior" and "Son of God" to depict Jesus as divine as it moved from the small Jewish arena into the giant Greco-Roman world. In general, earlier writings of Jesus show him as an apocalyptic figure, while later writings depict him as a unique type of miracle worker. John wrote after Christianity and Judaism had completed their separation, and he heightened this separation by portraying Jews as the enemies of Christians.

The evolving conception of Jesus can be seen by comparing the points at which the various books of the New Testament ascribe divine status to him. Paul equivocates on the actual divinity of Jesus the man, Mark thought that divinity began at baptism, and Luke and Matthew describe a divinity that began at birth. In contrast, the Gospel of John not only affirms the divinity of Jesus at birth, as do Matthew and Luke, but also asserts that Jesus, as an aspect of God, preexisted his human birth and was present at the beginning of Creation. This changing opinion of Jesus, with subsequent writings progressively elevating him, shows that the books of the New Testament were written for the specific purpose of supporting, not chronicling, early Christianity.

Johannine literature encompasses the Gospel according to John, the book of Revelation, and the three letters attributed to John. These works also describe the mysterious and enigmatic Holy Spirit, which is an aspect of the Creator representing his presence on Earth. John says that after Jesus ascended into Heaven, the Holy Spirit acts as a counselor until his return. The Book of Revelation portrays Rome as a great beast, and much of its abstractness may be a reference to Rome.

As is the case for the Tanakh — which would become the Christian Old Testament — the chapters in the New Testament follow a traditional form. The New Testament took a basic literary form, in common use at the time, and edited or modified it to serve as support for the new religion and a guide for early practitioners, and in the process created a new genre — the Gospels.

John Shelby Spong, a contemporary Episcopal bishop, building on the ideas of Michael Goulder, believes that the Gospels, or at least the synoptic Gospels, arose from commentaries on the Torah. According to his view, it is important to understand that the early Christian Church was fundamentally Jewish, and continued the Jewish practice of weekly Torah readings. Even in the Jewish tradition, it had been customary to accompany the weekly reading of the Torah with a sermon that translated the message of the Torah into advice for daily life. To the early Jewish Christians, this meant using the life of Jesus as an example of proper conduct. When the details of Jesus' conduct were absent, or needed to be embellished, these sermons became speculative, and Jesus rose in stature. In this view, the Gospels arose from the collection of these sermons. As Christianity and Judaism diverged, the early Church underwent a transition from basically Jewish to basically Gentile. As Christianity lost its direct connection to Judaism, these sermons became less connected to the Torah, and more concerned with promoting the greatness and divinity of Jesus. This argument makes sense, given that it was a priority for early Christians to make their religion appear continuous with the Tanakh, now called the Old Testament by early Christians, since they were now formulating a New Testament.

It should also be remembered that the standard technique for writing history at the time was to speculate on specific conversations and present them as verbatim accounts. For example, we see this in the writing of Thucydides. I believe that many of the quotes in the New Testament, though not verbatim, and possibly fictionalized, were honestly intended to portray what the writer believed to be the facts.

Another reason for the success of Christianity is that it appealed to women by offering more respect to them and to their domestic duties than other religions had. Christianity did not offer women full equality, but it came closer than its predecessors. Indeed, Christianity was the first religion to make a special effort to appeal to women and the poor. Its ability to transcend national and ethnic boundaries, its appeal to people of all classes and social stations, and the mutual support that early congregations gave each other were critical in the rise of the new religion. Christianity also offered certainty in place of distressing uncertainty.

Beginning in the second century CE, Christianity became more distinctly Gentile. Early Christianity never established the scholarly canon of Judaism, and was more concerned with specific religious beliefs than with general philosophy. Some early Christians wanted to simplify Jewish philosophy, customs, and behavioral codes, even to the extent of limiting the canon to Paul's letters and the Gospels. Eventually, however, philosophy crept into Christianity. Indeed, religion and philosophy have always been inextricable, and contemporary Christianity is based on a set of philosophical beliefs that is difficult to grasp, even for its followers. Today, a set of fixed beliefs, based on a greatly simplified understanding of Christian philosophy, is more important in Christianity than in other religions, which are likely to concentrate on behavior. For example, the Trinity is integral to Christianity, but few contemporary Christians understand the origins and true nature of this concept, and no early Christian would have understood the full contemporary expression of the relationship of God and Jesus.

Even with the relative tolerance of the Romans, proselytizing for the new religion in the days of occupation and widespread illiteracy was both difficult and dangerous. Because Greek was the common language of the Western world at that time, and because the Greek acronym for "Jesus Christ, Son of God, the Savior" spells the Greek word "fish," early Christians used a picture of a fish to surreptitiously communicate with each other (this symbol is still used today). In the second century CE, Christian apologists defended the new religion (the word "apology" in this case refers to a defense, not a confession). The apologists wrote after the writings of Paul and the Gospels, and specifically sought to separate Christianity and Judaism. One of the apologists was Justin Martyr (c. 100–165 CE), whose work *A Dialogue with Trypho the Jew* helped to differentiate Christianity from Judaism in the minds of most people. He also wrote the first apology intended to persuade the emperor that Christians were no threat to the Roman Empire. Origen (184–254 CE) was an instrumental early Christian thinker. He was a scholar well acquainted with Greek and Hebrew, and his early formulations of the Trinity were influential.

Ichthys

Ichthys (also spelled Ichthus) is the Greek word for "Fish". Tradition holds that because in Greek, "Jesus Christ, Son of God, the Savior" spells Ichthys, early Christians used this symbol, resembling a fish, to mark meeting places or to identify fellow believers. The Ichthys symbol has enjoyed a revival in modern times and can even be seen on bumper stickers.

It is a widespread misconception that Rome consistently persecuted Christians. As was the case with Jews and other groups, Roman authorities rarely mistreated any group unless it was perceived as causing trouble. There was a brief persecution of Christians in 64 CE. In that year, to divert attention from himself after a large fire, the emperor Nero blamed the Christians and instituted punitive measures. This was a short-lived persecution that was restricted to the city of Rome. After this, Christians were essentially left alone throughout the second century. Christianity was technically illegal, but the law was not generally enforced. Rome followed what we would now call a "don't ask, don't tell, don't pursue" policy. If a Christian were questioned and steadfastly held to his beliefs, some difficulty might have arisen, but it would be very rare for him to be questioned at all, and a denial would end the matter. In the third century, however, the empire fell on difficult economic and military times. To legitimatize their position, emperors claimed to rule by the divine right of the gods. Therefore, Christians, who refused to recognize these gods, potentially undermined the emperor's power and security. For this reason, anger at Christians was usually more political than religious. Even throughout the third century, however, Christians who did not advertise their beliefs were rarely harassed.

To the extent that the persecution of Christians was religiously based, a particular bone of contention was that Christians refused to take part in communal celebration of the gods. This was not only perceived as an attack on Roman values, but also led to concern that if the gods became angry at Christian non-participation, many good non-Christian Romans would be hurt. One such refusal, about 250 CE, is well documented. The Emperor Decius asked the Christians to participate in the communal celebration of the gods, but did not ask them to abandon their beliefs. Romans were more angered by the refusal of Christians to help them curry the gods' favor than by their beliefs.

There was also some suspicion of Christians because they met in secret, causing concern that they were more loyal to each other than to the state. As is the case for all groups of like-minded people, the perception of elitism and exclusion angers outsiders. Refusal to associate with outsiders fosters a sense of alienation and invites misconceptions and rumors. At one time, for example, there were stories of cannibalism in the Christian community.

By the late third century, the essential deification of emperors was an increasingly important means of claiming legitimacy in a time of rising tension and diminishing prosperity. In 299 CE, Diocletian introduced the only official persecution of the Christians throughout the empire. This lasted until 311 CE, but even though it was an official attempt to destroy Christianity, this policy was unevenly enforced. During this time, some Christians were killed in the Coliseum in the macabre ways that we have heard, but the number was not great, and most could have avoided this fate with a modicum of compromise and participation in Roman life. In 313, Constantine's Edict of Milan made all religions tolerated (contrary to popular belief, Constantine did not make Christianity the official religion, merely one that was officially permitted).

As was the case with Judaism, we must endeavor to be fair to both sides. On Rome's part, there was undoubtedly an overreaction to people who were different and not classically patriotic, but were nevertheless harmless. Persecuting them was neither necessary nor advisable. Indeed, the heroism of the martyrs increased the popularity of Christianity. On the Christians' part, none of them deserved any harassment, and certainly none deserved to die, but more often than not, there was an uncompromising stand and a poor choice of battles.

Like all religions, Christianity took centuries to fully develop, and it did so from innumerable influences, some remembered, and some lost to history. Different forms of Christianity became more evident in the second century after Jesus. This time also saw the rise of Christian asceticism, and an increased emphasis on dualism — the existence of a distinct figure of evil contemporaneous with God. Dualism had long been a part of many religions, including Judaism, but it gained immediacy with Christianity because of its emphasis on an afterlife and the belief that Jesus would be the final judge of the Apocalypse.

This was also the time of Gnosticism, a philosophy/religion that believed salvation was obtained by acquiring secret knowledge (gnosis) and using it to awaken the hidden divine spark that lay within all people. Most people are completely without Enlightenment or hope of ever acquiring the necessary knowledge (so-called "mud people"). Above them was a group that had some chance of acquiring the special knowledge and achieving Enlightenment, if they had a teacher. At the top was a small minority who possessed this special knowledge. The

Church specifically and robustly opposed Gnosticism for two reasons. First, Christianity held that anyone could be saved. Unlike other religions or philosophies, it did not appeal to or offer hope to a restricted segment of the population. Indeed, one of the selling points for early Christianity was that it was for everyone. Second, Christianity thought that salvation came from Jesus' death and resurrection, not from secret knowledge. It was correct beliefs, not arcane knowledge, that made salvation possible. Many of the Christian writings from this period are rebuttals to Gnosticism. Nonetheless, Gnosticism and the responses to it had a great influence on early Christian ideology because it stimulated Christian thinking and forced the new religion to rigorously codify its doctrines.

A rich lode of Gnostic scriptures was discovered in 1945 at Nag Hammadi, an Egyptian village near Luxor. The thirteen leather-bound volumes, now called the "Nag Hammadi Library," are regarded as a cornerstone in the search for alternative versions of Christianity. These volumes include *The Gospel of Truth, The Coptic Apocalypse of Peter,* and the *Treatise on the Resurrection.* Many of the works in the Nag Hammadi library had been known only because such church fathers as Tertullian of Carthage (fl. 200 CE) and Hippolytus of Rome (fl. c. 200 CE) referred to them in their diatribes against the Gnostics. The library not only verified much knowledge about Gnosticism, but also corrected several misconceptions (i.e., that the Gnostics were wildly licentious; in fact, they were ascetics).

The Gospel of Judas, which came to public attention in 2006, is a Coptic (Egyptian written in the Greek alphabet) manuscript dating to the early fourth century CE, but likely a copy of an earlier Greek text. It is a Gnostic work, and holds that Judas was the favorite apostle of Jesus and was therefore selected by him to receive the special knowledge of Gnosticism. It also indicates that Jesus asked Judas to betray him so that his body would no longer be a prison for his divinity. The major remaining question concerning the Gospel of Judas is whether it provides reliable new insight into early Christianity or was written simply to further the Gnostics' agenda. In an effort to overcome the Gnostics, some writers reinforced the connection between Christianity and Judaism, particularly Irenaeus (fl. late second century CE), who wrote *On the Detection and Overthrow of the So-Called Gnosis* (often called *Against Heresies*). Largely in an attempt to counter the Gnostics, early Christians developed a standard canon that consisted of the Hebrew Bible and the twenty-seven books of the New Testament. They developed professions of faith — now called Creeds — to emphasize that it is belief, not special knowledge, that leads to salvation. Early Christians also developed the doctrine of apostolic succession, the belief that the true Christian Church emanates directly from the teachings of the apostles. Bishops are thought to be the link between the apostles and the Church, and successive ordinations (bishop to bishop and bishop to priest) preserve the unbroken connection to the apostles.

Once Christianity moved out of the Holy Land, it entered a world of Greek thought, which it used as its philosophical model, just as it used the Roman government as its organizational model. In attempting to define the almost indefinable, Christians recognized that Greek thinking and literature could make their religion attractive to educated people. For example, it was Greek metaphysical thought, specifically Neoplatonism, that became the foundation for the discussion of the nature of God that would follow over the next several centuries.

To understand Neoplatonism, we begin by realizing that Plato postulated a material world — the everyday world we live in — and an ideal world of forms. Whatever existed in this world also existed in an idealized version in the world of forms. The two worlds were separate, but a Demiurge could interact with both and bring about more perfection in the material world. Middle Platonism (or pre-Neoplatonism) was a form of Plato's philosophy that developed in the first century CE and had a religious component. It postulated a supreme mind, and some Jews and Christians interpreted Plato's idea of forms as products of this supreme mind. Middle Platonism also adopted a dualistic view of soul and body, with the superiority of the former. Christian writers, such as Justin Martyr, Clement of Alexandria, and Origen, found in Middle Platonism the means by which they could understand the scriptures and reconcile them with rational thought.

Neoplatonism arose from Middle Platonism in the third century CE, largely from the work of Plotinus in Alexandria, and is sometimes referred to as the final form of Greek philosophy. The last of the great classical schools, Neoplatonism was based primarily on the metaphysical ideas of Plato, and viewed the concept of God as an incorporeal entity. Neoplatonists also believed in Monism, the view that all things belong to one universal reality and everything is a different manifestation of it. The Neoplatonist expression of Monism was that the universal reality was an omniscient, infinite, yet unknowable One, from which emanates *nous* (pure intelligence). Nous gives rise to the world soul, which in turn creates the lesser souls of people. These entities are part of and inextricable from the One. They are different manifestations of the One, not distinct creations of it. At the same time, however, these different manifestations can have different functions. The world soul, for example, is intermediate between the One and the material world even as it is consubstantial with both. This concept of oneness, yet separateness, greatly influenced the formation of the Christian Trinity.

The Neoplatonists' Demiurge provided a philosophical foundation for Christ as a preexistent entity involved in the creation of the world. Moreover, Neoplatonism established the example of one aspect of reality transmitting life to another, or mediating between two aspects, and influenced Christian thinking in the area of free will. Neoplatonists believed that each person could choose between good and evil. Poor choices, which included sensuality, arose from ignorance of our true nature, and must be corrected by a more appropriate exercise of free will, resulting in a reunification with the One (this correction often required a mystical experience). Neoplatonism also influenced Christianity in an uncompromising opposition between the spiritual and the carnal, even to the extent that the corruption inherent in the world of the senses should be mitigated by a rigorous ascetic discipline. More than any other religion, Christianity eschews carnal pleasure.

Neoplatonism surely took Plato's ideas far from any intent he may have had, but its followers thought they were rediscovering the true meaning of his teachings. It also borrowed from Pythagoras, Aristotle, stoicism, mysticism, and the occult. It furnished an interpretation of classical Greek Paganism that was palatable to early Christians, and simultaneously furnished them with a philosophical basis that legitimized their religion to skeptics. Until the rise of Aristotelianism in the Middle Ages, Neoplatonism had enormous influence on Christian thinking.

I believe the origin of Christianity illustrates how varied are the sources for all of our great ideas, and how little aware we are of the nearly infinite indistinct and subtle influences that shape all of the ideas we live under. Our lives are controlled by influences and ideas that most of us have never heard of. Most Westerners are convinced that Neoplatonism, if they have heard of it at all, is esoteric and remote from their lives, but from it came ideas that are critical to the daily lives of more than a billion people.

Christianity differs from other religions in that mysticism and metaphysics — especially the conception of the Trinity — are an integral part of the religion and are not relegated to the periphery, as is the case for Islamic Sufism and Judaic Kabbalah (which were also influenced by Neoplatonism). For this reason, Christianity has had to respond to criticisms of metaphysics raised by philosophers such as Hume and Kant.

Christian philosophy, spearheaded by Neoplatonism, had to grapple with the nature of Jesus vis-à-vis God. Arius proposed that Jesus was not exactly identical to the Father, but was of similar essence, was created by God, and was slightly subordinate to God. Athanasius argued that they were of identical essence. Constantine convened the Council of Nicaea (325) to settle this dispute. Athanasius' view won out, but the views of Arius persisted (the council also decreed that Easter would be the first Sunday after the first full moon after the equinox). The Council of Nicaea began the formulation of what would become the Nicene Creed, though this was not completed until the Council of Constantinople in 381 CE (the Catholic and Orthodox Churches uses the Nicene Creed, also called the Nicene/Constantinople Creed, while Protestants use the Apostles' Creed).

Many early Christian groups lost the struggle for legitimacy, largely because they lost the struggle for converts, and were eliminated entirely by the Council of Nicaea in 325 CE. The Gnostics were one such group; others were the Ebionites and the Marcionites. The Ebionites were Jews who kept their Jewish laws and customs while accepting Jesus as the Messiah. They believed, however, that Jesus was the Messiah because he was the messenger of God, not because he was personally divine (it is quite probable that this perception of Jesus was close to that of the apostles). The Marcionites rejected Judaism completely, and believed that the Jewish God of the Tanakh and the Christian God of Jesus were two separate Gods. They also believed that Jesus was a spirit and not a corporeal person.

All of these groups had their own books, which they claimed to have been written by apostles. Though these books were not included in the New Testament canon, they were influential. They include *The*

Gnostic Gospel of Truth, The Infancy Gospels, and *The Apocryphal Acts of the Apostles. The Gnostic Gospel of Truth* is a profound elaboration of the joy of salvation. *The Infancy Gospels,* such as the *Proto-Gospel of James* and the *Infancy Gospel of Thomas,* describe events before Jesus' birth and those of his early childhood. To the extent that they are credible, they are essentially our only source for the childhood of Jesus. *The Infancy Gospel of James* is our source for the idea that Joseph was an old man who was not married to Mary, an idea integral to Christianity despite the exclusion of its source from the Canon. *The Apocryphal Acts of the Apostles,* unlike the book of Acts that did enter the Canon, discusses the lives of individual apostles. Of all the alternative books, *The Coptic Gospel of Thomas* is the most intriguing. Supposedly written by a twin brother of Jesus, this book contains 114 secret sayings of Jesus that purportedly hold the key to eternal life. *The Secret Gospel of Mark* has not been found, but is referenced in a letter from Clement of Alexandria. If it exists, it may be a second Gospel of Mark that was written for a group of spiritually elite individuals.

In the fifth century, there were additional debates on the human and divine natures of the person of Jesus. Nestorius held that Mary gave birth only to the human person and that only the human person was crucified. The divine nature entered Jesus soon after birth, and was not crucified. This led to two separate and equal aspects of Jesus. The Monophysite position was that the two natures of Jesus were so completely intermingled that they were fused, and Jesus had only a single nature from the beginning. These sides differed on when and to what extent the two aspects of Jesus came to be integrated, but they did not disagree on the end result — Jesus was both human and divine. At the Council of Chalcedon in 451, there was confirmation of the dual nature of Jesus, but actually the council adopted a position that was different from either the Nestorian or the Monophysite view: Jesus had two natures, which were commingled from the beginning, but actually remained separate and not fused into one. The Council of Chalcedon also affirmed that Mary was the mother of both of these natures from the beginning. Many Nestorians moved to Mesopotamia, into Islamic lands, where they were much better treated, while the Monophysites were strong in Syria, Anatolia, and Armenia. The result was that these religious differences not only remained, but also became regional differences.

It soon became evident that not everyone could adhere equally to all the demands of Christianity, so a division was made between the clergy and the laity, but even this division was not completely successful because the clergy had to interact with the world. A few ascetics withdrew from the world completely to avoid all temptation. Anthony (c. 251–356 CE), a wealthy man from Alexandria who gave up a prosperous lifestyle to become an ascetic, wandered in the desert for a time, as is traditionally recorded, but actually spent most of his time in solitude in an abandoned Roman fort, where food and water were brought to him. He spent perhaps twenty years there before emerging as a man of great reputation and serenity. Anthony set an important early example for Asceticism and established the Eremitic tradition (based on total solitude), as opposed to the Cenobitic tradition (based on substantial, but not complete, withdrawal from society).

Monasteries arose as a more practical alternative to Anthony's endeavors. Christian monasteries began in Egypt, or perhaps Syria. Saint Martin (c. 336–397) was important in the monastic tradition in what is now France, as was Saint Patrick (c. 390–460) in Ireland. Saint Benedict (480–543) was influential in establishing the Western monastery, and he elaborated rules that institutionalized monastic life.

Many people, even many Christians, have difficulty understanding the desire to withdraw from society in favor of monastic life. A twentieth-century Trappist monk named Thomas Merton gave voice to the monastic desire for withdrawal with these words: "It is clear to me that solitude is my vocation, not as flight from the world, but as my place in the world."

Ascetics and monks also provided an uncomplicated view of Christianity that appealed to people who did not understand the full range of Christian philosophy, but were impressed with the simple lifestyle and peaceful living. Some of these ascetics and monks became saints, the successors to the prophets (like Judaism and Islam, Christianity believes that the days of prophecy are over). Saints are regarded as a triumph of God within human life. In addition to shaping early Christianity, they also served another function: most Christians considered God to be so complex and unapproachable that it became helpful to have a saint as an intermediary.

Judaism and Islam both have simpler sets of beliefs, and tend to define their religion more by behavior than belief. A set of absolute behavioral laws has not been as critical in Christianity as in Judaism and Islam. Paul, for example, argued that faith alone would lead to salvation. While this faith is generally held to imply behaviors that are consistent with the basic tenets of Jesus' life, and Christianity certainly affirms the Ten Commandments, the New Testament does not give as much day-to-day instruction about behavior as the Koran and the Torah do. Indeed, Jesus was not a lawgiver, and in fact broke Jewish law.

Christians focus more than Jews do on the unworthiness of man, on the forgiveness of God, and on the Paradise to come. Whereas the Jewish Covenant is based on the belief that humanity — or at least the Jewish subset of humanity — for all of its imperfections, could be worked with and improved, Christians believe that all people are inherently unworthy and can be saved only by the grace of God. By adopting this position, Christians shifted the focus from the worthy individual and the potential of man to the unworthy individual and the forgiveness of God.

The Torah continues to be a major influence on Christian morality, but unlike Judaism and Islam, Christian morality is not defined by virtuous behavior, but by sin. Sin is an affront to God, not to humanity. Whereas Judaism and Islam generally stress what its practitioners should do, Christianity often instructs its practitioners in what they must not do. Negative commandments are more prevalent in Christianity than positive ones because they are more definite and easier to follow. "Love your neighbor" is a little vague, but "thou shall not commit adultery" is unambiguous. Christians shifted the focus from behavior to belief, from the present to the future, and from intellectual activity as an integral part of the religion to a more simplistic ideology. In addition, Christians have always had difficulty accepting the body, particularly sexuality, and this has further complicated the construction of a moral code.

The period from 300 to about 600 is called the Patristic period, during which time the Church fathers took the biblical text and shaped it into Christian doctrine. They rendered an interpretation and elaboration of the Bible that has been very little questioned throughout history. The first of the fathers in the West was Ambrose (b. 339), a poet whose works still appear today in Christian hymns. He translated the work of Greek Christians, such as Origen, into Latin. Ambrose, like Origen, supported the use of allegory and symbolism in interpreting problematic biblical passages. Another great Latin father was Jerome (342–420), whose

Latin translation of the Bible, called the *Vulgate,* was used throughout the Middle Ages.

The most influential Church father of this period was Augustine (354–430), born Aurelius Augustinus in what is now Algeria. Though he was less influential in Orthodox Christianity, Augustine's thinking underlies much of the Western philosophical and religious tradition. Specifically, his thinking underlies much of existentialism. Augustine is an example of how subtle even great influence can be, and why it is important for students of history to understand that influences may not be readily apparent.

Augustine's temporal location allowed him to be a bridge between the classical and medieval worlds, partaking of the culture of the former and greatly influencing that of the latter. Augustine is an example of how interesting and important are those whose lives span two epochs, but we must remember that for many of these people, their position is not entirely fortuitous. Rather, they substantially shaped the epoch into which they bridged. Christianity and philosophy had long been intertwined, but Augustine was the definitive bridge, the link between introspection and Christianity. To him we owe the concept of an inner God whose grace and presence is within us at all times.

Like all great thinkers, Augustine was influenced by multiple sources. His first influence was his mother, Monica, a devout Christian. She was a continuing influence, and he even described a joint vision he had with her. His training in rhetoric was perhaps his next greatest influence. A third was Cicero, particularly his *Hortensius,* which concentrated more on philosophy than rhetoric. A fourth influence was Manichaeanism (or Manichaeism), a now-extinct religion founded in the third century CE by Mani. Manichaeans were dualists who combined thinking from Zoroastrianism, Christianity, and Gnosticism. They believed that God and his creations were light, while the creations of Satan, which included the material world and its contents, were dark. They posited that people were created by Satan but had a modicum of light from God. They had contempt for the body, but thought that the soul was a fragment of God's light that was trapped in the body. The Manichaeans appeared more spiritual than Christians, and also appeared more rational because they claimed they could prove their beliefs. That claim, however false it undoubtedly was, appealed to the intellectual Augustine.

Having merged these influences into an inquiring mind, Augustine then turned to the Bible, but was not particularly inspired by it. He was originally put off by the casual nature of its writing, which seemed significantly inferior to the formal Greco-Roman literature he was well familiar with, but he later came to realize that this informal style of writing was the Bible's strength, not its weakness.

As a young man, Augustine went to Milan, whose bishop was Ambrose. After reading and listening to Ambrose, Augustine was converted to Christianity in 386 and baptized in 387. From Ambrose, he learned that the Bible could be interpreted allegorically, making it much more palatable to him. It was also in Milan that he first came into contact with Christian Platonism, which was primarily in the form of Neoplatonism, and he probably read Plotinus. This continuing study merged with the catechism (instruction) he received from Ambrose, resulting in a philosophical/metaphysical approach to Christianity that was virtually tailor-made for Augustine. I suspect he would not have been captivated by any other presentation of Christianity because he would have considered it too simple. In Augustine, the four stages of development — education at home, formal education, contact with a few key mentors, and self-study and reflection — worked synergistically to generate a singularly powerful mind.

Able now to integrate Neoplatonism into the scriptures, Augustine conceived of true wisdom as emanating from God, analogous to Plato's forms, and earthly wisdom as analogous to the representations of forms on Earth. For Augustine, the divine forms are in the mind of God. Jesus made it possible for us to glimpse divine forms and thus to glimpse both true wisdom and our inner selves. This was the basis for his doctrine of divine illumination, which held that there were certain truths that were obtainable only from the direct action of God on the mind. Neoplatonism also made it possible for Augustine to form a link between his perception of God and the inner self. To turn inward is in fact to experience the divine mind. When we turn inward, we turn upward as well.

With this Neoplatonic approach to Christianity, Augustine arrived at satisfactory answers for such issues as non-bodily existence, the omnipresence of God, and the nature of evil. Following from the tenets of Neoplatonism, Augustine believed in free will, and expounded some of the first thinking on this topic. He believed that evil was not a distinct entity or a creation of God, but was the corruption or absence of good that resulted from the misuse of free will. He believed that the misuse of free will that resulted in evil stemmed from ignorance, which could be corrected.

After his time with Ambrose, Augustine returned to North Africa, founded a monastery, introduced Platonic Christianity, refuted the Manichaeans, and began writing in earnest. His first work of universal influence and greatness was *Confessions,* finished about 400 CE. It is perhaps the first work of personal introspection in Western literature. *Confessions* is a chronicle of an intellectual and spiritual journey in which Augustine shows us his humanity and the mistakes of his youth. He also shows that his path to Christianity was a philosophical one, in which Greco-Roman (pagan) scholars played a major role.

There are thirteen books in *Confessions,* the first nine of which discuss his past life. Augustine has an undeserved reputation for youthful promiscuity. He lived for about fifteen years with one woman and had a son with her. He was ultimately separated from her when he entered into an arranged marriage with a wealthy Christian, in accord with the customs of the time, and he wrote in *Confessions* of how this separation affected him. He also wrote movingly about the loss of a friend.

Book ten is devoted to his current life and is a movement away from the factual autobiography of his youth and toward self-analysis, which occupies the remainder of the work. Augustine asks why it took so long to find God, and reflects on God's love. In the last part of *Confessions,* he describes how our love for God, not a specific action of God, carries us into Heaven.

After his conversion, Augustine experienced a great joy in the longing for and the journey to God, and in *Confessions* he describes his life as an attempt to recapture that great moment of joy. He explains how faults and superficial values become habit forming, and how these habits then became necessity. In a line of thinking somewhat similar to Buddhism, he depicts how these superficial values impeded his search for the truth and for God's love.

After writing *Confessions,* Augustine spent considerable time refuting a group called the Donatists. Rome, while basically tolerant of Christianity, persecuted Christians briefly in the early fourth century, during the reign of Diocletian. During this time, Roman authorities demanded that Christian leaders turn over books for burning. The those who complied were called traditores ("those who handed over"). The traditores were shunned or expelled from the Church, but were restored during the reign of Constantine and forgiven by most Christians. The Donatists thought that the traditores had contaminated the apostolic succession, which is a central doctrine in the Catholic Church whereby bishops are a direct link to the apostles. Donatists considered any sacrament performed by traditore bishops invalid. Based in large part on Augustine's writings, the Donatists were suppressed.

The latter part of Augustine's career was largely spent refuting the Pelagians. The disagreement they had with the mainstream Church centered on the doctrine of original sin, which is the belief, to which most Christian Churches subscribe, that the sin of Adam and Eve changed human nature and forever tainted all people. Moreover, each individual personally shares in Adam and Eve's guilt, as if we ourselves had eaten the forbidden fruit. People sometimes overlook this second component to original sin. We are not only born unworthy, but we are also already guilty of this particular sin, which makes us so innately prone to sin that it is inevitable unless God intervenes. People are inherently unworthy unless specifically made deserving by God, usually through Baptism, which is a washing away of sin, making a fresh start possible. Original sin, by introducing people's inherent unworthiness, is one way in which Christians reconcile the problems of the world with an omniscient and omnipotent God (early Christians probably also introduced this doctrine to better explain the belief that Jesus died for the sins of humanity).

Pelagianism held that original sin did not forever taint humanity, and that our free will can choose good over evil without God's continuing help. All that was required was that we use our own free will to follow God's rules. In refuting Pelagianism, Augustine developed the concept of divine grace. He maintained that we cannot comply with God's rules without His continued guidance and help.

One of the arguments Augustine advanced in refuting the Pelagians is that we constantly sin. If people have the ability to follow a proper path, then why don't we? Indeed, we constantly ask forgiveness, which is a form of ongoing divine guidance. Augustine also argued that even if we could avoid evil on our own, doing so only out of fear of damnation would be insufficient. We must do so because we love God, and it is God who makes it possible for us to love Him. That gift from God, which makes our love for Him possible, is grace — Augustine's greatest contribution to Western Christianity. The doctrine of grace as set forth by Augustine is the key element in Augustinian Christianity. It held that good works alone cannot save us. Protestantism directly built on this doctrine.

For Augustine, faith came first. Faith then leads to grace, which makes it possible for us to love God. Understanding then emanates from this love. We start with faith, and then we pray for love. God grants this prayer through grace, and the love that follows makes understanding possible. We must not seek faith or love in exchange for reward or to avoid punishment. Neither should we expect to understand at the beginning. Rather, we are led to God through faith, and the sequence of faith-grace-love makes understanding possible. If we follow this sequence, we need not fear punishment; at no point in it are we driven by fear. True obedience and understanding come from love, not fear. Part of grace is to free us from fear and allow us to comply with God's wishes out of love. Always, Augustine focuses on the inner self and not on mere reward or punishment.

In his later writings, Augustine held that even faith, the starting point for the Christian, was a gift of God's grace and did not arise completely from our free will. This begs the question of whom God will bestow faith upon, which takes us into predestination. Though Augustine believed in free will, he also believed in predestination and eternal punishment. He may have been the originator of the doctrine of predestination, which a thousand years later would become crucial to Calvinist Protestantism. For Augustine, predestination is not just God's prior knowledge; rather, it is God's deliberate plan to bestow grace on some people and not others. This means that God predestines some, before they are born, to receive grace and be saved, and predestines others, also before they are born, not to receive grace, and to be damned. Though there is the possibility that one may practice Christianity in vain if he or she was not predestined for salvation, Augustine thought that people who believed and practiced Christine doctrines were very likely to have been predestined for salvation (Calvinists, when they adopted predestination, also thought that Christian beliefs and actions indicated selection for salvation, and they thought that true belief was an indication that the individual was chosen). Though it seems unfair to us that God would predestine some for damnation before they have a chance to believe and behave appropriately, Christians who accept this doctrine believe that the wisdom behind it is simply beyond our understanding.

In part because of his Manichaean roots, which held that humanity was created by a malevolent force, and in part because of the low opinion that Christianity has of people, Augustine adopted the philosophy of original sin. Augustine is not the source of that doctrine, which goes back at least to Paul, but Augustine popularized it and made it an integral part of Christianity, especially in his battles with Pelagianism. As part of his advocacy of original sin, Augustine taught that anyone, even an infant, who dies before being baptized, was damned. Prior to Augustine, traditional Catholic teaching was that unbaptized infants went to a place called Limbo, which was neither heaven nor hell. Because they were not baptized, original sin had not been erased, and they could not be admitted into heaven, but because they had no sin other than original sin, they would not go to hell. Augustine originally subscribed to this view, but his contemplations on original sin caused him to adopt a sterner position — without Baptism and the specific intervention of God's grace, hell was unavoidable. This doctrine has caused a great deal of anxiety over the centuries, and many Christians who otherwise cherish Augustine's thinking have departed from his teaching in the matter. It may be that so sharp and uncompromising a view was adopted as a specific refutation of the Pelagians, and that in different circumstances, Augustine might have reached a different conclusion regarding original sin and children.

The doctrine of the Trinity had been settled before Augustine reached his Christian maturity, but the power of his reasoning added weight to the principle. The Arians thought that God created Jesus in the same way that He formed the rest of the universe, and that Jesus was of similar, but not identical, substance to God. This is what the Nicene council had specifically rejected. In his very large *Treatise on the Trinity,* Augustine likened the Christian Trinity to the human mind, pointing out that the mind also has different aspects — such as memory, understanding, and will — each of which is simultaneously separate yet inextricably fused with other aspects. Augustine's position on the Trinity, still a hallmark of Christianity, is that God is simply incomprehensible, and cannot be approached with simple thinking. Ironically, it was Augustine himself who said that Christian beliefs must conform to what is known about the world, and they must be rational and comprehensible.

In *The City of God,* Augustine established much of the foundation for Christian philosophy, and here again, we see the indebtedness to classical, pre-Christian thinkers. Augustine argued that communities were not formed from a desire for justice, as Cicero had said, but by a common love. In the case of the Earthly city, that which is loved is false, and conflict over it will lead to friction in the community. In God's city, however, that which is loved engenders no conflict. Augustine not only absolved Christianity of responsibility for the Visigoth sacking of Rome in 410 CE, but also pointed out that Rome was not eternal. Rather, it was Christianity and God's kingdom that were eternal. The City of Man and the City of God are intermingled now, but will become separate at the last judgment.

Augustine also wrote *On Christian Doctrine,* which discussed the relationship of Christianity and classical thinking. Here, he argued that some aspects of antiquity could be comfortably embraced by Christians and were in fact indispensable to them. Augustine's writings are an expression of the multiple aspects of being a person. In them, we find literature that all of us can relate to, regardless of our religious beliefs.

The last of the great Church fathers in the West was Pope Gregory (reigned 590–604). He wrote a manual for bishops called *Pastoral Rule,* adopted and generalized the rules that Saint Benedict had written for his own monastery, and wrote a biography of Benedict.

In the early Church, the doctrine of apostolic succession required each bishop to show that he could trace his roots to the apostles. The two most important apostles were Peter and Paul, both of whom were connected to Rome. This meant that bishops of Rome could theoretically claim to be the successors of the two. In addition, these bishops acquired additional influence simply because of the status of Rome. Consequently, the Bishop of Rome came to be the leader of the church. In addition, the Emperor Theodosius decreed that the Bishop of Rome would have authority. The Bishop of Rome became known as the Pope (from the Latin word for "father"), but that word was never the official title of the leader of the Catholic Church. Later, the weakening of the Roman government permitted the Bishop of Rome to acquire civil authority.

Gothic Cathedral

Three artistic advances happily came together to create the monumental Gothic cathedrals: the pointed arch, the flying buttress, and stained glass. While Gothic cathedrals continued to be built into the 16th century, and there have been Gothic revivals in modern times, the truly great age of Gothic cathedral building lasted only about 150 years, from about 1150-1300 CE. This is Barcelona cathedral, but the center of Gothic cathedrals was in France.

Christian religious expression took a new form in the late Middle Ages with the Gothic Cathedral. In these giant houses of worship, the pointed arch (obtained from the Muslim world), the flying buttress (a new means of supporting high walls), and stained glass came together to provide an open space where the Christian could feel the power and grace of God.

Until challenged by the Reformation, the Catholic Church was much more tolerant than is usually remembered, but there were two moments in pre-Reformation Catholicism in which those perceived as different or threatening were persecuted. The Spanish Inquisition, a unique expression of this process in Spain, was under royal, not papal, control. While its harshness is legendary, it cannot be blamed on the Catholic Church. The Medieval (or Papal) Inquisition, under the control of the Church, was much more important because of its duration and extent.

The Medieval Inquisition occurred in Europe (with the exceptions of England and the Scandinavian countries) from the twelfth to the fifteenth centuries. While clearly a historic tragedy, its impact is often overstated, and an effort was made to ensure fairness. Medieval inquisitors traveled in pairs. On the day of their arrival in a new town, they would contact the local clergy and arrange for a town meeting. Attendance, while not technically mandatory, was highly advisable for the local residents. The inquisitors would preach to the crowd and promise that anyone who came forward at this stage and acknowledged wrongdoing would receive a very lenient penance — a promise that was kept. A number of people would accept this offer, and thereby avoid a confrontation with Church authorities. Part of the agreement, however, was that the confessing Christians, in exchange for their light punishment, had to divulge what they knew about other possible heretics.

When arresting a suspected heretic, the inquisitors were not required to state a reason for the arrest, and the accused could be held indefinitely without trial or even a charge. Inquisitors were also permitted to withhold any evidence that might be exculpatory and to sequester the property of the accused until final resolution of the case.

Accused persons were entitled to a trial, but could be imprisoned for months or years before it took place, during which time an inquisitor would visit periodically and offer the opportunity to confess. These confessions were taken with the accused still not knowing the reason for the arrest, so people trying to extricate themselves occasionally confessed to heretical deeds and actions that had not been suspected and may not have been true.

Inquisitors did insist on the testimony of two independent witnesses prior to a trial, and punishment was levied against those who accused falsely. Defendants were asked if anyone had a special dislike for them, and if anyone so named by the accused was an accuser, that person's allegation was thrown out.

By the 1250s, inquisitors were permitted to torture (as secular courts had long been). A confession obtained under torture was not admissible in a trial, but if an accused confessed under torture and then recanted, he faced the certainty of additional torture, so people learned that it was easier to maintain guilt even after the torture stopped, thus ultimately confessing in a manner that was admissible. Likewise, individuals had the right to an attorney, but lawyers absented themselves during trials because if they lost they would be permanently disbarred for having defended a heretic.

Trials of the Inquisition were conducted in secret. Verdicts were not announced immediately afterward, but rather were announced as a group at another town meeting at the end of the process. Though the process to this point was under Church control, those found guilty were turned over to secular authorities for punishment. While those convicted of heresy might be executed, the Inquisition tended to support confiscation of property and long-term imprisonment for a first offense (in fact, the Inquisition is important in history as a factor in bringing about imprisonment as a common punishment, versus the then-prevailing methods of punishment for serious offenses, which included torture, dismemberment, and death). A second conviction of heresy, or even a confession after a first conviction, would result in burning at the stake.

Inquisitors followed all the due process of the time, and were convinced they had adequate safeguards in place to prevent the conviction of innocent people. The real lesson of the Medieval Inquisition is that the perception of adequate safeguards is illusory. No set of safeguards or due process can fully compensate for our inherent weaknesses and prejudices. Following established procedures, however rigorous, does not protect us from repeating the mistakes of the inquisitors. Only tolerance, rational thought, and understanding — even when we are frightened or think that special circumstances apply — can guide us to a higher ground. Here again, we have a lesson of history that can help us with the uncertainty, fear, and anger that pervade the world after 9–11.

The organization of the Catholic Church continues to mirror that of the Roman Empire in which it formed. A parish is the area of one priest, and a diocese is the area of one bishop. The Virgin Mary is particularly important to Catholics, more so than to Protestants, and Catholics often say a particular prayer to the Virgin, called the Hail Mary. It is often recited in conjunction with rosary beads (a rosary consists of a cross and a string of beads that are used as prayer counters, and the word may also refer to a particular prayer). Individual Catholics often have a patron saint.

Rosary

The word "Rosary" is used by Catholics either to denote a particular prayer or a set of devotional beads. The Rosary prayer begins with a profession of belief called The Apostle's Creed, then continues with a portion of the Lord's Prayer alternating with recitations of the Hail Mary (a prayer asking for the assistance of the Virgin Mary), a profession called Glory Be To The Father, and reflections on the Mysteries of the Rosary (events in the life of Jesus or Mary). The Rosary beads are accompanied by a Cross and likely arose as a means of keep track of the number of Hail Marys said during the prayer.

The Eastern expression of Christianity gave rise to the Orthodox Church, which, like Catholicism, traces its roots to the first Christians and should be considered to be coeval with Catholicism. Orthodoxy is sometimes erroneously considered a type of Catholicism, and may inappropriately be called "Greek Catholicism," but it is a distinct expression of Christianity. Orthodoxy and Catholicism, sometimes called the Eastern and Western Churches, respectively, were the two forms of Christianity prior to the Reformation.

The beliefs and rites of Orthodoxy are based on the Church of Constantinople, which was the site of numerous ecumenical councils between the third and eighth centuries. Among these, the fifth council held that Jesus did not exist as an individual separate from the incarnate God. The sixth council held that Jesus had both a divine and a human will. The seventh council approved the worship of icons.

In Orthodoxy, patriarchates are considered the originating sites of the Christian Church. In addition to Constantinople, these are Rome, Alexandria, Jerusalem, and Antioch (the Patriarchate of Antioch moved to Damascus in the thirteenth century, but is still called by its original name). Orthodoxy does not have a single head, analogous to the pope. Rather, each of these patriarchates is led by a patriarch.

Monasticism was as important in Orthodoxy as in Catholicism, and even before Benedict, Eastern Christians such as Saint Basil (330–379 CE) had established rules for monastic conduct in the East. Basil was also known for his *Hexaemeron* (*Hexaemera* were treatises on the six days of creation; Saint. Augustine also wrote a famous Hexaemeron). In contrast to the Western Church, bishops in the Eastern Church usually begin as monks, not as priests, unless they were celibate priests. In addition to Basil, important fathers in the Orthodox Church include Gregory of Nyssa (c. 330–395), Gregory of Nazianzus (329–389), and John Chrysostom (347–407).

Orthodoxy is typically somewhat more conservative than Catholicism. Of the twenty-seven books in the New Testament, Johannine literature (the Gospel of Saint John, Revelation, and the three letters attributed to John) constitutes the main basis for Orthodoxy. By giving primacy to the teaching of John, Orthodox Christians conceive of Jesus as much more demanding and less personable than Catholics do. The Holy Spirit is more important in Orthodoxy than in Catholicism or most branches of Protestantism.

Though religious icons have always been more prominent in Christianity than in Judaism or Islam, they have had an even more prominent place in Orthodoxy than in Catholicism. Orthodox Christians worship icons that they consider to be representative of Jesus, and do not believe that such worship violates the commandment against graven images because the image is only a representation, not an incarnation. Though there were two periods, one in the eighth century and one in the ninth, in which the worship of icons was forbidden in Orthodoxy (these were the periods of iconoclasm and reflect the influence of Islam, which strictly forbids the worship of images of God), worshipping images is generally thought to comfort people and make God more accessible.

There has been less conflict between church and state in the Byzantine Empire than in the West. Because of the fall of the Western Roman Empire, secular authority had to form anew in the West, so the Church had a "head start" and could develop into a force equal to that of government. In the East, the government never faltered, and religious authority matured in an environment of strong central administration. The emperor was considered the head of both church and state. At the same time, however, he was not a priest, and was expected to defer to the patriarchs in matters of pure religion. As a result, the patriarchs acquired essentially full religious autonomy, but no secular power, and the conflict between church and state that characterized so much of Western European history was largely avoided. Interestingly, Orthodoxy was also largely free of the conflict between rationalism and faith that characterized both Catholicism and Islam in the late Middle Ages.

A breach between Catholicism and Orthodoxy occurred in 1040. This "Great Schism" resulted from disagreements over three issues. First, the worship of icons, which always made the Catholic Church uncomfortable. Second, the primacy of the pope. Orthodoxy accepted the pope as merely "first among equals," not as the sole leader of the Christian Church (the few Christians in the East who do accept the primacy of the pope are called Uniate Christians).

The third divisive issue was the filioque clause. *Filioque* is Latin for "and the son." Western Catholicism added this phrase to the Nicene Creed to reflect their belief that the Holy Spirit, the third component of the Trinity, emanated from both the Father and the Son. The primary motivation for adding the clause was to reinforce opposition to Arianism and to reaffirm that the Father and the Son are of identical substance. To Orthodox Christians, however, to say that the Holy Spirit emanated from both the Father and Son was to imply that the Father and Son were separate entities, which compromised their conception of the Trinity. Moreover, if the Father and Son gave rise to the Holy Spirit, it must follow that the Holy Spirit is diminished relative to the other members of the Trinity, again compromising the Eastern conception of the Trinity. The filioque clause is another example of the difficulty of reconciling the Christian Trinity with strict monotheism. Orthodox Christians were also concerned about the West's unilateral decision to change a fundamental creed without the knowledge or consent of their Eastern counterparts, and without a formal ecumenical council. Orthodox Christians have continued to adhere to the unmodified Nicene Creed.

In addition to these differences, there are also procedural differences in how Church officials are chosen. Orthodox bishops usually come from monasteries and are celibate (they may occasionally come from the ranks of priests if they are celibate). All of these religious differences were magnified by the ever-increasing cultural differences among the environments in which these churches found themselves, and the differences between Catholicism and Orthodoxy have always included cultural differences between East and West.

Today, there are about 200 million Orthodox Christians worldwide, including 3 million in the United States. The Coptic Christianity of Egypt is slightly different from Orthodoxy, but is usually considered to be an expression of it. While the tenets of Orthodoxy are invariant from country to country, there is slight variation in its expression due to national or cultural characteristics, resulting in Greek Orthodoxy, Russian Orthodoxy, etc.

In the late Middle Ages and Renaissance, a third form of Christianity emerged: Protestantism, which formed in the West from disagreements with Catholicism. Whereas Orthodoxy and Catholicism arose simultaneously and independently, Protestantism began as a breakaway movement from Catholicism. The Reformation was a long time in the making. Discontent with the Catholic Church had been common in northern Europe long before Martin Luther. People like John Wycliffe (c.1330–1384) and Jan Hus (1372–1415) insisted on the priority of scripture over the pope a century before Luther. Wycliffe was an Oxford professor and early dissenter from Catholic doctrines. The pope called for his arrest, but Wycliffe's support among academia and the court protected him, and he continued to write until his death. In the late fourteenth century, after Wycliffe's death, a group of followers called Lollards (a derogatory term meaning "mumblers") followed his example and became prominent in England. Their principal belief was that laypeople could perform Church rites because it was piety, not position, that conferred this power upon a Christian.

Though religious differences were the major bones of contention, cultural and linguistic differences also played a role in the Reformation. Northern Europeans felt alienated by the culture and language of the south, and were no longer willing to have so much of their lives dictated by Rome. Everyone wants a religion that is tailored for themselves and their culture. A personal relationship with the deity is key, and this was much more difficult for northern Europeans when another culture dictated the permissible interactions with God.

Martin Luther (1483–1546) was an Augustinian monk who did not see biblical justification for many of the institutions of the Roman Catholic Church. He thought that the church had strayed from its mission, and that it should return to the Bible and remove the needless complexities and incorrect thinking that had accumulated over the years.

The first major tenet of Luther's Protestantism is that man is inherently wicked and unworthy. To fully grasp the significance of this belief, we must put the Catholic view of man into perspective. It is true that all religion has the potential to diminish humanity, and the glory of God and the unworthiness of man had been an integral part of Christianity from the beginning, but the Catholic Church, until challenged by the Reformation, was not the obstacle to humanism and creativity that people commonly believe. While the idea that it was a principal instigator of the Renaissance is overstated, so too is the idea that it impeded and punished inquiry from its beginning. With the loss of the Roman economic and social structure in the early Middle Ages, a simplistic, rigid Christian view was both necessary and appropriate to provide societal cohesion. As social and economic times improved in the late Middle Ages, so did the Church's tolerance. The Church both shaped and was shaped by the larger world, the end result being an institution that, until the Counter Reformation, was as tolerant of innovative thinking as most other institutions and people of its time and place, if not more so.

In Catholicism, the unworthiness of man, while undeniable, was not an all-encompassing belief. People could become worthy and could earn salvation through proper beliefs and deeds. But now, Protestants took the unworthiness of humanity to an extreme. Luther thought it was impossible to overstate the unworthiness of humanity. People are so corrupt that they cannot even make the choices necessary for salvation, including the choice to have faith. Man is undeserving of salvation and too unworthy to even earn it. God must bestow salvation upon us, as a completely unearned, unearnable gift.

The core of Luther's teaching can be summed up in the phrases "faith alone," "grace alone," and "Bible alone." These three doctrines are linked, particularly the first two. In "faith alone," Luther held that people were justified only by faith (justification was the correction of a person's relationship with God and forgiveness for sinfulness). This belief has generated much controversy, in part because of the ambiguous meaning of "faith." Does faith include deeds? Historically, charitable deeds were a requirement of faith. It is unlikely that either Paul or Augustine would accept belief alone as sufficient for salvation, and the requirement for concomitant charitable deeds had always been an inescapable part of Catholicism. Traditional Catholic thought was that people, though defective, could, and must, choose to perform charitable actions. Because such actions are within our abilities, faith must include deeds.

In Luther's eyes, however, man's great unworthiness changed this, leading Luther to a different conception of justification by faith. People were too corrupted by sin to exercise free will, so they were incapable of voluntarily performing the deeds associated with faith and salvation. Salvation could not be earned by deeds because people were too unworthy to choose correct behavior. All human actions, even those that appear altruistic, were motivated by selfishness. This meant that people could not even assist in their own redemption. The one and only pathway to salvation was faith in God and in His Son Jesus. This faith and this alone makes possible the grace of God. In turn, this grace alone can bestow worthiness to man. God, through the death of Jesus, makes available the grace required to make man worthy. Faith is a gift from God that leads to grace, another gift, which in turn allows us to be saved. While this thinking has similarities to that of Augustine, it is much simpler, much more extreme, much less compromising, and much less humanistic.

Luther never denied the importance of good deeds, but maintained that they are the result of the faith and grace that God bestowed to permit justification, not the cause of justification. Good works were acts of faith. This was the principal problem Luther had with indulgences, money paid to the Church that was said to bring about justification. Given that only God can bestow the faith and grace necessary for enlightened behavior or salvation, indulgences were useless. Words emanating from the Church were an arrogant usurpation of God's unique ability to bestow grace. What was needed was not individual action to change God's mind, but rather faith to receive His grace. As an aside, Luther also had two other problems with indulgences: he knew that indulgence money from Germany went to Rome, which rankled his sense of nationalism and patriotism, and he felt that the greater ability of the rich to afford indulgences was contrary to Christian egalitarianism.

The "Bible alone" portion of Luther's thinking held that everything people need to know was in the Bible. Luther also believed that God has ordained for each of us a specific calling or task that we must perform — doing so is our individual covenant with God, a personalization of the long-standing Covenant in Judeo-Christian religion — and individual study of the Bible can lead a person to his calling. The Bible is the sole authoritative source for both religious and personal knowledge, which people can read and understand for themselves. Whereas the Catholic Church actively opposed private ownership of Bibles and believed that people could understand scripture only through the clergy, Luther felt that all "interpreters" of the Bible, such as popes, councils, and clergy, were unnecessary and undesirable because the experience of God must be personal. Because this required that the Bible be readily available to people, Luther translated it into German. He also took advantage of the new printing press to increase the number of Bibles that could be disseminated.

Today, with Catholicism and Protestantism sitting more or less comfortably side by side in most areas of our culture, we may not immediately grasp the magnitude of Luther's agenda. In a time when there was poor separation of church and state, his proposals were as revolutionary as a contemporary proposition that people could interpret the law for themselves and that the judicial system was not needed. In particular, the belief that salvation came only from faith, which implied that the dispensation of the Sacraments was unnecessary, and the belief that the Bible, not the Church, was the primary authority, struck at the heart of Catholicism.

It is not completely established that Luther literally nailed his *Ninety-five Theses* to the Wittenberg church door in 1517, but he may have. At the time, before the widespread use of printing, ideas were often promoted in such a manner, rather like putting something on a community bulletin board or the Internet today, and such an act would not have been overly belligerent given the practices of the day. In either case, Luther certainly mailed them to the local archbishop.

In 1520, Luther published three treatises. The first was the *Address to the German Nobility,* in which he urged noblemen to oppose payments to Rome, requiem masses, pilgrimages, and clerical celibacy. These practices implied that human acts could influence God, and therefore gave humanity undeserved value and power. The second treatise was *On the Babylonian Captivity of the Church.* Here Luther argued that the Church was imposing the doctrine of transubstantiation improperly. Transubstantiation held that during the Eucharist (communion), the piety of the priest transformed the bread and wine into the actual blood and body of Christ. Luther accepted the transformation, but rejected the idea that the priest had the power to effect it. Rather, it was God alone who did, and no human action, thought, or devotion, however sincere, could replace God's power. Luther held that only Baptism and the Eucharist were valid Sacraments. The third treatise was *On the Freedom of a Christian Man,* in which he argued that salvation occurred from the faith of the individual and the grace of God alone, and that good works were not sufficient. Later in the 1520s, Luther published his *Greater Catechism* and his *Lesser Catechism,* were treatises addressed to the clergy and to the laity, respectively.

Luther was a monk, and his initial intent was undoubtedly to reform the Church from within. The Church was partially receptive to change, but slow progress and Luther's dogmatic and fiery temperament, superimposed on a long-standing and widespread discontent with the Church that predated even Wycliffe, transformed his goal into essentially the destruction of the Church as it then existed.

The Church excommunicated Luther, but otherwise tolerated him for a number of reasons. First, Catholic authorities were slow to realize the full power and threat of the Reformation. For example, his *Ninety-five Theses* were not officially condemned until 1521 (the year of his excommunication), four years after their promulgation. Second, though Luther was the leading spokesman of his time and place, many agreed with him, and the ideas he voiced had been in the air throughout northern Europe for many years. He was not a lone voice whose silence might end the reform movement. A third reason for Luther's successful defiance is that he had the protection of some secular leaders. This protection only partially stemmed from religious sympathy; much of the support that secular rulers gave Luther came from a desire to weaken the papacy so as to augment their own power, and to free German states from papal (Italian) domination. Moreover, many secular rulers realized that a successful Reformation would permit them to confiscate Church lands, have a free hand in the appointment of religious officials, and exercise greater influence in religious education.

John Calvin (1509–1564) was born in France, and apparently encountered Protestantism when he was a law student. He officially broke with the Roman Catholic Church in 1533. Shortly thereafter, King Francis I of France began to identify and sequester Protestants, so Calvin fled to Basel. In 1536, he published the first edition of *Institutes of the Christian Religion.*

The Calvinist tradition is sometimes called the Reformed Protestant tradition. In many ways, it began with Huldreich Zwingli (1484–1531), who attacked a number of traditional Catholic doctrines, such as monasticism, the celibacy of priests, the authority of the pope, the belief that Christ was actually present in the Eucharist, and the belief that the mass was a reenactment of the sacrifice of Christ.

Guillaume Farel (1489–1565) secured power in Geneva, and invited Calvin to participate with him in the creation of a Protestant state. Together, Farel and Calvin wrote *Articles of Church Government,* and in 1541 they successfully instituted a strict Protestant regime in Geneva. Public morality was under the control of the consistory, which comprised both laypeople and ministers, but Calvin became essentially a dictator. In 1539, Calvin published another edition of his *Institutes,* which was intended to serve as the literary foundation for Protestantism. In writing the *Institutes,* Calvin may have drawn inspiration from a twelfth-century work by Peter Lombard called *Sentences,* which was a long series of questions and answers, with commentaries. *Sentences* was regarded as a literary foundation for Catholicism, and it is likely that Calvin sought to create a counterpart work for Protestantism. Like Martin Luther's *Catechisms,* the *Institutes* concerns reflections on the Ten Commandments, the Apostles' Creed, and the Lord's Prayer.

Calvin's theology is often summarized by the acronym TULIP. The "T" stands for total depravity. Like Luther, Calvin believed that man was so wicked, sinful, and incapable that he cannot even contribute to his own redemption, either by proper beliefs or proper actions. Echoing and expanding the theme of unworthiness, Calvin said that a human being is "a five-foot worm" and that babies were "wiggling snakes." This is a new and frightening demotion of the status of humanity to a level significantly below that accorded it by the Catholic Church.

The "U" stands for unconditional election. The word "election" refers to salvation; to be elected is to be saved. Calvin thought that God predestined for salvation all those who would be saved, and that this predestination was absolute, unconditional, and unalterable by the individual's beliefs or actions. God doomed the vast majority, before birth, to damnation. Indeed, Calvin held that Jesus died for only a small number, the elect, whom God had chosen for salvation. Calvin insisted that no one could know whether or not he was elected. This generated enormous anxiety, as people wondered whether they were among the anointed; paradoxically, it also comforted a small number who could not control their behavior, because in this doctrine, their behavior was irrelevant. In anticipation of the idea that people may take up hedonism since their fate is predetermined and independent of their actions, Calvin offered the "signs of election": regular church attendance, leading a godly life, and public profession of faith. These signs might indicate predestination for salvation. The hope was that no one wanted to appear as if he or she had not been elected.

The "L" stands for limited atonement, meaning that Jesus died only for the elect, not for all of humanity. The "I" stands for irresistible grace, meaning that the elect cannot resist God's grace, nor can they claim in any way to deserve or to have earned His grace. The "P" stands for permanence of grace. No matter what a person does, if he is predestined to have God's grace, it stays with him forever. God has absolute power — even beyond what is indicated in scripture — while man is absolutely powerless. These opinions were not only much less liberal than the prevailing Church doctrine, but were also antithetical to Renaissance Humanism.

Calvin and Luther both agreed on the primacy of scripture over Church authorities, the lack of free will, and justification by faith alone. They differed in that Calvin placed the sovereignty of God above even scripture. They also differed in that Luther did not accept absolute predestination (though he accepted a lesser form). Luther also did not think that the grace of God was necessarily permanent; God could perhaps grant and then withdraw it. Luther believed that Jesus was present during the Eucharist — though God, not the officiating priest, brought about his presence — whereas Calvin thought that Jesus' presence during this time was symbolic. Perhaps most important, Calvin believed the Church was also the supreme political unit, whereas Luther thought that political power still belonged to the state.

Calvin stressed the importance of the Old Testament and the significance of the Protestants as God's new chosen people, replacing the Jews and certainly the Catholics (this view is integral to contemporary American fundamentalist Christians). Not all of Switzerland was Protestant, but Calvinism was the rule in the part that was. The Protestants in France (called Huguenots) and in Scotland were also Calvinist.

Protestantism is often perceived as having "liberalized" religion, and in the sense that alternative viewpoints are inherently constructive, it did. Protestantism also offered a more direct connection to God, and was the religious expression of the desire to "see for oneself" that revolutionized science. But Protestantism was considerably less humanist than Catholicism, and it impeded, rather than enhanced, an inquiring outlook. Indeed, a selling point for Protestantism was that it adhered more strictly to scripture than did Catholicism, which had tolerated unorthodox thinking, not just in religion, but also in science and the arts. Neither Luther nor Calvin supported scholasticism, a major means for integrating the newly rediscovered Aristotelian thinking into religious thought, which Catholicism did accept (Saint Thomas Aquinas, a Catholic theologian, was a leading proponent of the integration of the new knowledge). Likewise, the Catholic Church substantially accepted the new Humanism of the Renaissance, but neither Luther nor Calvin did, because they did not believe that people could be made better. Indeed, it is possible that the Reformation would not have occurred were it not for the relative secularization of the Renaissance, which led some to believe that the Catholic Church had become too lenient. When the Protestants' low opinion of humanity is considered in conjunction with their aversion to innovative thinking, and the little-remembered tolerance of the Catholic Church, we can see that it is impossible to argue that the Protestant Reformation was good for innovation.

The Catholic Church was somewhat receptive, and had in fact had begun to change even before the Reformation. The Council of Trent, which met periodically from 1545 to 1563, primarily confirmed existing Catholic teaching, but did make some refinements, such as better training of priests. The Society of Jesus (Jesuits), founded primarily by Saint Ignatius of Loyola (1491–1556) and Saint Francis Xavier (1506–1552), not only presented the "new face" of the Church, but also fostered excellent education. The Jesuits were essentially a new monastic order, but rather than being confined to monasteries, they moved freely throughout the world.

Saint Ignatius published *The Spiritual Exercises* in 1548. These affirmed the primacy of Catholicism and the role of discipline, but offered a practical, understandable approach that laypeople could follow. The *Exercises* cover practical matters such as when and how to pray, confession, advice for living within the rules of the Church, etc. It was a "how-to" manual for Catholics at a time when many needed simple instructions and reassurance that Catholicism was both superior to Protestantism and practical to follow.

Angela Merici (1474–1540) founded the Ursulines, and Teresa of Avila (1515–1582) revitalized the Carmelite order (Teresa wrote a prominent autobiography, and is the subject of the famous Bernini sculpture *The Ecstasy of Saint Teresa*). The Church also reached out to its (largely illiterate) following by sponsoring art and music in what is now known as the Baroque Era.

Sadly, however, the Church eventually felt threatened and embarked on the Counter Reformation (sometimes called the Catholic Reformation), which lasted from roughly 1550 to 1650. Its terrible highlights included the bloody Thirty Years' War and The Roman Inquisition, which was a different process from the earlier Medieval and Spanish Inquisitions. The Roman Inquisition was a specific reaction of the Catholic Church to Protestantism, and it specifically targeted Protestants. In large measure, it was intended to demonstrate that the Catholic Church could be as adamant on scriptural matters as the Protestants, thereby removing the perception that Protestants were truer to biblical intent. The Thirty Years' War (1618–1648) devastated the region that is now Germany, and eventually forced the Church to accept Protestantism.

There is a greater history of internal conflict in Christianity than in any other religion. A fascinating aspect of the study of any time, place, event, or institution is that it offers us profoundly general lessons. From the Reformation, we can learn that change takes time, and that those who wish for change should be patient and careful that they do not adopt the same intransigence that they oppose. Dogmatism, extremism, infighting, and a view of opponents as completely corrupted delays, rather than hastens, change. From the Counter Reformation, we can learn that overreaction to a threat can be a greater peril than the threat itself. Had the Church not embarked on the Counter Reformation, the Protestants' fanatical dogmatism would have been its best ally. As it was, the Church's own rigidity and extremism damaged it more than the Reformation had. In the Counter Reformation lie lessons that can help us deal with the terrorist attacks of September 11, 2001, if we are wise enough to hear them.

The conflict between Catholicism and Protestantism spilled over into politics. Beginning in the sixteenth century, it became common for the religion of a nation or a region to follow that of its ruler. This superimposed religious differences on political differences, and European wars of the seventeenth and eighteenth centuries were fueled in part by religious differences. One of the factors in the rise of the Enlightenment was that the conflict between Catholicism and Protestantism, and the ensuing involvement of political entities, convinced many people that church and state must be separate. Certainly, the founding fathers of America, as well as their counterparts in France and Russia after their revolutions, were satisfied that church and state had to be separated. Enlightenment leaders could see that the separation not only removed the yoke of religion from their own citizens, but also made fighting over religion less likely. The Russian Revolution went even further: to achieve a classless society, Russia believed that religion must be abolished altogether.

Although different forms of Protestantism diverge in their precise beliefs, the common denominator is a belief that the two-tiered structure of worshippers in the Catholic Church — monks, nuns, and priests on one hand, and the laity on the other — could be replaced by a single tier of devoted Christians. Protestantism is a set of simple yet profound changes that redirected Christianity, very much as Upanishadic Monism redirected Hinduism, the Mahayana view redirected Buddhism, or Rabbinic Judaism redirected that religion. All of these are examples of the fluidity and dynamism that characterize all great religions. In the cases of Christianity and Buddhism, the original versions remain vibrant, whereas few Hindus and Jews practice a version of their religion that predates the *Upanishads* and Rabbinic philosophy, respectively.

Baptism and the Eucharist are the Sacraments agreed on by all Christians. Baptism is an acceptance into the Church and a washing away of original sin, while the Eucharist is a confirmation of Christ's making it possible for us to achieve salvation.

Communion

Communion (the Eucharist) is a Christian sacrament that is a reenactment and commemoration of the Last Supper. The bread that is served celebrates the moment in the Last Supper when Jesus served bread to his Apostles and told them "This is my body", while the wine celebrates the moment when Jesus gave wine to his Apostles and told them "This is my blood". Communion reminds the Christian that Jesus gave his body and his blood for their salvation.

Many Christians also recognize some or all of the following additional Sacraments: confirmation (where acceptance of Baptism and entry into the Christian community is confirmed; this replaces circumcision, which represents acceptance of the Covenant in Judaism), ordination, marriage, penance or reconciliation, and extreme unction (last rites).

Protestantism recognizes Sacraments, saints, and the Virgin Mary, but to a much lesser extent than the Catholic Church does. In their desire for a simpler expression of Christianity, Protestants rely less on images than Catholics do. For example, whereas Catholic crucifixes depict the dead Jesus, Protestant crosses usually do not. The primary artistic expression of Protestantism is music, which is thought to uplift the mind and prepare the individual to receive God. Moreover, music is a shared experience that allows the congregation to seek God both communally and individually. Protestantism has always made little distinction between religious and secular music, as both are spiritual and either can express the glory of God. It is no coincidence that Protestant composers such as Bach, with their vast output of both religious and secular music, became prevalent in the aftermath of the Reformation. The sermon is of greater importance in Protestantism, and replaces the Mass as the high point of the service. Sermons are in the vernacular, which long ago replaced Latin, and are usually based on a verse from the Bible.

Though the composition of the New Testament is universal in Christendom, Protestants use a slightly different version of the Old Testament. The Orthodox and Catholic versions of the Old Testament are based on the Greek translation of the Jewish Tanakh (the Septuagint), and have seven additional books that are not found in the original Hebrew text. These additional books are called deuterocanonical writings or the Old Testament Apocrypha. In keeping with the Protestant desire for a more direct text that was free of what they regarded as extraneous material, their Old Testament does not contain the Old Testament Apocrypha, and is nearly identical to the Tanakh (though it is arranged somewhat differently and ends with the prophets, whereas the Tanakh ends with First and Second Chronicles). In the United States, a 2008 survey found that Protestants very slightly outnumber Catholics, but worldwide, Catholics account for more than half of all Christians, alone numbering about 1 billion.

The Radicals were a division of Protestantism. This division included Puritanism, the brand of Reform Christianity that most closely followed the ideas of Luther and Calvin. The Puritans never became an established church — the recognized Protestant Church of England was the Anglican Church — nor were the Puritans a generally accepted group in England, so they set their sights on America, believing that God had given up on Europe and established America as the new Promised Land. Many Puritans thought that America's discovery during or just before the Reformation was not a coincidence, but a reflection of God's divine plan. Some Puritans even saw England as the new Egypt and the Atlantic Ocean as the new Red Sea.

We were taught in school that the Pilgrims, who were Puritans, came to America for religious freedom because they were persecuted in the Old World. There is a certain amount of truth to this in that they were never welcomed into the community of the Anglican Church. There is, however, much more to this story than this simple belief: the Puritans were never actively persecuted, and their rabid fundamentalism made them very difficult for even enlightened people to accept. Ironically, the Puritans, both in Europe and the United States, were more intolerant than the Anglican Church from which they fled.

Roger Williams (1603–1684) first attracted attention in Massachusetts when he opposed the attempt of secular authorities to enforce observance of the Sabbath in the Puritan manner. This has led to a common misconception that Williams supported separation of church and state so that people could worship or not as they chose, and that he was an Enlightenment figure of the same fabric as Thomas Jefferson who supported the right of people to be more secular. This is not the case; in fact, Williams wanted civil authority removed from religious matters only because he was afraid that the state would weaken the Church. He was a strict Calvinist and no paradigm of tolerance. Driven out of Massachusetts, he founded Rhode Island. Ironically, traditional Puritans became more tolerant, while the Rhode Island tradition moved to the South and became the Southern Baptists.

Though Western Christianity could be broadly classified into two major groups — Catholicism and Protestantism — by the end of the seventeenth century there were in fact many evolving forms of Christian worship in Europe. While all major religions have diverse expressions and are actually families of related beliefs, there is probably more diversity in contemporary Christianity than in any other religion. The Episcopal Church is a hybrid between the English Anglican Church and the Catholic Church. It is more willing to supplement scripture with reason than are some other types of Christianity. The Lutheran tradition is perhaps most directly linked to the "scripture alone" and "faith alone" doctrines of Martin Luther. In the eighteenth century, John and Charles Wesley, with George Whitfield, founded Methodism, which began as a branch of the Anglican Church in England. As it matured, it established a particularly strong musical tradition, beginning with hymns composed by Wesley. Contemporary Presbyterians are the most direct heirs of the Calvinist tradition, although few contemporary Protestants of any denomination, including Presbyterian, are comfortable with predestination. Most mainstream Protestants have come to believe, as Catholics always have, that through their beliefs and behaviors, people play a decisive role in achieving salvation.

The Anabaptists began as a group of radical Protestants who believed that other Protestants had not gone far enough. For example, they did not even have the limited church hierarchy of the Lutherans or the Calvinists. Each Anabaptist congregation is freestanding, with no hierarchy in the church (this helped to establish a tradition of free churches in other denominations). They did not believe in infant baptism, but rather baptized people only after they had professed their faith as adults. Those who had been baptized as infants must be re-baptized as believing adults (hence, the name of the movement, meaning, "to be baptized again"). Unlike the Calvinists, the Anabaptists believed that the elect could be identified if they had undergone an obvious conversion (what we might now call being "born again"), and that an adult baptism was a sign of that conversion.

Many Anabaptists believed in separation from the world. Contemporary Amish and Mennonites are descendants of the Anabaptists. Though a direct lineage is controversial, the Anabaptists influenced contemporary Baptists. Today, there are about 30 million Americans who follow or are influenced by the Anabaptist tradition, making it the largest Protestant tradition in the United States. Some denominations that have been influenced by the Anabaptists — such as the Southern Baptists — are the most evangelical and proselytizing denominations in America.

There is also diversity among the versions of the Bible that are in use today. The King James Bible was published in 1611 and intentionally used archaic language for that time. It is the most influential modern Christian work. It remains in wide use and is the basis for most subsequent Bibles. Published in 1901, the American Standard Version is a revision of the King James Bible. The Revised Standard Version, loosely based on the American Standard Version, was published from 1946 to 1977. The New Oxford Annotated Bible is a current work based on the Revised Standard Version.

The eighteenth-century Enlightenment saw the advent of Deism, the view that God had created the universe but then took little further role in its workings. As we have seen as far back as Confucius, the change in status of any deity from one actively involved in human affairs to one who is remote is a first step in understanding that the deity might not be required at all. It would be two centuries, however, before Europe seriously considered this idea, and even longer for the United States.

In the New England colonies, the Great Awakening (also called the first Great Awakening) occurred in the 1730s and 1740s as a response to a belief that America had become somewhat degenerate. Leaders included John Wesley, George Whitfield, and the fiery preacher Jonathan Edwards. The second Great Awakening was from 1797 to 1801. American businessmen later participated, creating the Businessman's Revival of the 1850s. In the first half of the nineteenth century, the United States may well have been the most Protestant nation in the world, but by 1850, immigrants started coming from Catholic countries, such as Italy and Ireland, changing the face of American Christianity.

The last decade of the nineteenth century was an exciting time in intellectual history and saw the origin of many new disciplines, such as sociology and anthropology. During this decade, Max Weber and Ernst Troeltsch analyzed the sociology of religion, particularly the concepts of church and sect. A sects is a group that separates from a larger body, usually with the belief that its members are truer to the original ideals than the parent body is, and that the parent body must return to the primary sources from which they have strayed. Weber and Troeltsch expanded this greatly, and provided a number of defining characteristics: Sects are cut off from society and have to be voluntarily joined with deliberate action, whereas churches are a mainstream component of society into which most people fall simply by birth. Sects view mainstream society as evil, and try to avoid it except insofar as contact with it results in converts or change.

Churches have well-trained clergy, whereas sects do not. In fact, members of a sect have very little formal training. There are established mechanisms for dealing with sin in churches, but for sects, sin is a more personal problem requiring more direct divine intervention. Sects originate from churches, but then develop structure and become established churches, ironically, in the process, adopting all the attributes they initially despised. In fact, the entire Protestant Reformation began as a sectarian movement. Sects may also give rise to other sects, with the newer sects often being more fundamental. In this manner, many well-established contemporary Protestant denominations arose.

The last twenty years have seen a revival of religion and a return to fundamentalism in four major religions — Judaism, Christianity, Islam, and Hinduism. These revivals began as sectarian movements within their respective parent religions. Fundamentalism is now an important force worldwide, and a major threat to global stability.

Fundamentalism is easier to characterize than to define. The word itself is problematic because fundamentalists of different religions have a variety of beliefs. For example, fundamentalist Christians have opinions of Jesus that are not shared by fundamentalists of other religions. But fundamentalists of all religions are united by a shared rejection of modernity, a simplified belief that the troubles of the world will disappear upon literal adherence to ancient texts without regard to contemporary context, and a refusal to see a differing viewpoint. These same beliefs separate them from the mainstream religions they arose from. Though it initially seems strange, and the fundamentalists of these religions would disagree, fundamentalists of all religions have more in common with each other than they do with their parent religions. Ironically, a fundamentalist Muslim and a fundamentalist Christian make the strangest companions on the world stage.

Christian Fundamentalism is a Protestant movement that believes in the literal interpretation and infallibility of scripture. Modern Christian Fundamentalism arose in the latter part of the nineteenth century as a sectarian response to what was considered the corruption of modernity, as scientific progress replaced life's simple certainties with discomfiting new information whose uncertainties outweighed its potential in the minds of many. Fear fuels fundamentalism. That fear can stem from economic concerns or from the belief that the world is changing too rapidly with no substitute for what is lost. Modern Christian Fundamentalism arises from fear caused by science's displacing religious underpinnings, without providing a commensurate feeling of inner peace. It is largely a response to progress that was not perceived as offering an adequate substitute for what it replaced.

The discoveries that most threatened fundamentalist Christians were those in geology and evolution. Mainstream churches accommodated these new scientific ideas, but fundamentalism viewed them as intensely menacing. Some conservative Christians even thought that the devil had placed supposed pieces of evidence in these scientific disciplines to mislead us. Like Orthodox Judaism, fundamentalist Christianity is a response to reform thinking, not the cause of more liberal beliefs.

In a significant difference from other Christians, fundamentalists have made the Apocalypse a major focus of their movement. Early Christians thought that the world was about to end, and were undoubtedly puzzled when it did not. Mainstream churches have, for the most part, moved away from this opinion and do not dwell on the end of the world. Mainstream Christians (and practitioners of other religions) may accept that the world will end one day, but the immediacy of it is not part of their daily thinking. Indeed, the Book of Revelation was nearly excluded from the New Testament because there was fear that it would encourage people to focus too much on the Second Coming of Jesus.

Fundamentalist Christians stress being "born again" because they seek an intensely personal experience with God while they are believing adults. Fundamentalists also have a much harsher view of Jesus. Both mainstream and fundamentalist Christians see him as the final judge at the time of the Apocalypse, but fundamentalists see him as an uncompromising, demanding judge who will condemn most people to hell, whereas mainstream churches tend to believe that the Second Coming will bring a savior similar to the teacher, friend, and confidant that was on Earth before.

Christianity accepts the doctrine of original sin — that the sin of Adam and Eve taints all people, even newborns, making us all intrinsically sinful — but it is on the periphery of mainstream churches. For most

Christians, sin, whether original or specific to the sinner, is unfortunate, but does not necessarily mean that people are intrinsically evil. Even the Protestant churches most directly connected with the doctrines of Luther and Calvin have eased considerably over the years on man's inherent unworthiness. For fundamentalists, however, sin indicates that people are inherently evil. To them, sin means that one is not in touch with Jesus and will not be saved unless there is a radical change in one's thoughts and actions.

For mainstream churches, redemption is a slow, lifelong process, with two steps forward and one step back. For fundamentalists, redemption is instantaneous, seized upon in a moment of revelation and forever changing the individual's life. I believe this simplified view of redemption is one reason that fundamentalism has become an important movement. It prospers for the same reason that Christianity itself prospers — it offers people hope, a degree of stability, and a form of certainty in a way that can be quickly understood and attained. While many cringe at the oversimplification and political consequences of fundamentalism, we must acknowledge that people are entitled to seek, and will seek, that which provides hope and certainty.

Political goals are an integral part of fundamentalism and distinguish it from simple evangelicalism. For example, Billy Graham's crusades emphasized many of the ideas of fundamentalism, and his followers have very similar religious beliefs, but they are not generally considered fundamentalists because they have no publicized political agenda. This distinction is quickly blurred, however. Many fundamentalist Christians who fully subscribe to a political agenda prefer to be called "evangelical" because the term implies concern for the salvation of others, whereas fundamentalism connotes dogmatism and rigidity to some people.

Because fundamentalism appears to be a quick and easy path to certainty in this world and paradise in the next, it will always have its appeal, especially to those who have not been exposed to more complex thinking. In addition, fundamentalism seems to exhibit periodicity, surfacing approximately every fifty years. We must remember that these are resurgences of fundamentalism, which never goes away, not a complete rebirth. Because God's relationship to humanity is a concept that individuals must settle for themselves, each generation has to deal with uncertainty and make its own peace with a higher power. Roughly every generation, fundamentalism becomes temporarily attractive until enough individuals in that generation are satisfied that the proposed solution is too simple and not directly applicable to daily life. The extent, significance, and manifestation of these revivalist cycles are a reflection of how people react to uncertainty.

Few American Christians opposed the teaching of evolution in 1900, but in large part this was because many rural students had little access to education and therefore were not exposed to the theory. In the first several decades of the twentieth century, public education in the United States increased enormously, particularly in rural areas, and many more young people were exposed to evolution theory. Conservative Christians then felt they had to react. The climax of the conflict was the 1925 Scopes trial. Teacher John Scopes agreed to be a defendant, and the American Civil Liberties Union deliberately picked that case so that it would lose, the goal being to win on appeal, thus overturning the Tennessee statute against the teaching of evolution. The intent was a small, obscure trial that would lead to a precedent-setting appellate victory, but as fate would have it, William Jennings Bryan passed through that area of Tennessee and volunteered his services. Subsequently, the famous defense lawyer Clarence Darrow volunteered his time, setting up the dramatic confrontation. At one point, Darrow, thinking about the importance of an appellate victory, demanded that Scopes be found guilty, which he was.

The Tennessee Supreme Court did overturn the case, but not on the constitutional grounds that the ACLU had hoped for. Rather, it was overturned because the judge had fined Scopes $100, and under Tennessee law, only a jury could impose a fine exceeding $50. So the ACLU did not get the constitutional victory it sought, and the law stayed on the Tennessee books until the 1960s. Not until 1968 did the US Supreme Court strike down a similar law in Arkansas, ruling that religious thinking could not prevent the teaching of scientific theory.

The ultimate result of the Scopes trial was a great increase in Darrow's national reputation, a victory for evolution, and national defeats for Bryan and fundamentalism. After the trial, fundamentalism flourished only in the Bible belt of the Deep South. The American South today has an evangelical movement and a fundamentalism that has not been seen anywhere else in the world in living memory. Part of the reason for this is that the denominations that were close to the Calvinist tradition, such as southern Baptist, Methodist, and Conservative Presbyterians, are primarily located in the South. The South also had less immigration than the North, and the immigrants it did have came from Protestant countries — mostly England, Scotland, and Ireland — that were more receptive to fundamentalism. In addition, until recent times, most of the American South was predominantly rural and poor, with minimal industry, and has therefore lacked both the economic security and the influx of new ideas that form the foundation of change.

After the 1968 Supreme Court decision removed obstructions to the teaching of evolution, conservative Christians demanded equal time for their viewpoint — Creationism. There are several varieties of Creationism, but the common denominator is the belief that God created the universe and everything in it without the need for evolution or scientific principles. In 1987, the Supreme Court ruled that Creationism is a religious theory, not a scientific one, and therefore is not entitled to equal time in the public schools. In the latest round, conservative Christians then introduced the doctrine of Intelligent Design, the belief that the universe may have been born and developed along scientific principles, but that a creator must have begun the process. At this writing, it is unclear whether Intelligent Design will be ruled a scientific teaching that merits equal time, or will be rejected as attempting to teach Creationism under another name.

It appeared that America was becoming secular in the 1960s. In the 1970s, there was a profusion of mystic cults that appeared to be Eastern. Although not truly Eastern religions, they did indicate America's willingness to explore non-Christian ways of thinking. In the 1970s, however, America took a decisive conservative turn that defies explanation. The current revival of Christian Fundamentalism began in the US and has been particularly powerful and prolonged. It can be largely dated to one year, 1979, because this was the year when the Moral Majority was founded. No one can say why the revival of fundamentalism occurred at this time. There was no severe social crisis that undermined confidence and caused people to turn away from rational thought. I believe scientific progress had engendered a sense of disconnectedness from the world without offering a matching peace of mind. Beyond a few specialized situations, such as better treatment for certain medical conditions, progress has not resulted in discernible advantages in the daily lives of most people.

Rather, it has created a vacuum that it has been unable to fill. The rapid changes of modernity have troubled many, causing the current wave of fundamentalism to persist longer than previous ones.

Another factor was the perception by fundamentalists that liberal legislation interfered with, or might interfere with, their lives. Could enforced separation of church and state mean loss of protection of church by state? In addition, I believe that people have traditionally (rightly or wrongly) associated liberalism with secularism, and in the 1970s, people began to be disillusioned with liberalism. The 1980 election saw not just the victory of Ronald Reagan, but also the defeat of a number of long-time liberal congressmen. There was a much stronger message being sent than just the election results. A thorough analysis of the failure of liberalism in the minds of Americans is beyond the scope of this work, but suffice to say that many thought it was not working. Many billions of dollars had been spent on liberal programs, such as the anti-poverty program, with few demonstrable results, and people were reluctant to allot more time or money to liberalism. Given the association of liberalism and secularism, if the former had been overrated, perhaps it was time to re-examine the latter. Why give liberalism and the secular programs it espoused more time and money when God can set things right immediately?

Fundamentalist Christianity has clashed not only with mainstream Christianity, but also with science, in areas such as stem cell research and evolution. We cannot yet know what the result will be, but I believe it is a lesson of history that the need for security and understanding in changing and turbulent times forces people to do one of two things: they either do the necessary work to bring about understanding, or they oversimplify. The former response has enriched our lives immeasurably, but the latter is much easier and faster. Watching the cultural evolution of humanity is like watching the development of a child. There are many times when one would like a realization to dawn more quickly, but there is enormous joy and satisfaction in recognizing that however slowly, maturation and understanding are slowly emerging. We must be grateful that it is happening at all, and we should believe that the timetable, though occasionally frustrating, is unfolding as it should.

Christianity's responses to modernity include ignoring it (most mainstream Christian churches), more actively embracing it (liberal congregations, such as Unitarianism), and fighting it (fundamentalism).

While the varieties of Christianity still differ in many ways, including their response to modernity, recent years have seen an attempt to find common ground. The Ecumenical Movement, which began in the twentieth century, works toward unity among different Christian denominations. In 1948, the World Council of Churches, a Protestant organization, sought reconciliation among denominations. The Catholic Church resisted this until the second Vatican Council (1963–65), which was arguably the most significant Vatican action since the Counter Reformation. After the second Vatican Council, Catholicism gave up much of its fundamentalist approach, became more accommodating to modernity (with the notable exceptions of abortion and birth control), and joined the Ecumenical Movement. Even more recently, Orthodoxy has joined.

The impact of Christianity is perhaps the most elusive question in our history, and a profound challenge to historians. Arguably, Christianity is now entering its fourth stage (after its early tenuous beginnings, its establishment as a solid religion, and its dominance of Europe). Today, much of the most significant Christian activity occurs in developing (formerly called Third World) countries, and it is these nations that may determine the future of Christianity.

Chapter 10

ISLAM

ISLAM, WHOSE FOLLOWERS ARE called Muslims, or Moslems, is the world's most misunderstood religion. To many Westerners, Islam condones violence, but as I discussed in *Who We Are: A Chronicle of the Ideas That Shaped Our World,* when practiced as it was intended, as it usually is, Islam is brilliant and beautiful. Let us begin our examination with a look at Islam's founder.

At the time of Mohammed (or Muhammad, 570–632 CE), Arabs were polytheists, with a social organization centered on the clan. Mohammed was born into the clan of Hashem, which to this day enjoys special significance. Certain members of the Saudi royal family are from this clan, as was the late King Hussein of Jordan (which is why the full name of the country is the Hashemite Kingdom of Jordan). Though nothing was written about his life until the period from 750 to 900, we know more about Mohammed than about any other major religious figure. His father died before the future prophet was born, and his mother died when he was six years old. His grandfather took over his care, but died soon thereafter. Ultimately, Mohammed was raised by an uncle, Abu Talib.

Sixth-century Arabia was largely rural, with only a few towns, such as Yathrib (now Medina) and Mecca. The economy was based predominantly on commerce. Their geographical position allowed them to not only trade with the two great empires of the day — Sassanid Persia and the Byzantine Empire — but also with sites in the Indian Ocean. Mohammed became involved in trading, and married an older widow named Khadija.

When he was about forty, Mohammed began to hear what he came to regard as the Archangel Gabriel relaying to him the direct word of God. Based on these revelations, Mohammed came to believe that one of the Arabian gods, Al-Lah, was in fact the only god, and identical to the Judeo-Christian God. Since he could not write, Mohammed recited these revelations to others, who recorded and collected them into a work that became the *Koran* (or *Qur'an,* Arabic for "recitation"). Some refer to Mohammed as the "Messenger" rather than the "Prophet." I agree with this because the term prophet has a specific meaning to Jews (as advisors to kings) and to Christians (as those who foretold the coming of Jesus), neither of which is appropriate in referring to Mohammed. In deference to tradition, however, this work will use the term "Prophet."

From a religious perspective, Muslims believe there is no other source for the *Koran* than the pure word of God, but from an historical and sociological perspective, Mohammed was the only great religious thinker who directly recorded his ideas, and it is possible that his travels as a merchant may have allowed him to integrate into the revelations some thinking from the few Jews and Christians that visited the area.

Mohammed united his people into a single faith with a common mission. Many were threatened by his message because he challenged the sacred belief that primary loyalty was to one's clan, but he gave his people a sense of belonging, and filled them with a self-esteem that was previously unknown. Indeed, the *Koran* says, "You are the best community ever brought forth from mankind." Let us contemplate those words from the viewpoint of their intended audience. To a tribal, rural society with minimal influence, yet well aware of the much greater power of adjacent empires, those words from a charismatic figure united and empowered. Never before in history, and never again, would so many diverse people be so quickly united by one person. I believe it is a lesson of history that much of the success of religion is because it provides a sense of belonging, a belief in a shared purpose. Mohammed, in the *Koran,* provided this masterfully.

While Muslims believe that God created the Koran, by being the instrument of its creation Mohammed was also one of history's great literary figures. The Koran illustrates what we have consistently seen in our examination of religions and their literature: the canons of the world's religions, while conveying a message we can accept or not, are incontestably great literature. Anyone who doubts the power of words to move people need only look at religious literature.

In 619 Mohammed lost both his wife and his uncle. The death of the latter — a senior man in a paternalistic, tribal society — deprived him of some protection that the fledgling Muslim community had enjoyed in Mecca. Mohammed's followers — fewer than one hundred — left Mecca for Medina in 622 CE. The Prophet joined them shortly thereafter. This journey is called the *Hijra* (or *Hegira*). The details and timetable of the Hijra are difficult to reconstruct, but it does not appear that the early Muslims suddenly fled Mecca for their lives. It is known that in 620, people from Medina became Muslims, came to Mecca, and asked Mohammed to arbitrate in their tribal disputes, so the Meccan Muslims knew that Medina would be a safe haven. The Hijra is the central date in Islam and the starting point for the Muslim calendar. Muslims use the term "AH" to denote their years, referring to the time after the Hijra. For example, Mohammed died in 632 CE, which is 10 AH. Because the Muslim year is lunar, consisting of 12 months of 29 or 30 days, without a leap month, the Muslim year is 354 days. For this reason, we cannot simply subtract 622 from the Christian year to get the corresponding Muslim year. Most of 2008, for example, was Muslim year 1429 AH, though 2008 minus 622 would suggest a Muslim year of 1386. Muslim holidays, though fixed in their calendar, rotate among the months of the Christian calendar with passing years.

Mohammed and the first Muslims were forced to defend themselves against their Meccan adversaries (the *Koran* prohibits initiating a conflict, but permits self-defense). The last of several key battles with the Meccans was the Battle of the Ditch (or Trench) in 5 AH (627 CE). As soon as the immediate danger had passed, Mohammed adopted a nonviolent philosophy. For example, during a time of pilgrimage in 6 AH, he and his followers entered Mecca entirely unarmed, having confidence that the prohibition against violence during this time would not be violated. Mecca surrendered peacefully to the Muslims in 7 AH (629 CE).

"Islam" means submission and peace (the words "Islam" and "Muslim" have the same root). Westerners often use the words "Muslim" and "Arab" synonymously, but this is a mistake. The first Muslims were Arabs, to be sure, but today, there are approximately 1.2 billion Muslims in the world, and only about 25 million people in Saudi Arabia. Even if we broaden the definition of "Arab" to anyone speaking a form of Arabic, thus allowing inclusion of those in North Africa and many in the Middle East, it would still be true that only about 20 percent of Muslims are Arab. As Islam spread, many nations, such as Iraq, Egypt, and those in North Africa, adopted Arabic as their language, but many Muslim nations, such as Iran, Afghanistan, Indonesia, Pakistan, and Turkey do not speak Arabic (though most scholars in those countries can speak and read Arabic, just as many Jewish scholars of any nation speak and read Hebrew). There are fifty-seven nations whose primary religion is Islam. Of these, twenty-two can reasonably be classed as Arabic in their language, culture, or history. The remaining thirty-five are not Arab nations by any reasonable criterion.

Many Westerners do not understand the nature of the *Koran.* Muslims view it as having been created by God; Mohammed was merely the instrument of transmission through which the *Koran* came to humanity. Whereas traditional Jews believe that only the Torah, the first five books of their Bible, is the direct word of God and truly divine, Muslims believe that the entirety of the Koran comes directly from God. This is why the *Koran* is said to be uncreated — meaning uncreated by man. Mohammed was the prophet who received the revelation.

Most Westerners also harbor a serious misunderstanding about Mohammed. In Christianity, Jesus is considered divine, the Son of God. But Muslims do not have this view of Mohammed. In Islam, Mohammed is not considered a messiah. It is not Mohammed, but the Koran that is divine. Roughly speaking, it is the Koran, not Mohammed, that is the "counterpart" to Jesus in Islam. Mohammed is a prophet, just like those of the Tanakh/Old Testament, and is completely human. This is why Muslims must not be called Mohammedans.

Another misconception among Westerners is the failure to understand how deeply Islam respects Judaism and Christianity. Muslims revere Judaism and Christianity as wonderful religions, complete in their own right for those who follow them, but brought to completion for Muslims by Islam, just as Christians revere Judaism and the Tanakh as excellent and complete for Jews, but brought to completion for Christians by the New Testament.

Especially in today's political climate, many Westerners think that Islam is a completely different religion, with no connection to their own beliefs. After the attacks of 9–11, one prominent American evangelist even went so far as to say that the Muslim and Christian gods were different. In fact, acceptance of and respect for Judaism and Christianity is an integral part of Islam (Islam and Bahá'í, more than other religions, specifically acknowledge their debt to preceding religions). The Koran says there are four "people of the book" (meaning that they have a common heritage from the Old Testament) — Muslims, Jews, Christians, and Sabians (about whom little is known). Indeed, the word "infidel" refers only to those who do not believe in a single god, and was never applied to Jews or Christians.

Jesus is also a revered prophet in Islam. Whereas Christians have no doubt that Jesus was greater than all those who came before him, Muslims do not consider Mohammed greater than the prophets who preceded him, nor is he considered greater than Jesus. Though Muslims often refer to Mohammed as "The Prophet," he is simply regarded as the final prophet, bringing the last, triumphant, uncorrupted form of God's word. He is not greater than the prophets who came before him any more than the author of the last chapter of a book is greater than those who wrote the first chapters. Islam has always had more respect for Jesus than Christianity has for Mohammed. For example, in the *Divine Comedy,* one of the great works of Christian literature, Dante placed Mohammed in hell, as a corruptor of Christianity. In contrast, no great work of Islamic literature has treated Jesus in this manner, and I am not aware of a single Muslim, including the very few who are terrorists, who ever made a disparaging remark about Jesus.

Along with Judaism and Christianity, Islam has become a vital Western religion, and the debt of the West to the Muslim preservation and extension of Greek knowledge is incalculable. When we speak of the Judeo-Christian legacy, we should be speaking of the Judeo-Christian-Islamic legacy. Perhaps the best way to refer to what are sometimes called "the three Old Testament religions" is "the Abrahamic religions," because all are directly or indirectly based on the figure of Abraham, the patriarch of Judaism, which is the "parent" of Christianity. The same man (Ibrahim in Islam) was the father of Ishmael, believed to be the common ancestor of the Arab people. Ibrahim and Ishmael are said to have built the *Ka'ba,* the house of God in Mecca.

Islam readily accepts those worthy individuals who lived before the Prophet as full and complete members of their religion. The status and fate of worthy pagans who lived before Jesus has always been a problem in Christian thinking. Christians recognize and respect the righteous conduct of these people, but by definition, one cannot be a Christian if he or she lived before Jesus. In Islam, however, all righteous people of the past, including the Jewish and Christian prophets, and Jesus, are immediately accepted as good Muslims, even if they lived before the religion's founder. Muslims respect Jews and Christians and believe that their prophets laid the groundwork for Islam. These prophets delivered important messages, but, through no fault of the prophets who brought them, these messages were incomplete, imperfectly transmitted, and had to be completed by the final Prophet for his people. The Koran confirms the Torah and the Gospels, but Muslims believe that the previous revelations of Judaism and Christianity were imperfectly recorded and transmitted. For example, Muslims revere Jesus as a great prophet, and believe he was born of a virgin, but they believe that his divinity and the doctrine of the Trinity compromise strict monotheism. Likewise, the Koran indicates that God rescued Jesus from the crucifixion at the last moment. To correct the misunderstandings that generations of imperfect transmission had caused, Muslims believe that God revealed the entirety of his message in the Koran, thus erasing any possibility of confusion. Islam is the culmination of the Judeo-Christian tradition. The Koran is an extension and correction, not a repeal, of these revered earlier scriptures.

There are 114 chapters (surahs), of very unequal length, in the Koran. Each begins with "In the Name of God, Most Gracious, Most Merciful," a phrase common in the Muslim world. Though there is repetition, with the greatness of God reaffirmed throughout, there is also an overall structure and direction in the Koran. The surahs are not organized chronologically, in the order of their revelation, as we might expect. The earlier Surahs are thought to represent later revelations, after the Hijra, when the new religion was well established and the Muslim community (called the "Ummah") was secure in Medina. These early surahs are sometimes called the Medinan portion. The later surahs, for the most part, are thought to represent the initial revelations, shared by the Prophet with the then-small number of followers in Mecca before the Hijra. These later surahs are sometimes called the "Meccan Surahs." Because the longer, chronologically later Medinan surahs concern the philosophical and political questions in the daily lives of Muslims, they go well at the beginning of the work.

Surah 1 contains only seven verses, which are so central to Islam that they are called the seven oft-repeated verses. They are an affirmation of faith and of the greatness of God. Surah 2, the longest in the Koran, contains a broad outline of Islam, including its basic tenets and beliefs, and the basic obligations of its practitioners. More than any other single chapter, surah 2 is a "summary" of Islam. Everyone should at least read these first two surahs.

The first seven surahs, comprising about a third of the Koran, discuss the early history of humanity, the formation of the Muslim community, and the place of the new religion as a completion of Judaism and Christianity. These surahs affirm these earlier religions as valid, but in need of completion, and indicate that some (not all) Jews and Christians have become corrupt.

Surahs eight and nine describe the defense of the Ummah against external hostility, while later surahs, written when the Ummah was more secure, describe the obligations and laws that the new community should observe, while always reaffirming the greatness and glory of God. Still later surahs describe particular issues, such as the treatment of women. The Koran ends with a series of short surahs, the Meccan surahs, which describe spiritual life in mystical, lyrical verse. They have been compared to the psalms of the Jewish and Christian Bibles.

Like other religious works, the Koran has been misunderstood because parts of it have been taken out of context. The so-called "sword verses" appear to give permission to fight nonbelievers, but when properly judged in their temporal context, they refer to the Meccans who were early opponents of Islam and sought to crush the new religion. The "sword verses" must also be judged in their literary context because they are immediately followed by an admonition to be merciful to opponents if they cease to be a threat.

Not all of the Koran was recorded at one time. As the people who remembered the recitation of portions of it developed conflicting recollections and died, different versions of the Koran became available. About twenty years after Mohammed's death, an effort was made to bring together the surviving people who had knowledge of the revelations and to record an accurate version. Probably by the 650s, and certainly by the 670s, a standardized Koran had been achieved. The Koran has been central not only in Islam, but also in Arabic literature and language, making Mohammed the only person in history to have had a decisive influence on religion, intellectual history, and military history.

The Koran is meant to be read aloud, preferably in its original classical Arabic. Many Muslims believe that only the Arabic version of the Koran is the true word of God, and that translations are only approximations. Some, however, feel that a good translation can capture the essence, if not the full glory, of the Koran.

There are six articles of faith in Islam. These are as follows:

> *1. Belief in one God, the creator of everything. Unlike other religions, including Christianity, there is very little speculation in Islam about the nature of God. Muslims think that God is inherently and absolutely unknowable and that such speculation is therefore pointless. They do not believe that God has a gender, although the Koran uses the masculine pronoun for him (interestingly, God is also referred to as "We" in many places in the Koran).*
>
> *2. Belief in angels (Muslims also believe in four archangels).*
>
> *3. Belief in scripture. While Muslims deeply respect the scriptures of Judaism and Christianity, the Koran is held to be the final, direct, personal revelation of God, and belief in the Koran is a key article of faith in Islam. Other important writings for Muslims include the Sunna (or Sunnah, the practices of Mohammed) and the Hadith (the sayings of the Prophet). The Sunna is considered second only to the Koran, but it is known that the Hadith was edited into the ninth century, so not all of it is directly from the Prophet, and Muslims differ on its authority.*
>
> *4. Belief in prophets. These are essentially the prophets of the Tanakh/Old Testament, with the inclusion of Jesus and Mohammed. Jesus is revered in Islam, but like Mohammed, is considered a prophet and a wonderful man, but not part of God.*
>
> *5. Belief in a Day of Judgment. The Koran makes it clear that only God knows when the final judgment will be. We occasionally*

hear a Christian or a small group of Christians claim to know when the final judgment will be, but no Muslim would allege such knowledge.

6. Belief that God has ordained human life, and takes an interest in the welfare of people.

Although not a specific article of faith, most traditional Muslims also believe in the devil. Notice how remarkably similar these articles are to Judeo-Christian thinking. Traditional Muslims also believe in Adam and Eve, but not in original sin or collective punishment for the sins of Adam and Eve. Unlike Christianity, Islam does not believe in the intrinsic unworthiness of people, but more in their perfectibility through internal struggle.

Like Judaism, Islam emphasizes orthopraxy (correct practice) rather that orthodoxy (correct beliefs), while Christianity emphasizes the latter. In addition to the six articles of faith, there are five pillars of practice in Islam. These are individually alluded to, both directly and indirectly, in the Koran, and have been assembled from consensus opinion and traditional practice over the years.

The first pillar of Islam is the profession "There is no God but Allah and Mohammed is his Prophet." This is called the *Shahada.* The sincere proclamation of the Shahada is sufficient by itself to make one a Muslim, even if the other pillars cannot be performed.

The second pillar is prayer, and is called *salat.* Muslims are to pray five times a day, but these are perhaps better understood as periods of worship. An official known as a *muezzin* issues the call to prayer — the *Adhan* — from a minaret adjacent to the mosque. The precise form of the Adhan varies according to the form of Islam (*Sunnah* and *Shia,* discussed subsequently), and from country to country within the Muslim world, but an approximate English translation is:

God is most great (repeated four times)
I testify that there is no god except God (repeated three times)
I testify that Mohammed is the Messenger of God (repeated three times)
Come to prayer (repeated two times)
Come to salvation (repeated two times)

Prayer is better than sleep (with the morning prayer)
Come to the best of work (added by Shiites)
God is most great" (repeated two times)
There is no god except God.

The name of God is written on the top portion of the minaret, so that when people look up in response to the Adhan, they will see God's name. When a Muslim hears the Adhan, he or she will repeat it, or a portion of it, in a soft voice. They may also respond, "There is no strength or power but in God," or "You have said what is true."

The five prayers are called *Fajr, Dhuhr* (or *Zhuhr), Asr, Maghrib,* and *Isha.* The prayers are slightly different from each other. They have a fixed text, but afterward, individuals may add their own text or make requests. The prayer times depend on the position of the sun in the sky and therefore vary among locations and different times of the year. Fajr takes place between dawn (defined by the presence of sufficient light to discern a black thread from a white thread) and sunrise. Dhuhr occurs after the peak of the sun, in the early afternoon. Asr is performed in the late afternoon and must precede sunset. Maghrib takes place after sunset, but while there is still twilight. Isha takes place after the last of twilight and before midnight. The times for these prayers likely originally arose to fit the rhythm of the workday. Several techniques are used to determine these times, but the times at which each prayer can be begun are published for each locality, so Muslims rarely determine their own prayer times.

Most Muslims perform each prayer at the beginning of the appropriate period, but each prayer can be performed anytime between the beginning of its time period and the time for the next prayer. When praying, Muslims face Mecca (the first Muslims faced Jerusalem, but when Jews refused to convert, Mohammed's new revelation was to face Mecca). Prayers need not be performed in a mosque; they can be performed in any location, provided that the practitioner does his or her best to face Mecca. The exception to this is that the Dhuhr on Friday is replaced by a special service called the *Jumu'ah,* which contains a short sermon. Muslim men must make a reasonable effort to go to a mosque and participate in the Jumu'ah. Muslim women are welcome to participate, but are not required to. If participation in the Jumu'ah is not possible, a regular Dhuhr is performed.

Shoes are removed before entering a mosque, and there is a place for washing prior to praying. In every mosque, there is an empty alcove called the *mihrab,* which points to Mecca. The mihrab conveys the impression of a doorway to Mecca, and by facing it, the Muslim faces Mecca.

The third pillar is *zakat,* or tithing, a 2.5 percent assessment of one's total assets to be given to charity. At one time, the government collected zakat, but it is now generally left to individuals. The zakat is paid during the month of *Ramadan.*

The fourth pillar is observance of Ramadan. The holiest month in the Muslim calendar, Ramadan commemorates the month in which the Prophet received the first revelations. It is also a time when Muslims remind themselves of what it is like to be poor and hungry (hence the payment of the zakat during Ramadan). During this month, Muslims fast from sunrise to sunset (the fast is called the *Sawm),* but travelers, heavy laborers, the sick, pregnant women, and children under ten are exempted. Muslims may eat a pre-dawn meal called a *suhur.* Fasting begins at dawn. The *iftar* is the meal that breaks the fast at sunset. Depending on the cultural tradition, the iftar may be a small meal, to be followed by a larger meal later, or the fast may be broken with a large meal.

During Ramadan, the 114 chapters of the Koran are divided into segments, one of which is read every night, so that the entire Koran is read during the month. The "Night of Power," considered to be the time of the first revelation, occurred during an odd-numbered night on one of the final ten days of the month (i.e., the 21st, 23rd, 25th, 27th, or 29th), and is the first of two special nights in Islam. Some Muslims celebrate a particular night during this ten-day period (most commonly, the 27th), perhaps praying throughout the night, while others will hold the entire period in special significance. Ramadan ends with a festival, *Id al-Fitr* (or *Eid-al-Fitr).* Celebrations and gifts follow.

The fifth pillar is the pilgrimage, *Hadj* (or *Hajj).* The Hadj should be made at a common time to reinforce the sense of commonality and community. An important part of the Hadj is to circumambulate the Ka'ba (or *Kaaba),* a small building in Mecca that is regarded in traditional Islam as the house of God. Indeed, when Muslims face Mecca to pray, they are actually facing the Ka'ba, which is considered the oldest building on Earth, built by Ibrahim (Abraham) and his son Ishmael, the patriarchs of the Muslims. Used as a pagan shrine in the time before Mohammed, the

Ka'ba retained its holy status in Islam. This continuation may have been a compromise. Since pilgrimages to the Ka'ba in pagan times generated great revenues for the region, it is probable that some of the opposition to Mohammed stemmed from fear that the new religion would impede these benefits. Islam could more easily be accepted if pilgrimages to the Ka'ba, with their economic advantages, continued.

The Ka'ba has been periodically renovated, most recently in 1996, and is covered by a black cloth called the *Kiswa,* which is changed after every Hadj. Within the Ka'ba is the Black Stone (*Al-Hajarul Aswad* in Arabic), which is about twenty inches (fifty cm) in diameter, now fragmented and held together by a silver band. The current Black Stone is believed to be a remnant of the original Black Stone, said to come from Heaven, and is symbolic of God's covenant with humanity.

In another portion of the Hadj, pilgrims walk between two hills to commemorate Hagar's search for her son Ishmael. They cast pebbles at a stone pillar to symbolize Ibrahim's rejection of Satan. They gather on the plain of Arafat, where Mohammed delivered his final message. Those who have completed the Hadj can refer to themselves as *Al-Hadji* (masculine) or *Al-Hadja* (feminine).

Jihad (struggle) is sometimes thought of as a sixth pillar. It is defined as the struggle to fulfill God's will. Although Westerners think of a Jihad solely as a holy war, usually directed against the West, most Jihads are internal struggles, wherein the Muslim simply attempts to make himself better.

Except for the Shahada, Muslims can be exempted from any of the five pillars if they are unable or if such performance would be inappropriate. For example, one should not pray if he or she is not first of a pure mind. Women who are menstruating should not pray. Ill or indigent Muslims are exempt from the Hadj. The fast of Ramadan can be broken for medical reasons. Islam allows each individual to determine whether the circumstances are appropriate or not.

The second special night in Islam is the *Mi'raj* (or *Miraj,* the Night Journey), during which some Muslims believe that Mohammed briefly ascended to heaven (others believe the journey was a dream). The site of this ascension, the contemporary Dome of the Rock in Jerusalem, made Jerusalem the third holiest city in Islam, after Mecca and Medina, and helped establish a connection with Judaism and Christianity. After the

Ka'ba, the Dome of the Rock and the tomb of Mohammed in Medina are Islam's most sacred sites.

A mosque (often called by its Arabic name, *masjid*) is often a place of social gathering as well as worship. In addition, Muslims have *madrasas,* religious schools that usually also have secular curricula.

Blue Mosque

The Blue Mosque in Istanbul (also called the Sultan Ahmed Mosque), built between 1609 and 1616, is one of many beautiful mosques and testament to Islam's enduring achievements in architecture. Like many mosques, it houses a school (madrasah).

Like Christianity, Islam held to a compelling egalitarianism. Rich or poor, male or female, slave or free, all who believed had an equal opportunity for a lifetime with God's love and an afterlife of Paradise. A commitment to egalitarianism and social justice was one of the most revolutionary aspects of the Koran, virtually tantamount to monotheism in the degree of its progressive nature. Upon returning from battle, Mohammed turned his attention to social reform and is said to have uttered, "We have returned from the lesser Jihad; now for the greater Jihad."

In assessing the treatment of women by Islam, many Westerners not only fail to compare it to the treatment of women by Christianity and Judaism, but also fail to take into account that even though Islam was born in a patriarchal culture, it still afforded women huge gains over what preceded it in Arabia and compared to feudal Europe.

While the Koran permitted polygamy, it limited the practice to four wives, and required that all be treated fairly, unprecedented for that time and place. Prior to the Prophet, there was no limit on the number of wives a man could have, nor was there any requirement that he be able to take proper care of them. Contemporary Muslim countries usually require a man to have court permission for a second wife. The Koran also restrained what had been the male prerogative to divorce on whim, requiring a man to pronounce his intent to divorce once a month for three months. While this is hardly egalitarian by today's standards, it made divorce less capricious by introducing what we would call a waiting period or a cooling-off period. The Koran gave women access to divorce through the courts, equally unprecedented for that time and place. It also greatly improved women's right to inherit. Previously, land simply passed to the nearest male relative. After the Koran, women were guaranteed a percentage of an inheritance. Importantly, the Koran addresses women as well as men, something unheard of prior to Mohammed, and indicates that men and women will be judged equally. Although one can reasonably argue that traditional Islam has not kept pace with the progress of history, this is likely true of any religion, and those who regard Islam as misogynistic might do well to examine their own religion's progress.

Westerners are familiar with the concept of the veil, but they may not realize that the Koran does not specifically require that a woman's head or face be covered. Muslim women did not adopt the veil until several generations after the Prophet's death, at which time it was assumed voluntarily, and primarily by higher-class women to distinguish themselves from those of lower social standing. Very conservative countries like Saudi Arabia are exceptions, but in most Muslim communities, wearing the veil is voluntary. In fact, one of the major passages discussing the covering of women's heads is preceded by a similarly worded passage making a very similar recommendation for men. Islam asks both sexes to dress modestly, and the precise details are more a reflection of cultural mores and individual preference than an intrinsic command. Another passage alluding to women's dress suggests that this is intended largely for women's benefit: "that they be known, but that they not be molested." Some women dress conservatively simply to spend less time and money on cosmetics, or to deflect the attention of men. Still others view their attire as a resistance to Western domination. While some Muslim feminists believe that the veil entails subtle discrimination, those women who voluntarily wear it maintain that it helps them be true to the ideas of Islam without any personal diminution.

In the generations after Mohammed, the status of women fell below what the Prophet had envisioned. Mohammed probably qualified as a feminist by the standards of his day, but those who have retreated from his egalitarianism, rather than broadening it, now appear to be misogynists. I believe that the treatment of women by contemporary Islamic fundamentalists shows how important it is to keep alive the spirit of an innovative idea, and expand it as times change and society advances. It is a lesson of history that the most progressive thinking, such as the treatment of women in the Koran, will regress with the passage of time and the progress of society, unless it is kept fresh by constant rejuvenation and extension. Innovators give us building blocks, but we err if we perceive them as permanent buildings, and we err again if we judge great people or great ideas from the past by contemporary standards.

Throughout its history, Islam has had only minimal numbers of guiding patriarchs similar to Catholic and Orthodox fathers, and it has no significant clergy. Rarely, a Muslim might recognize a Catholic saint, but in general, human intermediaries are discouraged, and Muslims certainly would not name a saint. The religion is based on the individual practitioner's relationship to God. An *imam,* a local person who leads the prayer service, can be any adult male from the community who understands Islam, but in recent times, many mosques have their own full-time imams, who are roughly analogous to the Jewish rabbi, the Catholic priest, or the Protestant minister. *Sheikh* is a word that initially referred to the leader of a village or tribe, but is now used in a general sense to denote a person who is distinguished or respected. Imams and sheikhs have respect at a local level, but neither is analogous to a higher Christian Church official such as a bishop. Imams and sheikhs may explain and clarify the Koran for someone else, but they may not mandate a specific interpretation. In Islam, the individual believer is the final interpreter for her- or himself because the Koran is the direct word of God made directly available to each individual. Neither an imam nor a sheikh can confer forgiveness of sins, as a priest does during confession. Only God can forgive sins, and only God can guide the individual to a correct understanding and course of action. A hallmark of Islam has always been a personal and direct relationship between God and the individual. Islam has had from its beginning a philosophy similar to Protestant Christianity in this regard.

After Mohammed's death, most Muslims thought that his spiritual authority could not be replaced and that no attempt should be made to do so, but that an institution of political authority was needed. They also thought that this authority should be vested in the Muslim community as a whole, not with descendants of Mohammed. They therefore began the institution of the *caliphate,* wherein an individual was chosen from the general Muslim community to be its political leader. The first caliph was Abu Bakr, a confidant of Mohammed who solidified control of Arabia.

About 85 percent of Muslims are *Sunnis,* or *Sunnites.* The other major subdivision in Islam is *Shiite* (also written Shi'ite). All Muslims, including Shiites, follow the *Sunna,* which discusses the practices of Mohammed, so despite the name "Sunni" for the majority, the importance of the Sunna is not a distinguishing feature between Sunnis and Shiites. Shiite Muslims differ from Sunnis in two major ways. First, they believe that succession of leadership should stay in the family of the Prophet. This is why they supported Ali, Mohammed's cousin and son-in-law, for caliph after the Prophet's death (the term "Shiite" is derived from *Shiat Ali,* meaning the Party of Ali). Because Abu Bakr was chosen as the first caliph instead of Ali, Shiites did not recognize the caliphate. Second, in contrast to the Sunnis, Shiites felt that anyone who succeeded Mohammed must be a religious as well as a political leader. Shiites studied Islamic history and literature, and the life of the Prophet, and concluded that the Sunnite interpretation was flawed, in large part because it did not take into account the proper succession.

Ali finally did become the fourth caliph, but this did not quiet the Sunni-Shiite dispute, and not all Muslims accepted him. After Ali's death in 661 (probably by assassination), the Shiites rebelled against the newly founded Sunni Umayyad Dynasty. Ali's son, Husayn (also Hussein or Hossein), was killed by Yazid, a Sunni caliph, and is remembered as a martyr. The annual festival of *Ashura* commemorates him. After this, Shiism was largely an underground movement, but it resurfaced in the eleventh century.

In contrast to Sunnis, early Shiites believed that every generation has an individual who is to serve as both the political and spiritual leader of the Islamic community. This individual, a descendant of Ali, was called an Imam (all Muslims use this term to denote a leader of prayers or a respected scholar, but the term has a special meaning to Shiites). In the eighth through the tenth centuries, Shiism fractured into several groups that differed over the succession of the imamate. The two major branches were the Twelvers and the Seveners — names that derive from the number of Imams who are recognized. Today, almost all of Shiites are Twelvers. They accept the legitimacy of the first eleven Imams of Shiism, and further believe that the eleventh had a son, usually called Mohammad al-Mahdi, who is regarded as a hidden Imam and who will return to Earth someday. In the meantime, there is no earthly Imam, but Mohammad al-Mahdi communicates to people via intermediary figures called *babs* (bab is Persian for "gate" or "door"). In his absence, these Shiites believe that a handful of people on Earth can substitute for the Imam. They are called ayatollahs, scholars who are accorded special respect by popular consent. Ayatollahs are accorded greater status than the Sunni Muslims give their scholars, but they are by no means considered divine or infallible. Individual Shiites have the right to accept or reject the advice of an ayatollah or to seek the counsel of another ayatollah. To Westerners, the most famous ayatollah of recent times was the Ayatollah Khomeini, who ruled Iran during the hostage crisis of the late 1970s.

The Seveners, also called *Ismailis* (or *Isma'ils)*, split with the Twelvers after the death of the sixth Imam. They believe that Isma'il, oldest son of the sixth Imam, should have become the seventh Imam, and unlike Twelvers, Seveners accept no Imam after the sixth. Like the Twelvers, they believe that their last Imam, Isma'il, will return to Earth someday. Like all Shiites, Seveners respect ayatollahs, but unlike Twelvers, do not recognize them as substitutes for their Imam. There is an even smaller group of Shiites called the Fivers (or *Zaydis)*, found mostly in northern Yemen, who accept only the first four Shiite Imams. Their fifth Imam, Zayd, will someday return to Earth. Today, the Seveners and Fivers are largely of historical interest.

The Koran does not specifically address a savior or messiah figure, and the concept of such a person (called a *Mahdi)* is peripheral to Sunni Islam, but is more central in Shia Islam because of its belief in a hidden Imam. As we will see, the belief in the coming of a hidden Imam played an important role in the rise of Bahá'í.

Shiite Islam is more mystical than Sunni Islam, assigns higher status to Sufism (Islamic mysticism), and more directly addresses the injustices of the world. Though Shiism is largely found in Iran and Iraq today, there are interesting regional differences within countries. For example, until the fall of Saddam Hussein, the ruling power in Iraq was Sunni, and the majority of Saudis who work in the oil industry are Shiites. Hezbollah, the resistance (some would say terrorist) movement based in Lebanon, is a Shiite group.

The first several caliphs saw a huge expansion in the Islamic Empire. After conquest, a subject people were permitted to convert to Islam or to retain their existing cultural and religious identity in exchange for a tax. Either choice would permit protection from other potential conquerors. Because Muslim rule was often more lenient than Byzantine or Persian rule, voluntary conversion was common. One of the several terrible misconceptions about Islam in the West is that it forcibly converted those it conquered. Indeed, there is even an unfortunate catch phrase that appeared in some Western history books: "Islam spread by the sword." This is patently false. Acceptance of the social preeminence of Islam was expected, and a tax was levied on non-Muslims, but Islam has always been tolerant of other religions, and Muslims never forced others to convert. Indeed, the point of these early conquests seems to be territory and a tax base rather than converts. It would have been economically foolish for Muslims to force conversion of Jews and Christians, because then they could not have collected a higher tax. Though Zoroastrianism is not specifically mentioned in the Koran, it too was well tolerated by the expanding Muslim Empire. Indeed, as long as three centuries after the conquest of the Persian Empire, half of its residents continued to practice Zoroastrianism without difficulty.

The Umayyad family ruled from Damascus until about 750. Many of the administrators of the Umayyad Muslims were Byzantines, to whom the Muslims turned for their administrative experience. The Abbasids seized power from the Umayyads, with Shiite assistance, and moved the capital from Damascus to Baghdad (they founded the latter city in 762). The Abbasid success shifted power in the Muslim world toward Iran and Iraq. The caliph began to acquire significant religious authority. The Abbasids also employed non-Muslim administrators, particularly Persians, who had not yet converted to Islam. Many voluntarily converted so that they would have the protection of the caliph, for greater success in business, or to enjoy the lower taxes and greater privileges that Muslims enjoyed (for example, non-Muslims were forbidden to learn how to ride a horse or to carry arms).

The Abbasids allied with the Shiites when overthrowing the Umayyads, but did not remain loyal to them after they attained power, and ruled as Sunnis. The Abbasid Dynasty lasted five hundred years before falling to the Mongols in 1258, but began to fragment in the ninth century, resulting in semiautonomous states within the Islamic world. One of these was the Shiite Fatimid Dynasty, which arose in Tunisia in 910, spread eastward, eventually settled in Egypt in 969 (establishing the city of Cairo), and threatened the Abbasids. In addition to the Fatimids, there were other semiautonomous dynasties in different parts of the Muslim world that diluted Abbasid authority. For example, Morocco had a series of independent dynasties, one of which established the contemporary Moroccan city of Fez. Another such dynasty, established in tenth-century Spain by a member of the Umayyad family, was centered in Cordoba (the weakening of this dynasty in the eleventh century was a factor in the eventual Christian victory in Spain). In 1171, Saladin replaced the Fatimids in Egypt, in the process replacing Shiite rule with Sunni rule, and founded a dynasty that lasted until the mid-thirteenth century. Though Saladin's victory temporarily bolstered the Abbasid Dynasty, continued diminution of central authority weakened the caliph, resulting in the eventual demise of the position.

In the tenth and eleventh centuries, Turks migrated into Muslim lands and converted to Islam. The largest group of these was the Seljuks (or Saljuqs), who migrated into western Asia in the ninth century and accepted Sunni Islam. They were established in Baghdad by 1055. The Seljuks established a tolerant empire in which scholars like mathematician and poet Omar Khayyam (c. 1048–1123) and Rumi (1207–1273), a great poet, theologian, and philosopher, flourished. The height of the Seljuk Empire was in the thirteenth century. In the eleventh through the fifteenth centuries, Persian and Turkish became important languages for secular events in the Muslim world. There were roughly three important regions during this time: Iran and Iraq, Egypt-Syria-Arabia, and North Africa. As political differences became evident in these regions, Islam was no longer sufficient to completely unify the Muslim world.

Islam settled over the northern part of India, but was never firmly seated in the south. When Islam came to India, Islamic raiders destroyed the Buddhist monasteries in the northern part of the country in the eleventh and twelfth centuries, severely compromising the continuation of Buddhism in India. When Islam abutted Hinduism, important differences between the two religions became apparent. First, Islam had a strict prohibition against depicting God, and nearly as strict a prohibition against depicting the human figure, whereas human figures were common in Hinduism, and even God could be represented in numerous ways. Second, Islam was more transcultural than Hinduism, which tended to reflect only Indian culture. Third, though Islam is much more tolerant than most people think, it does have a stronger conception of heretics than Hinduism does, and has much more of a sense that it is a final revelation to humanity. Islam essentially believes — as does Christianity — that it has the absolute truth, directly from God, while the belief that humanity does not and cannot know the definitive story is an integral part of Hinduism. Even the most ardent followers of Hinduism have considerable uncertainty about the nature of the universe and what will happen in the future. Fourth, Hinduism, based on the caste system of general Indian society, is much more hierarchical than Islam.

Within four decades of the death of the Prophet, Islam, under the Umayyads, had spread over an enormous geographic area. This put the early Muslims in physical proximity with different cultures at precisely the time that the first disciples of the Prophet, who could transmit his direct words, were beginning to die. Also at this time, disagreement arose within the Muslim community concerning exactly how the Koran translated into a code of conduct. Muslims believe the Koran has answers to all ethical questions, but they believe that some of these answers are implicit and not explicit, and not all Muslims came to the same conclusions regarding the Koran's instruction in ethical matters. These events engendered a desire for a standard code of behavior, called the *Shari'a* (also written Sharia or Shari'ah).

To assist in the creation of the Shari'a, it was decided that the Sunna would also be a legitimate and compelling guide, second only to the Koran. Whereas the Koran is the word of God as recited by the Prophet, the Sunna discusses the practices of the Prophet. The difficulty was to decide the precise composition of the Sunna. Those who had personally observed the Prophet were gone, so there had to be a group of scholars to determine a standard form of the *Sunna*, just as there had earlier been agreement on a standard form of the Koran. This was the origin of the *Ulama* (or *Ulema*), scholars appointed by the Muslim community to define proper conduct. "Ulama" means "seekers of knowledge" and refers to those individuals who have the best knowledge of the Koran and the Sunna. It was to these people that the Muslim community entrusted the formulation of the Shari'a. The Ulama are not specifically alluded to in the Koran, but have been established and maintained by tradition, beginning with a need for a standard Shari'a. Some of the finest buildings in the Muslim world were built for the deliberations of the Ulama.

The first task of the Ulama in the formulation of the Shari'a was to determine the legitimacy of the Sunna. To do this, they relied upon the Hadith, the sayings of the Prophet, as recalled by his few surviving followers. Biography and history were also studied, including the recorded history of the Prophet (called the *Sira*). Though the scholarship behind the formation of the Shari'a is theoretically ongoing, it had been reasonably well codified by about the twelfth century, at least in the minds of Sunnites. Shiites accept some of the conclusions of the Ulama, but for them, the hidden Imam, or an ayatollah, fulfills much of the Ulama's function.

Shari'a is often translated in the West as Islamic Law, but it is more properly thought of as God's law, and refers to what Muslims must and must not do in order to live according to God's will. The two categories of Shari'a are conduct with regard to God and conduct with regard to other people. Shari'a covers some desirable attributes that are not matters of law, such as manners and courtesy. At the same time, it omits many aspects that must be included in legal codes. After all, the Koran and the Sunna could not have foreseen every aspect of contemporary life. For example, in the time of the Prophet, homicide was a matter between the families involved and did not concern the state or the community. So Shari'a is not completely synonymous with Islamic law. Today, there is debate in the Muslim community over the role of Shari'a in secular law and daily life. Another question that all Muslims face is that of the relative roles of the individual Shari'a versus that of a communal Shari'a, since Islam has always been based on the individual interpretation of the Koran.

Fiqh is the Islamic system of jurisprudence (Islamic law) as developed by the Ulama, and can be thought of as the legal codification of those aspects of the Shari'a that are required in a legal code (i.e., those aspects of God's law that must also be in man's law), with the addition of necessary legal aspects that are not covered in the Shari'a. As an example, discourteous behavior is a violation of Shari'a, because it violates how God would have us behave, but it is not a violation of Fiqh because it is not criminal conduct. Counterfeiting is a violation of Fiqh because it is a criminal activity, but it is not specifically addressed in the Shari'a. Another way to look at Fiqh is that it is the human understanding and implementation of Shari'a.

Fiqh was developed in the seventh to the tenth century by the Ulama, not by elected officials or courts. The origin of Islamic law was not only an attempt to integrate the will of God into daily life, but also an attempt to limit the power of rulers. Because there is little separation of church and state, Fiqh is a fusion of religious and legal law. This seems odd to contemporary Westerners because they forget that the integration of religious and civil law was an integral part of Judaism and Christianity throughout most of their histories. Until the Enlightenment, religious and secular laws were inextricably linked in Western culture as well. After all, prior to the Enlightenment, why would anyone have wanted to separate human law from divine law? Islamic civilization has always been much more humanistic and scholarly than Westerners believe, but did not experience the distinct Renaissance and Enlightenment that were important in the separation of religious and secular power in the West. As is the case for many other aspects of Islam, or for any religion that might be foreign to us, we must evaluate its beliefs and evolution in their historical context. The Koran and Islamic law simply mirror the standard practices of the time and place of their creation.

The two most important sources of Fiqh are the Koran and the Sunna, but there are two other foundations. The third source for Fiqh is *ijtihad,* which is independent judgment by scholars, based on reasoning by analogy from information in the Koran and Sunna (this form of reasoning is called *Qiyaas*). The fourth source is *ijma,* consensus opinion. National and cultural mores also contribute. Although the Hadith is a guide to individual Muslims in daily life, it is not an integral part of the formulation of Fiqh because of the disagreement on which parts derive directly from the Prophet and which have been added later or edited. Shiite Muslims accept Fiqh, but also include the traditions of Ali.

Four slightly separate forms of Fiqh came into existence in the eighth and ninth centuries in Sunni Islam. These were based upon the name of its founder and are called the *Malikite, Hanifite, Shafi'ite,* and *Hanbalite* Schools. Each became predominant in a particular region. For example, the slightly more conservative Hanbalite School came to predominate in Saudi Arabia. *Faqih* is a general term referring to someone who has legal training. A *mufti* is an individual who furnishes an informed legal opinion, called a *fatwa* (also *fetwa)* for the benefit of individuals, courts, and judges (these judges are called *Qadis,* also *Cadis)*. Fiqh is not as monolithic as Westerners might believe; occasional exceptions to law are permitted.

Today, members of the Ulama are university educated and specifically trained for their position as religious scholars. A member of the Ulama is associated with most mosques. The influence of the Ulama has been great, but their actual power varies. Members of the Ulama may shape community standards, or they may be part of a collective that publishes treatises to shape general Islamic opinion. However, neither individual Muslims nor the larger Muslim community are obliged to follow the advice of Ulama members. In theory, members of the Ulama are to elucidate or interpret Fiqh, which is then put into play by political rulers. In practice, government officials often institute their own brand of Fiqh without consulting scholars, or after consulting only that subset of scholars with whom they agree. Modernity has brought the Ulama into conflict not only with Muslim political leaders, many of whom are Western educated, but also with an increasingly educated Islamic lay society.

Beginning in the late eleventh century, Islam came under pressure from the Crusades, its first experience of being on the receiving end of conquest. Few Westerners realize how much more brutal the Crusaders were than Muslims had ever been. Both Muslims and Jews, who had been living peacefully together in Jerusalem, were massacred in the First Crusade. Crusaders also destroyed numerous Muslim holy sites. In contrast, when Saladin recaptured Jerusalem in 1187, civilians were not harmed, and Christian holy sites were not desecrated.

There were eight canonical Crusades (initiated by the Catholic Church), but from the late eleventh century on, a continuous stream of Europeans traveled to the Middle East, bent on the destruction of Islam. In general, the Crusades were ineffective from a military viewpoint. The only permanent territory the Crusades established was in Spain, where successful expeditions in the twelfth and thirteenth centuries ultimately resulted in the expulsion of the Muslims. The major effect of the Crusades in the West was the establishment of new trade routes and the importation of some aspects of Islamic artistic expression.

Beginning in the eighth century, Islamic scholars translated the works of classical Greece into Arabic. As it had in the West, this led to dissent within the Islamic community as to whether these works should be accepted or not, and what their place was with regard to the Prophet's revelation. The newer thinking was accepted more quickly than in the West, and Islamic scholars became the custodians and extenders of Greek knowledge. They incorporated the Socratic method and dialectic reasoning into their teachings. *Kalam* is a term used to indicate independent secular thought and is essentially a secular counterpart to ijtihad.

Images of God are forbidden without exception in Islam because it is thought that these might lead to the independent worship of these images, thus compromising the religion's passionate monotheism. Because Christian art so readily depicts Jesus, many Christians do not realize that Islam also forbids any representation of the Prophet, not because he is considered divine, but out of respect for the Messenger of God. Islam generally prohibits the creation of images of people or animals as well, because it is thought that any attempt at lifelike representation infringes on God's unique creative power, but this prohibition may be relaxed somewhat in secular settings, especially in non-Arab Muslim nations such as Iran, Turkey, and Muslim areas of India. Where this restriction is relaxed, people and animals are often expressed in the form of miniature paintings, often as illuminations in books. Large paintings, so common in the West, are rare in the Muslim world.

The relative prohibition against images of living creatures, in conjunction with the naturally decorative nature of Arabic script, and especially in conjunction with the fact that the Koran was revealed in this ornate script, led to the use of calligraphy as a primary form of artistic expression. Many Westerners believe that calligraphy is simply beautiful writing, but the nature of Arabic writing makes calligraphy a true art form. The Arabic script has much more flexibility than Western scripts and can be written in many ways. Individual letters can change shape depending on their location within a word. Calligraphy is therefore not simply beautiful writing, it is art, and is additionally valued because God revealed himself through words. Even where the prohibition against portrayal of living creatures is strictly observed, Islamic art demonstrates how beautiful art can be without depiction of life. Color, design, detail, and calligraphy uniquely combine to render rich and moving works.

Calligraphy

Because Islam generally forbids the depiction of people or animals and absolutely forbids any depiction of the Prophet, artistic expression has taken a different path in the Muslim World. Calligraphy, geometric designs, and architecture have been principal means of creative expression in the Muslim World. This script is an example of meticulous and creative calligraphy. It depicts a portion of Surah 2 of the Koran.

Also important in Islamic art is the use of repeating geometrical patterns. These may be simple shapes, such as squares, or they may be more elaborate, curvilinear designs called arabesque. The result is an art form that represents the order of nature, is mathematically precise, yet pleasing, and appears to continue beyond the immediately visible object into infinity. Arabesque art is seen in architecture (especially in mosques), on textiles, carpets, and on handwritten documents.

Architecture is another form of artistic expression in Muslim countries. The Taj Mahal is well known, but many other buildings in the Islamic world — both mosques and secular structures — are also ingenious, striking, and precise in their design and construction. The influence of Islamic architecture on the Western world, particularly during the Gothic period, is enormous.

It is a misconception that music is discouraged in Islam. To the contrary, the Koran is chanted in a musical manner, as is the call to prayer. Islam has long recognized that music, even secular music, can guide the spirit toward a higher goal, but secular music that arouses passions such as lust, blasphemy, and violence is discouraged. Pipe instruments and strings were historically forbidden because they were associated with drunkards, but this restriction is often relaxed today.

Literature has also been critical in Islamic history. Indeed, it was from a great work of literature that the religion began. From the eleventh century, biographical dictionaries (short alphabetical descriptions of the lives of famous people) became an important literary form in the Islamic world, apparently arising from transmission of the Hadith.

Although Christians and Muslims routinely hold their Holy Books to have all of the answers, in actuality, practitioners of both religions have sometimes looked beyond the books. As was the case in Europe, some Muslims believed in spirits or in the ability of certain people to influence others through rituals. Likewise, dreams and visions have sporadically been accepted in both West and East as a means to understand reality or predict the future. Islamic mysticism, called Sufism, arose in about the eighth century. As was the case with early Christianity, Sufism was based in part on Greek thought, specifically Neoplatonism.

Sufism's importance in the history of Islam is out of proportion to its actual practice for two reasons. First, Sufism was important in the spread of Islam. As Islam grew, many potential converts were attracted to the mystical aspect of the religion. Second, Sufi literature was influential in the development and evolution of subsequent literature throughout both the Western and the Islamic worlds.

Like practitioners of mysticism in other religions, Sufis believe that meditation can focus the mind, and, while still accepting the fundamentals of Islam, they seek a more personal relationship with God through meditation, rituals, and spiritual thinking. Sufis believe that there are both spiritual and material manifestations of God, and that it is essential to see past the material manifestations to allow the spiritual to become apparent. Sufis believe that the closer they are to God the more He speaks through their bodies, but bodily motion is only a way of preparing the mind, never the sole means of seeking God. Poverty is the rule, to overcome the temptations of the daily world in order to understand the divine nature. Some Sufis used erotic language to express their love for God because this language offered a means of going beyond daily speech and conveying the intense feelings of their individual quest for God.

Mevlana Jalaluddin Rumi (1207–1273) is a revered Sufi poet whose writing, though often abstruse, speaks of tolerance, kindness, love, and the awareness that these bring to life. Rumi's major works are the *Masnavi-ye Ma'navi* (also called *Spiritual Verses* or *Spiritual Couplets)* and the *Divan-i Kebir* (or *Dīwān-e Kabīr,* meaning "Great Work"), both voluminous and influential works of mystical poetry that illuminate the individual's search for God.

Most Sufis practiced within the bounds of traditional Islam, and attempted to integrate Sufism and traditional Islam, but a minority thought that Sufism could supersede traditional Islam, and that a direct relationship with God through Sufism or spirituality was an alternative to the Shari'a. The willingness of some Sufis to bend the letter of the law for what they believed to be a direct relationship to God brought them into occasional conflict with established Islam. It is difficult for traditional practitioners of a religion to realize that wise practice of a great religion permits individuals to step away from it and adopt a different approach because the religion is powerful and resilient, and can withstand supplementary ideas and occasional skeptics.

Once again, relief came from a person who could reconcile apparent disparities. Abu Hamid al-Ghazali (1058–1111) was instrumental in resolving the conflict between Sufism and traditional Islam. He supported

Sufism, but argued that traditional Islam should be afforded primacy. He also understood Greek thought and held that much — but not all — of it could be accepted into Islam. By rejecting a portion of Greek thought and insisting upon the primacy of traditional Islam, Al-Ghazali was able to make both Sufism and Greek thinking palatable to traditional Muslims, and was responsible for an integration of both of these areas into Islam. For this reason, Al-Ghazali is often remembered as a renewer of Islam, a title of great honor because only one person each century can be so designated. In achieving this synthesis, Al-Ghazali bears a striking resemblance to Moses Maimonides and Saint Thomas Aquinas, who integrated Greek thought into Judaism and Catholicism, respectively. Though Sufism is far removed from the lives and thoughts of Christians and most Muslims, in its history we find a striking lesson: People who can view new knowledge without fear or threat can integrate it into the existing body of knowledge without compromising essential principles. The result strengthens rather than weakens existing thinking. As different cultures and religions of our burgeoning world come face-to-face, we need many more people who can synthesize as al-Ghazali, Maimonides, Aquinas, and others have done.

Because of people like al-Ghazali, Sufism became more legitimate in the twelfth century. Also at this time, Sufi orders emerged, examples of which are *Qadiriyya, Mawlawiyya,* and *Chishtiyya.* Founders of Sufi orders became saints in many cases (very unusual in Islam). Today, not all Sufis are mystics, and Sufism can be thought of as an emotional supplement to Islam and as a means of enhancing a sense of community. Some, but not all, Sufis use music and dance or song or repeated body motions. Dervishes, famous for their repetitive whirling or rolling motions, are Sufis. Some Sufis participate in magic and superstition, but it must be remembered that these beliefs were an integral part of the times in both East and West when Sufism was born. Likewise, some Sufis withdraw from the world, but others do not.

Sufi monasteries became prominent sites of learning and study. Sufis were a significant force in conversion, surpassing the military in the dissemination of Islam. Indeed, Sufis led the way in the conversion of Hindus because they reminded the latter of their respected Bhaktas. Like the Hindu Bhaktas, Sufis stressed devotion and love more than ritual and dogma, and shared an antiestablishment persona. Sufis were also important in conversion because they worked in vernacular languages.

By 1250, the Mongols had swept across Asia and conquered many Islamic lands, including Persia and northern India (although they never conquered Arabia itself). Much more than during the Crusades, Islam was on the defensive, but it weathered the storm, partially because of the dissolution of the Mongol Empire and partially because of conversion of Mongol leaders to Islam. After Islam was re-established, regional autonomy, which had begun earlier, accelerated, resulting in a number of Islamic states called sultanates. Three of these stood out: the Ottoman Empire (1281–1924), the Persian Safavid Empire (1501–1722), and the Mughal (or Moghul) Empire of India (1528–1857). Leaders of these were called sultans, or in the case of Persia, shahs. These sultanates generally practiced an enlightened Islam, and demonstrated that there need not be a conflict between different religions or between religion and innovation. The Mughal Empire, in particular, has a well-deserved reputation for tolerance and prosperity (the Taj Mahal was built during Mughal times) until the reign of Aurangzeb (1648–1707), who reasserted both Islamic orthodoxy and hostility toward Hinduism. Beginning in the seventeenth century, Islamic power began to wane, largely because of European colonialism, which was particularly injurious to the sultanates.

The influence of European colonialism was so great that many contemporary nations were literally carved out of Islamic lands by European powers. Western powers controlled the leadership of many of these countries, installing puppets loyal to the West. Western-educated leaders in Islamic society often had a different conception of law from the traditional Ulama. This not only disrupted the indigenous culture, but also introduced a schism between the leadership and the people; independence movements in these countries, seeking a return to traditional values and religious practice, became a major historical force.

It is a lesson of history that no outside power, however well-meaning, can reformulate a culture. There are too many nuances and details with which an outside power cannot be familiar. A society must change from within. A well-intentioned outside power can provide the prosperity and stability to allow reasoned internal voices to be heard, but there is no such thing as external "nation building." European colonialism and cultural interference have been one of the great tragedies of the last half millennium, resulting in the virtual destruction of many nations.

Islam has a tradition of scholarship and innovation unknown to most Westerners. Indeed, the Koran specifically instructs its readers to study and learn. Because of this tradition, the Muslim world in large measure made the Western Renaissance possible by preserving, transmitting, and extending Greek knowledge. Paradoxically and tragically, the Muslim world has not experienced a distinct Renaissance or Enlightenment of its own. The beautiful religion of Islam, one of the most innovative and humanistic ideas in history, has not generally kept pace with the march of time, and remains substantially imprisoned in many Muslim countries by a union of religion and state, which neither affords individual liberty nor is conducive to new ideas. But might this also be truer of Judaism and Christianity than many realize?

Nevertheless, Islam has responded to changing times more than most Westerners believe. Islamic renewal is called *Tajdid* and reform is called *Islah.* These are carried out by practicing ijtihad, wherein the Koran and the Sunna, though critical guides, are supplemented by reasoned independent thought. Islamic countries are not only struggling with how much reform to institute, but also with how to do so. As is the case with other religions, some reform movements have been fundamentalist, while others have been more moderate. Wahhabism, based on the teachings of Muhammad ibn al Wahhab (1703–1792) in Saudi Arabia, is a fundamentalist Islamic movement that arose in response to modernism. There is a natural tendency to believe that fundamentalist movements have always been present, and constitute the "native" form of that religion. In actuality, each of the most conservative expressions of the Abrahamic religions — Orthodox Judaism, fundamentalist Christianity, and fundamentalist Islamic movements, such as Wahhabism — arose relatively recently as a specific response to modernity.

Wahhabism is a conservative form of Islam, practiced primarily in Saudi Arabia, but it is no more representative of Islam in general than fundamentalist Christianity is of that religion. Sufism is a particular target of the Wahhabis, and they have consistently clashed with Shiites because of their greater emphasis on Sufism. Even in Saudi Arabia, however, there is a slow change in the perception and practice of Islam.

Other Islamic reform movements have been more liberal. Mohammed Ahamad (1848–1885) founded the Mahdi movement in the Sudan. He outlawed many Western practices such as gambling and music, but he sought to reform rather than destroy Sufism. Additional Islamic reform movements are the Fulani in Nigeria and the Sanusi in Libya. Sayyid Ahmad Khan (1817–1898) and Mohammed Iqbal (1877–1938) were important reformers of Islam in India.

Islamic modernists have never been in the majority and have never been able to institute a significant amount of overt change, but like all great ideas that ostensibly were not adopted, their influence was subtle and greater than initially apparent. Modernist thinking has quietly crept into traditional Islam. Westerners should remember that modernism came more quickly to us because of the Renaissance and Enlightenment, but it is also coming to Islam.

It is another lesson of history that the health of a society or a movement or a religion can be judged by its tolerance of peripheral thought. To have the adaptability that is essential for survival, any set of beliefs must allow for those who will make changes. We as a society, and any subset thereof, must accept and even welcome those who may at first appear to tread upon our cherished beliefs. If we do not, the set of beliefs will either die, or the society based on it will effectively become a police state. I believe that a major problem with contemporary Islam and Islamic countries — but also found in the West — is their failure to accept new ideas. What could have been an expansive, adaptable combination of religion and government has instead often encased its citizens in an unchanging tradition. The problem is exacerbated by the union of church and state, which prevents new ideas from forming and getting a fair hearing in either.

The tension between modernity and Islam is particularly evident in the role of women. Some view the failure of rapid and complete acceptance of Western values in Islamic countries as a great disappointment of the last century, but we must never underestimate the importance of traditional religious, cultural, and nationalistic ideas. It is simply not reasonable for a developed, industrialized, influential nation to expect Muslim nations to think and behave in a Western manner. In addition, Westerners must remember that they and their culture came uninvited to Islamic lands.

Christianity and Judaism have modernized more than Islam because these religions have had more time to adapt to modernity. Most technological changes occurred in Christian lands, and have been ongoing for several centuries. In contrast, these changes were dumped on Muslim countries in just the last couple of generations. Muslim reformers have had only a few decades to do what took Christianity and Judaism centuries.

Although some fundamentalist movements, such as Wahhabism, date to the eighteenth century, fundamentalism did not sweep over the Muslim world until the failures of the Islamic states that succeeded the Ottoman Empire, and the subsequent domination by Europe. Just after WW I, most of the Muslim world was under Western control — domination more complete than that during Mongol times, and certainly infinitely greater and more threatening than ever occurred during the Crusades. Indeed, many Muslims view European colonialism and Zionism as a continuation of the Crusades, but this time much more successful. Faced with a sense of powerlessness and a need to preserve their culture and religion, some Muslims have turned to fundamentalism. Like fundamentalist Christianity, Fundamentalist Islam demonstrates that political or economic insecurity, fear, or domination by an external power causes some to seek a "purer" expression of their religion.

We often do not realize how intimidating we, either as nations and cultures or as individuals, can be to others. The West needs to realize that despite the best of its intentions, it has often virtually manhandled the rest of the world, and has often been insensitive to the thinking of other cultures, resulting in damage that was unintended, but could have been avoided with more cultural sensitivity. Though this behavior represents a common human frailty, not a specific Western shortcoming, and the West has often been genuinely benevolent, Western foreign policy cannot be intelligently constructed until we understand the intimidating and bullying effect we have had on the world. Westerners should imagine what it would be like if most of the Christian world were under Muslim domination, or what it would have been like at the height of the Cold War if most of the West had been under Soviet economic and cultural influence. A similar situation actually exists for most people in the non-Western world. Why should their feelings be any different from a Westerner's?

It is always instructive to place yourself in the position of others and see events from their perspective. The Muslim world had spread with astonishing rapidity and formed the most important and stable empire in history. The Muslim Empire was much longer lived and much more influential than that of either Alexander the Great or the Mongols. Even the Roman Empire matched the longevity of the Islamic preeminence only if we count the Eastern portion.

With rare exceptions, such as southern Spain, Islam eventually won virtually every conflict in its history. Even the Mongols, the only people to have significantly defeated the Muslims, either converted to Islam or faded from the scene within two or three generations, making the Muslims the de facto winners of that clash. But after 1800, it became obvious that Muslim nations were being dominated by a power that is far stronger and more permanent than any it had previously seen, and that will neither go away nor convert. It is no surprise that Muslims are fearful of the sudden changes in their worldview.

The watershed event of Muslim disillusionment was Israel's decisive victory in the 1967 Middle East war, and the ensuing Israeli occupation of the subjugated lands. Foremost among the catastrophes of the war was the loss of Jerusalem. This exacerbated centuries of waning Muslim influence caused by declining military power and internal social difficulties, resulting in a crisis of identity and confidence. The painful situation was made much worse by Israeli settlement of the occupied lands, making it extraordinarily difficult to negotiate their return to Muslim countries. Non-Muslims, and Americans and Israelis in particular, must understand the frustration and concern that this causes in the Islamic community.

It is another lesson of history that ignoring or belittling others' opinions enrages them and fills them with resolve to cling to those opinions all the more tenaciously. This is illustrated by the worldwide outrage in the Muslim community over the widespread publication of caricatures of the Prophet in February 2006. Incredibly, several European newspapers republished one of those cartoons in 2008. If, in any dispute — personal, cultural, or national — we understand the history of the other side, respect their beliefs, and put ourselves in their position, the door is opened to dialogue. Surely, it is not asking too much of our leaders to understand that powerlessness breeds a fanaticism that can never be controlled with force. People will pay any price to obtain a degree of control over their destiny, and fundamentalism and fanaticism are forms of self-empowerment.

It is critical that we understand that the lesson of fundamentalist Islam is not that Islam is bad, but that fundamentalism in any form is extreme and uncompromising. When people in the modernized West hear of Muslim terrorists, they often undertake what they believe is a fair comparison of Islam and Christianity, but it is in fact a comparison of an extreme and unrepresentative subset of Islam to a more moderate and representative subset of Christianity. Fundamentalists of all religions resemble each other more than they resemble mainstream practitioners of their own religion. The only significant difference between fundamentalist Christianity and fundamentalist Islam is that the latter is in power in some countries. If you want to see what the United States would be like if the fundamentalist Christians win, just look at Saudi Arabia.

Literal interpretation of scriptures is an overriding theme in fundamentalism of all religions. Fundamentalists believe that modernity has caused a straying from the wisdom of the past, while more liberal religious people of all faiths find that the true wisdom of their scriptures is precisely that they speak more elastically in language that is valid to all ages, and that it is the spirit of the texts that should be held sacred. Religious thought is not inherently intolerant, and is among the finest thought in history, but practiced with inflexibility and intolerance, religion sets the stage for worldwide conflict. In my view, all three Abrahamic religions need to conduct their own Jihad to live in peace with both modernity and other religions. Christians will have to ensure that fundamentalists do not translate their opinion into law in the United States. Jews will have to vacate the occupied territories in the Middle East and have more sensitivity for the plight of the Palestinians. Muslims, both as individuals and as nations, must decisively and unequivocally renounce terrorism and universally adopt nonviolent means of protest.

Because there are secularists and fundamentalists in the Muslim world, with a range of gradations in between, there are a variety of responses to Western intrusion in the Muslim world. The first is to ignore or resist the West. Traditional fundamentalism holds that the ideas of the West are intrinsically at odds with those of Islam, and that there must be a return to basics in an inherently Muslim way. A second response, from mainstream Muslims, has been partial acceptance and a degree of emulation, including an attempt to incorporate some Western ideas, without their corruption, to exist side by side with tradition. This attempt has, however, still imported many aspects of the West that even some of the more liberal Muslims are uncomfortable with. A third response, from more liberal Muslims, has been the facilitation of reform movements within Islam. These are not mutually exclusive, and mixed forms may occur. For example, a more liberal fundamentalism holds that there is not necessarily a conflict with the West, and that the Islamic world must change, but in a way that remains true to the basic tenets of Islam. These Muslims are willing to update Islamic law and to believe that the sources of the past may not be divine or directly applicable to all contemporary situations. They insist, however, that the traditional canon should remain the driving force in all Islamic societies. Neo-traditionalist Muslims seek a return to the past, but they accept some ideas from other cultures, such as some form of elected government, and they support some Western-style social and educational programs within the context of traditional Islam.

Another effect of Western contact was the importation of concepts that are not religious. For example, the ideas of nationalism and communism came into the Muslim world from the West, and some Islamic countries adopted them as a response to the West. Beginning in the mid-twentieth century in Syria and Iraq, the *Ba'ath* (or *Ba'th)* movement was a response to Western domination, and focused on nationalism, secularism, and a pan-Arab union. Though the Ba'ath movement generated excitement and hopes for an Islamic Renaissance, it also had many critics because it was not inherently Muslim. Resistance to reform was great, and Ba'athist leaders were never able to fully modernize their countries. The movement then drifted away from its egalitarian leanings and became more totalitarian and militaristic, especially in Iraq under Saddam Hussein. One still sees references to Hussein's regime as Ba'athist, but in practice, it moved away from the original Ba'athist ideology long before its downfall. The Ba'athist movement came to an end in Iraq with Hussein's overthrow, and continues in Syria in a nearly unrecognizable form. We can never know how the Muslim world might have been different had a generalized, uncorrupted Ba'ath movement become reality.

Today, the leaders of all Muslim countries except for the Sudan, Iran, and Saudi Arabia are theoretically modernists. Only in those three nations is the government one of professed fundamentalism. In much of the Muslim world, there is now a disconnect between leaders, who are often relatively secular, and the people, who are more religious and who question their leaders' support of the West. Modernism has lost much of its appeal for the rank-and-file Muslim for the same reason that fundamentalism has grown in Christianity — there has been a loss of something comforting and precious without a satisfactory substitute.

The Muslim Brotherhood was founded by Hassan al-Banna in Egypt in 1928. Its official position is that it is an international, moderately fundamentalist form of Islam that is peaceful, dedicated to the rejuvenation of the Ummah, and to giving it priority over national boundaries. Some have questioned the completeness of its commitment to peace, and believe its members are more willing to resort to violence than the organization admits, while others believe that it is committed to peace and that its members have been unjustly persecuted. As large as the organization is, it is inevitable that there has been variation in thinking among its members, with some more moderate and tolerant than others, and some more willing to engage in dialogue than others. In general, most members are dedicated to a peaceful renewal of Islam, through education, in a rapidly changing world dominated by the West. There is no compelling evidence that the Muslim Brotherhood is fundamentally violent. We must avoid stereotyping the entire group based on the actions of a few. The Muslim Brotherhood has also championed political freedom and been active in social programs. It is particularly visible in Egypt and actively opposed the Mubarek government prior to its downfall.

Between 15 and 20 percent of slaves brought to the United States were Muslims, and there has been some immigration from Muslim countries, but most American Muslims are converts. Today, there are about 5 million Muslims in the US. The Nation of Islam was founded in the early 1930s by Wallace D. Fard Mohammed, and subsequently headed by Elijah Mohammed. It did not initially practice the Five Pillars or make an effort to be mainstream Muslims. The most famous member of the Nation of Islam was Malcolm X (the "X" referred to the fact that his actual African name was lost. It also signified that he was an ex-drinker, ex-Christian, and ex-slave; after his pilgrimage to Mecca, he changed his name to El Hajj Malik El-Shabazz). After the death of Elijah Mohammed, his son Wallace D. Mohammed moved the Nation of Islam closer to traditional Islam, and its members became known as Black Muslims. Louis Farrakhan was left as the head of a much-reduced Nation of Islam, but even Farrakhan has moved that organization closer to orthodox Islam. Today, though the term "Black Muslim" has specific historical significance, its members are essentially an American expression of Islam.

Europe is also being challenged by an increasing number of Muslims. There are about 15 million Muslims in Europe, including 5 million in France, which received international attention, mostly negative, for banning the *hijab* (head scarf worn by some Muslim women) in schools. This was part of a larger prohibition of all religious clothing, but it was the hijab ban that ignited debate on the separation of church and state versus religious freedom.

Let us close our consideration of Islam by returning to the statements made at the beginning of our discussion — that it is the most misunderstood religion and that many Westerners believe it condones violence. As I hope this brief exploration has made clear, nothing of the sort is true. Those who believe that Muslims are uniformly hatemongers and terrorists make two mistakes. First, they fail to understand that the real problem is fundamentalism, not Islam. Fundamentalism exists in other religions, and in any religion, leads to oversimplifications that breed fear and hate. Second, they fail to understand that the Prophet was far ahead of his time. Among his many egalitarian and humanitarian beliefs, his concern for the welfare of women and orphans is evident throughout the Koran. Who among us, and who among those who criticize Islam, has done so much to advocate for defenseless people? Is it fair to compare contemporary beliefs with those of a person who lived fourteen centuries ago, and then draw conclusions about a whole religion? A little understanding and a little empathy will allow Westerners to avoid these mistakes. To the extent that Islam is more fundamentalist than Christianity — if that can even be said — it is only because it has changed slightly less over the centuries in some countries than Christianity has, and because it has been stressed by reduced power and influence in international affairs. The violent fundamentalists who make today's headlines are Muslim because terrorism, always the refuge of the small minority, is more common in groups that face a stronger adversary.

There is no faster way to get someone's attention than to address and heighten their fear, and there is no surer pathway to conflict than to present an oversimplified argument of sweeping generalizations, conflations, and stereotypes. The progress of history has been the triumph of understanding over stereotypes and the recognition of commonalities over differences. This is the challenge facing America as it ponders Islam.

Chapter 11

BAHÁ'Í

BAHÁ'Í IS THE NEWEST of the world's major religions. It arose in 1844 in Iran from Shiite Islam. We recall that Shiites believe that until their last Imam returns, he communicates via intermediaries called Babs. In 1844, Siyyid 'Alí-Mohammed (1819–1850), known in Bahá'í as the Báb, proclaimed himself such a Bab and almost certainly also believed he was the hidden twelfth Imam himself.

The *Persian Bayan* is the Báb's major writing. He foretold the appearance of a divine messenger, who would be a World Teacher, and who would bring unity and peace to the world. In 1848, he and his followers proclaimed their independence from Islam. The Báb was imprisoned and executed in 1850 (his execution almost certainly stemmed from his claim to be the hidden Imam, and from the separation of his community from mainstream Islam, rather than from his claim to be a Bab). Persian authorities massacred as many as 20,000 of his followers two years later.

Before his death, the Báb appointed a disciple named Subh-I-Ezel as his successor, but this position was actually assumed by that person's older half brother, Mirza Husayn Ali (1817–1892; also written Mirza Huseyn Ali Nuri), another disciple of the Báb. In 1863, Mirza Husayn Ali declared himself the Messenger and World Teacher spoken of by the Báb. He then took the name "Bahá'u'lláh," meaning "the glory of God." In the hands of Bahá'u'lláh, the doctrine of Babism became the religion of Bahá'í, which was further promulgated by his eldest son Abdu'l-Baha (1844–1921).

There are currently about five million Bahá'ís in the world. Bahá'í has an established governing structure at the local, national, and international level, but there is no clergy. Its central administrative center, called the Universal House of Justice, is near Haifa, Israel (also near Haifa are the shrines of the Báb and Bahá'u'lláh).

The principal belief of Bahá'í is that humanity is a single group and that the time has come for the unification of all people into a single global society. Enlightened people of all faiths have long hoped for the unity of all nations and religions, but Bahá'í, more than other religions, incorporates a deep and abiding conviction in the oneness of humanity as an integral and intrinsic attribute of its belief system.

The Bahá'í believe that historically, God has given humanity successive revelations through a series of divine messengers. Until now, these revelations have taken the form of founding or supporting separate religions, but now humanity is mature enough to be guided into the establishment of a single global society with one set of beliefs. Whereas Judaism, Christianity, and Islam all believe that the age of prophesy and messengers ended long ago (with Jesus in the case of Christianity and with Mohammed in the case of Islam), the Bahá'í believe the Báb and Bahá'u'lláh are additional divinely inspired teachers to continue God's revelation, and to guide us to the unification that is our ultimate destiny. Though Bahá'í recognizes its origin in Shiite Islam, and believes in a single, eternal, personal God, it differs from its parent religion in many respects and is equally concerned with a humanistic agenda. Basic Bahá'í beliefs are:

- The elimination of all prejudice;
- The full equality of women;
- Elimination of poverty and extremes of wealth;
- The provision of universal education;
- The right of each person to believe as he or she desires, and the right and responsibility of each person to seek the truth for himself or herself;
- The establishment of a global nation;
- The recognition that true religion does not conflict with reason or scientific progress.

The Bahá'í embrace science without fear. Abdu'l-Bahá, son of Bahá'u'lláh, addressed the matter in these words:

> *Religion and science are the two wings upon which man's intelligence can soar into the heights, with which the human soul can progress. It is not possible to fly with one wing alone.*

Let us hope that the beliefs of Bahá'í fly on the wings of eagles into our history and into our legacy.

Ring Stone

The Ring Stone is a symbol of the Bahá'í faith. The top horizontal line refers to the World of God. The middle horizontal line refers to the World of His Manifestations. The bottom horizontal line refers to the World of People. The vertical line joins the three worlds and represents the linking of God, his manifestations, and humanity. The two five-pointed stars on either side represent the two messengers of this age who brought the Bahá'í faith into being, the Báb and Bahá'u'lláh.

Nine-pointed Star

The nine-pointed star is a common symbol of the Bahá'í faith. Although the number 9 is not regarded as magical in any way, it does have special significance in Bahá'í for several reasons. First, as the largest single-digit number, 9 represents completeness and perfection. Second, in Arabic, every letter also has a numerical value. Letters are not used in this way anymore, but at the time of the founding of Bahá'í, it was common to employ letters as substitutes for numbers. The numerical value of Bahá, the root of Bahá'í, is 9. Third, the Koran uses 99 names for God.

Epilogue

BEYOND OURSELVES WITHIN OURSELVES

We have now examined all of the major religions that have shaped our history and are still practiced. Two religions — Judaism and Hinduism — arose from the works and teachings of many people. No religion in its present form arose entirely from one person, but three — Buddhism, Confucianism, and Islam — have arisen primarily from the teachings, compilations, or expansions of one person. Others — Sikhism and Daoism — arose from the teachings of a small number of people, and to this list we should add Christianity, in recognition of the enormous contributions of Paul, Augustine, and the Reformationists.

God is not anthropomorphic in Hinduism, though manifestations of the Supreme Being are. God has no body or form to Sikhs. Daoism recognizes a supreme force that is not anthropomorphic. Two religions — Confucianism and Buddhism — do not necessarily recognize a supreme entity, though Mahayana Buddhism believes in celestial Buddhas and Bodhisattvas. Among the Abrahamic faiths, while Genesis indicates that God created man in his own image, many Jews do not interpret this as a simple anthropomorphic God. Likewise, Islam does not have or teach a simple anthropomorphic view of God. Christianity has the most anthropomorphic view of God of any religion. Indeed, one component of the Trinity is the corporeal person Jesus. Christianity is the only major contemporary religion that believes in the divinity of a corporeal person (though this belief is not rare in history, and a number of extinct or "minor" religions have recognized the divinity of a person, such as the Egyptian belief that the Pharaoh was the son of the Sun God, and the deification of the Egyptian scientist and architect Imhotep). Even in Christianity, however, while depictions of Jesus abound in art, there are few depictions of the father aspect of God (Michelangelo's Sistine Chapel is a notable exception) and one aspect of the Trinity — the Holy Spirit — is not anthropomorphic.

Three religions — Buddhism, Jainism, and Sikhism — began as modifications of Hinduism (there is also Muslim influence in Sikhism), while Christianity began as a modification of Judaism. Bahá'í is indebted to Islam.

The Eastern religions of Hinduism, Buddhism, and Daoism surrender the self, while the Abrahamic religions of Judaism, Christianity, and Islam place more emphasis on the self, holding it inviolate throughout eternity. In particular, the concept of a final, definitive truth is more a part of Christianity and Islam than of the Eastern religions, and reflects the Western desire to dominate, whereas the Eastern religions generally believe in living in harmony with the world. The curious opinion of absolute rights and wrongs, black and white, truths and falsehoods, has sent Western history down a much bloodier path than was necessary. We have much to learn from the East, for we lack the inner peace, harmony, and reverence for life that the East has achieved.

We have seen that all religions are much more similar than dissimilar, and we can discern five common threads. First, every religion, Eastern or Western, with or without a deity, seeks to make the world more understandable and assist in coping with life's complexities and vicissitudes. Second, all religions accept an incomprehensible force (deity or otherwise) that is more powerful than daily human existence. Third, all require their practitioners not to covet or seek worldly possessions. Fourth, all advocate a time of quiet and setting aside worldly concerns to achieve a fuller awareness of nature. Fifth, all stipulate compassionate treatment of other people. Though Christianity, as practiced through the doctrine of justification by faith alone, is unique in placing as much emphasis on correct beliefs as on correct actions, in practice, all religions have codes of conduct.

It would be wrong to believe that each religion has given only one gift to humanity, for all have rendered many, but I will state the most important lesson I have acquired from each of them. To traditional societies, I am grateful for the idea that nature is not to be dominated. To Hinduism, I am grateful for the concept that all things are different manifestations of the One. To Jainism, I am grateful for the doctrine of harmlessness. To Buddhism, I am grateful for the Four Noble Truths. To Sikhism, I am grateful for the belief in egalitarianism and the rejection of castes. To Daoism, I am grateful for the recognition that in many ways we are passengers in life; we should accept what cannot be changed and go with the flow. To Confucianism, I am grateful for the recognition of the value of constancy, and the need — for all of our explorations — to occasionally return to a familiar place. To Judaism, I am grateful for the tradition of scholarship and ethical behavior. To Christianity, I am grateful for the belief that the weak will eventually triumph. To Islam, I am grateful for the verification of the essential goodness of all people, even those who are misunderstood or persecuted. To Bahá'í, I am grateful for the belief in the oneness of humanity.

Religions provide a sense of peace, comfort, and understanding, and our history is richer for them. But in partaking of their treasures, we must be careful in two respects. First, though religions afford a unifying sense of purpose and belonging, they may deflect attention from the present and make us less eager to improve the world and ourselves. The promise of an afterlife may reduce the importance of the here and now. Religion may lessen the individual and collective self-confidence that are the key components of creativity and the foundation of our prosperity and progress. This is particularly true of religions that are based on a deity, because they arose from the belief that people alone cannot fully understand or perfect the world. Religions are not, however, necessarily incompatible with individualism, a collective self-confidence, or effective social change if they are expressed humanistically and with a concurrent belief in human potential. History shouts that progress and religion are potential, *but not invariant,* adversaries.

Second, even minor differences between their respective religions may divide societies. Concomitant to facilitating uniformity *within* societies, religions generally accentuate the differences *between* societies. Almost all wars have been fought over religion, land, or both. History proclaims that religious differences and war are common, *but not invariant,* allies.

Some people believe that the final phase in our religious development will be the understanding that deities of all types are not required, and that our own intelligence and basic goodness will one day be sufficient to give us the power and ability we had thought to exist only in gods. This opinion holds that religion is a consequence of our continually developing cultural evolution. I am among those who hold that there is hope and good news for humanity, but it need not lie with a savior or a supreme being, but rather lies within us, individually and collectively, and with human ingenuity and strength of spirit. We believe it is possible to find one's way in the world, and to find happiness, without a deity, the threat of eternal damnation, or the promise of immortality. We cherish the religious thought that is beyond ourselves, and we are grateful for the inner peace and the many wonderful lessons of the world's religions, but we believe that now is the time to look within ourselves to better understand each other.

The belief in God or the holding of any religion does not by itself impede progress. All of these beliefs are precious and can be among the best of our thought. What is dangerous are the opinions that too often follow: that one way of thinking is the only correct way; that the use of rational thinking to understand the world or better our lot clashes with the will of the Creator; or that any one religion has a more noble origin, a superior history, or a greater destiny than another. As we face a resurgence of fundamentalism in many religions, now is the time to affirm that all of us have much to learn from others, and that all of us have the freedom of — or from — any religion. It is the weakness of our nature — and the tragedy of our history — that we desire our ideas and religions to be universal, rather than becoming *personally* universal in our experiences and tolerance. All religions have been forces for kindness and social reform, but many have also been forces for cruelty. Indeed, today's social reformers often must contend with religion.

Secular humanism is not intended to replace religion, but to sit beside it — as one sits beside a friend — to share and to complement, and to work together with it to complete and to fulfill us. Secular humanists respect all religions and believe that all of them have added, and will continue to add, enormously to our development. Religions need not be and cannot be replaced with secular thought, but now is the time to look within us, join hands, and supplement the comfort and security of religion with our own confidence. When we are young, we need simple answers, but as we mature, we understand that life has many shades of gray, and if we are fortunate, these illuminate new pathways that provide as much comfort as simple answers did earlier. We also develop in stages collectively, and as a people, it is time to receive religious shades of gray. Simple, final answers are gratifying in the short term, but cheapen our development and our potential in the long term. We need not accept tragedy as a part of an unquestioned divine plan, nor should we submit to any authority — celestial or terrestrial — unless it conforms to the rational principles that have been the triumph of our species.

The realization of our potential requires better educational and economic opportunities for all of us, so that the necessary understanding currently available to only a small segment of our society can be extended to all. Now is the time to take the first steps toward a new understanding of religion, not as obsolete, but no longer as primary; not as separate sets of beliefs, only one of which can be correct, but as families of related beliefs that all have much to offer; not as a threat to rational thought, or to be replaced by it, but to stand equal to it as the twin pillars of who we are. The secular humanist view of religion recognizes its great and continuing role in providing comfort and security, but asks that the critical day-to-day decisions be made through intellect. We will have matured as a species when we understand that while there may be a God, improving the world is our job, and we are up to it. We can believe in the divine origin of the world if we wish, but we must never believe that only the divine can make it better. This new understanding of religion can be initially frightening, but it empowers us without diminishing the beauty or importance of any faith.

Secular humanists believe that people are basically good and do the best they can, where they are, with what they have. We believe that the evils of the world stem not from the evils of individuals, but from an individual and collective ignorance, which is remediable. Secular humanism can be summarized in a modification of the Four Noble Truths. First, people are basically good. Second, most suffering comes from ignorance, which arises from poor teaching, poor example, and diminished opportunities. Third, societal improvement is through greater understanding of the nature and origins of problems, an acceptance that only people can make the world better, and a farsighted approach. Fourth, until there is a time of greater understanding, we can cope with ignorance and its consequences by accepting of it as part of life, and by accepting that people do the best they can. Understanding history and historical wisdom are very helpful in this regard.

Religions have lit up history, they light up the world today, and they will light up posterity, but now is the time to make that light the soft glow of understanding and tolerance, not the harsh glare of dogmatism and absolutism. Dogma is a poor tool to shape a better tomorrow, but tolerance is the master sculptor for posterity. Understanding is the first step to tolerance, so I humbly offer this work, as the world still heals from the horrors of 9–11, as a gateway toward understanding and tolerance.

Preparing this book has enabled me to feel a part of all religions, and I hope that reading it has done the same for you. We are all practitioners of all religions because we are all members of the fabric of humanity. Preparing this work has also taught me that life is a pilgrimage. For all of the mistakes that we make, for all of our flaws and fallacies and cruelties, with each step of this pilgrimage we affirm who we are. We affirm that humanity is worth preserving and worth improving. As long as there is movement along the slow and winding pathway of our individual and collective lives, there will be goodness, hope, affirmation, and love. We are neither good nor bad, but some of each as we continue to mature during our pilgrimage. We are both good and bad with every step, and we will neither ignore the bad, nor become disillusioned by it, for this is who we are.

We walk with countless varieties of courage, many so subtle we are not aware of them. With every step, we make mistakes, but with every step we affirm goodness and kindness, love and curiosity, and that we have value. We are quiet heroes, traveling down small roads, believing that even the steps we take alone are a shared journey, and that shared journey — in all its forms, down all of those roads, with all its mistakes — is the pride and the hope and the affirmation of our species.

I dream of the day when all of us can step in our different ways, along our different paths, and still walk hand in hand on the shared journey that is who we are. I dream of the day when we will look within ourselves for the guidance and answers we seek. I dream of the day when we will reach out to each other, across the differences and rough spots in life, with understanding, respect, kindness, and unity. Profound diversity has indeed emerged from the single species of humanity. I dream of the day when diversity and unity will exist together in peace, when we will understand each other and all the many ways in which we look beyond ourselves. I hope that this work has moved you to dream the same dreams, and if I am very fortunate, it has perhaps moved us a little closer to those goals.

Afterword

FUNDAMENTALISM: A PERSONAL VIEW

THE CONTEMPORARY RISE OF FUNDAMENTALISM in four religions — Judaism, Christianity, Hinduism, and Islam — is perplexing and alarming to many people. Those devoted to secular scholarship wonder if the current wave of fundamentalism is a blip on the radar screen of history, or the end of centuries of slow progress for the dignity and worth of humanity.

Why do we see fundamentalism at a time when science and technology have given us so much? In my opinion, the reason is that people depart from rationality when they are fearful. The fear can come from economic difficulties or from a perceived threat to a way of life. In the case of contemporary fundamentalism, it is the latter. Never in our history has there been such rapid change, with so many time-honored and treasured institutions and ways of thinking under pressure to change. To some of us, this change is exciting and welcome, but to some, it comes uninvited and unwelcome because it shakes the foundations of their lives.

In understanding the rise of modern religious fundamentalism, we must first remember why there is religion at all. The needs for security and a sense of understanding are visceral and are as basic to our species as the need for food. Religion arose to fulfill these twin needs. Fundamentalism is a heightened expression of these same needs. All of us — including secular scholars — return to the familiar if threatened or confused. For some, religious fundamentalism is that return. We will never understand the rise of fundamentalism, its implications, or how we should respond, until we understand that it is driven by fear and uncertainty.

Science is the most conspicuous expression of secular scholarship and the form that is most threatening to fundamentalists because it directly challenges the need for God as the creative and sustaining force of the universe. Christian fundamentalists believe in Creationism — the belief that science plays no role at all in the existence of the universe, that there is no evolution, and that God's hand created everything in the proverbial six days — or in Intelligent Design, a belief that grew out of Creationism and accepts some elements of science, but believes that there must be a guiding force behind the creation and evolution of the universe and everything in it. There is an inherently thin line between Intelligent Design and Creationism. But now, perhaps, that line can be widened, and in the process, room for negotiation and compromise might be found.

While some fundamentalists accept some aspects of science as a mechanism of Intelligent Design, all are afraid that science will replace religion altogether. Fundamentalist insistence that Intelligent Design be part of science education horrifies secular scholars, who perceive the two as incompatible with three centuries of progress. But those not familiar with the myriad possibilities of gradual change over eons might very reasonably conclude that Intelligent Design is the only way for the universe to have arisen.

We must also recognize that our progress of the last few centuries, while amazing, has not been able to replace the security of religion. Modernity has been much more effective at displacing religion than replacing it. Modernity has not provided an adequate substitute for the sense of understanding, security, or belonging inherent in religion. All of us — again including the secular — have sustained tragedies that modernity has been unable to prevent or ameliorate.

Secular scholars should examine the situation from the point of view of fundamentalists. Fundamentalists have — and are entitled to have — a siege mentality. As everything around them changes, as anchors are pulled up, their world disappears before them. Fundamentalists are not stupid people who are incapable of understanding modernity. They are people who have been overtaken by a fear of the unknown, who feel the foundations of their lives threatened by changes they cannot control, and who do not see those changes providing an adequate substitute for the familiar. Secular scholars should ease their fear by affirming that there will always be a place for them and their worldview.

Fundamentalists are also influenced by group dynamics that are superimposed on individual needs. In the Fundamentalist community, individual fear is magnified by the fear of others, and a collective sense of anxiety ensues that is greater than the sum of individual anxieties. But at the same time, the group provides a deep sense of belonging and community that makes its members feel empowered. Others like themselves are anchors in turbulent times. There was safety in numbers in confronting a saber-toothed cat, and fundamentalists have learned that in coping with the modern world there is safety in numbers. Indeed, secular scholars should be half as good at extending a feeling of belonging to their own people.

Secular scholars must be careful to avoid the dogmatism and close-mindedness that they decry in fundamentalists. They must also be careful not to overstate their own contribution. While the progress of the last centuries has made our lives richer and better, no form of rational thinking — including science — has substantially changed how most people think, how they dream, or what they want for their children.

Fundamentalism is a test for the heirs of the Enlightenment and the champions of tolerance. It is easy today to foster the ideals of the Enlightenment, but the challenge for this generation of enlightened people is to extend the fabric of understanding and tolerance to those who disagree with or threaten them. Secular scholars must respect fundamentalism as they would any other set of religious beliefs. They must acknowledge the concerns of fundamentalists and the legitimacy of their beliefs, and they must reassure them that secular scholarship is not a threat to their beliefs or their way of life.

Secular scholars should do a better job of picking their battles. Most confrontations with fundamentalists are not worth fighting because they pose no threat to the march of scholarship. Secular scholars should fight for the right to teach evolution as the established and irrefutable fact that it is, and they should oppose any attempt to present Intelligent

Design as a closeted form of Creationism. Likewise, they should oppose any attempt to permit Intelligent Design to engender skepticism about evolution. But they should permit fundamentalists to propose, in a single short statement at the conclusion of the teaching of evolution, that evolution does not preclude a creator and that Intelligent Design may work through evolution, provided such a statement stipulates the absolute fact of evolution.

If Intelligent Design is presented in a way that threatens the teaching of evolution, then its introduction should be rejected. That is a battle worth fighting. But if it is presented in a way that does not impede the teaching of evolution, and people are able to make an informed decision regarding the coexistence of evolution and Intelligent Design, then where is the harm in teaching students that evolution does not preclude a supreme being? Nowhere in all the triumphs and potentials of science is there a disproof of God or Intelligent Design. A reasonable compromise is to accept both the fact of evolution and the possibility of Intelligent Design — if one believes in a creator — in exchange for the abandonment of any attempt to present Creationism in any form. Making sure that evolution is taught as a fact is the only battle worth fighting in the matter of evolution versus Intelligent Design. Evolution does not need to be protected from religion. It will not melt away when placed beside the idea of a creator. The heritage and strength of secular scholarship in all its forms are strong enough to sit beside religious expression in all its forms. But scholarship and the society it serves cannot withstand a dogmatism and dichotomy caused by the belief that fundamentalists are stupid.

Likewise, secular scholars should fight for the right to be exempt or to have their children exempt from mandatory expressions of *their own* religious beliefs in public, but they must understand that attempting to restrict the public religious expression of others causes them to retrench and makes life more difficult for everyone. Where is the harm in other people professing a belief in God in public if there is no requirement for you to do so? Where is the harm in leaving "under God" in the Pledge of Allegiance, as long as children are concurrently taught that there are different and equally valid opinions concerning the existence and nature of God? The fact is that the United States *was* founded under God — be He real or imaginary. To fight those battles is to lose even if you win, because the conflict alienates people and transforms different opinions into eternal enemies.

Surrender these battles, then gently explain why stem-cell research takes tiny collections of cells that probably will never even attempt the long journey to humanity, and allows them to help millions of people. Fundamentalists may not fully understand what is and is not involved in stem-cell research, so inform them respectfully, suggest that God would want us to help so many millions of people, and offer a compromise that preserves the essence of what each side hopes for. Fighting over small matters makes it very difficult to reach accord over the issues that can make all of our lives better.

Fundamentalism is related to the general conservative trend in political life. It is the extreme example of the general fear of change and the widespread belief that progress has not satisfactorily replaced the religious and cultural foundations of simpler times. Those who are less afraid or have less religious background are relatively secular conservatives, while those whose uncertainty is united with and augmented by a strong religious background have become fundamentalists. We must understand this continuum. The most appropriate response to fundamentalism is much the same as that to conservatism in general — a show of respect and a willingness to communicate and compromise.

Fundamentalism teaches — or should teach — secular scholars what they must do to appeal to more people. It has been the tragedy of secular scholars — my people — that they have often been arrogant, condescending, and elitist. I and many like me have been driven away from a wide variety of secular humanist causes — including the Unitarians, the women's movement, and public broadcasting — by dogmatism, arrogance, apathy, and elitism. The great ideas of Humanism and secular scholarship — beginning in the Western world with that marvelous period we call the late Middle Ages, and continuing through the Enlightenment to the present day — are strong enough to hold their own against opposing views and have done so since their inception. They do not need arrogance and belligerence to survive. They need only to be presented as quiet truths so that they can speak for themselves. Hamas upset the more moderate Fateh party in the Palestinian elections of January 2006, but even here, only 45 percent of Palestinians voted for Hamas, and most oppose a militant agenda. People are inherently inclined to moderation, but this predisposition can be undone by arrogance, ineffectualness, and poor communication. Herein is a sobering lesson for secular scholars throughout the world.

Preparing this book has taught me that any religious belief, however strange, alien, or threatening, is to be respected. Fundamentalism must be a protected set of beliefs like any other because everyone is entitled to a sense of belonging and security. Secular scholars seek a unity of humanity, but that unity must begin with a bridge to those with whom they most strongly disagree. Confrontation and belittling breed retrenchment and dogmatism. Acceptance and communication foster reconciliation and integration. Dialogue can only begin when both sides feel safe, and conveyance of a feeling of safety and respect must start with secular scholars because the recent historical threat to fundamentalists has been more direct and immediate than the threat to secularism.

Secular scholars must show fundamentalists that their sense of belonging and security will be protected, both now and in the future. All we ask in return is the same for ourselves. The depth and breadth of human diversity permits both views without threat, fear, or conflict. Faith and reason are the twin pillars of who we are. Surely this can be agreed upon before my two small children find their place on the world stage.

To return to the question posed at the start of this essay — will modern religious fundamentalism be a blip on the radar screen of history, or the end of centuries of slow progress for the dignity and worth of humanity? Much of the answer depends on how secular scholars respond. As is so often the case in life, the real enemy is within.

Bibliography and Suggestions for Further Reading

THE RELIGIOUS TEXTS MENTIONED in this work are the best sources for further reading. These are the primary sources that form the foundation of their respective religions. Because all religion is a personal experience, there is no substitute for studying the holy books themselves. They are an irreplaceable connection to the past and an incomparable learning opportunity for all who wish to understand each other.

The body of religious writing, including commentaries, is probably the most voluminous in history. The complete canon of each of the religions discussed in this work, combined with their principal commentaries, is beyond the scope of anyone. But I recommend the reading of selections from each of these religions' most important works because religions live and breathe through their literature. The religions of traditional people are usually oral and generally do not have a written canon. From Hinduism, I recommend the Bhagavad Gita. In its few pages is a summary of the ideas of Hinduism. From Jainism, I recommend the following simple passage, which summarizes the religion and serves as a guide for all of us:

> *I ask pardon of all living creatures. May all of them pardon me. May I have a friendly relationship with all beings and unfriendly with none.*
>
> *Friendship to all living forms, delight in the qualities of the virtuous ones, unlimited compassion for all suffering beings, equanimity toward all who wish me harm, may my soul have these dispositions now and forever.*

From Buddhism, I recommend the Dhammapada, selections drawn from the Pali Canon. In this short work is the essence of Buddhism and wisdom that no Westerner should be without. From China, I recommend the Analects, the sayings of Confucius, and the Dao De Jing, a short work of enormous depth. From Sikhism, I recommend the Japji, the first portion of the Guru Granth Sahib. From Judaism, I recommend the Torah, which sets forth the ethical monotheism and the unique history and culture of the Hebrew people, and a few moments with the Talmud, which breathes life into Jews and Judaism. From Christianity, I recommend the Gospels, which make the case for Jesus as the Son of God, and Paul's Letter to the Romans, which sets forth the basic tenets of the then-new religion. From Islam, I recommend the first two surahs of the Koran. The first of these is only seven verses. These verses have lifted the heart of Muslims for centuries and are called the oft-repeated verses. The second surah, more than any other, sets forth the basic principles of Islam and the beliefs and responsibilities of Muslims. From this relatively modest set of works, the reader can feel the strength and power of the religions of the world and can greatly magnify his or her experience of life.

In addition, there are many fine secondary sources that provide further commentary and explanation. A representative sampling is listed below.

Armstrong, Karen. *A History of God.* New York: Ballantine Books, 1993.

Basham, A. L. *The Origins and Development of Classical Hinduism.* Boston: Beacon Press, 1989.

Bowker, John. *God: A Brief History.* London and New York: DK Publishing, Inc., 2002.

Bowker, John (ed.) *The Cambridge Illustrated History of Religions.* Cambridge: Cambridge University Press, 2002.

Bowker, John. *World Religions: The Great Faiths Explored and Explained.* New York: DK Publishing, 1997.

Greenberg, Irving. *The Jewish Way: Living the Holidays.* New York: Simon & Schuster, 1988.

Hattstein, Markus. *World Religions.* Cologne: KönemannVerlagsgesellschaft, 1998.

Parrinder, Geoffrey (ed.). *World Religions: From Ancient History to the Present.* New York: Facts on File Publications, 1971.

Smith, Huston. *The World's Religions.* San Francisco: Harper, 1991.

Spong, John Shelby. *Liberating the Gospels: Reading the Bible with Jewish Eyes.* San Francisco: Harper, 1996.

Because all religions are living entities, one must actually experience the services, festivals, holidays, and ceremonies of a religion to truly understand it. Religions resemble languages in that even the finest books can take a student just so far, after which only personal experience can bring true familiarity. I encourage all who wish to learn of other religions to attend the services in their community. If there is one particular religion that is of interest, I recommend obtaining its calendar and practicing its holidays, festivals, and daily activities, preferably in conjunction with others so that the fellowship of the religion is evident. This is living the religion and integrating it into your life.

PERMISSIONS

PAGE	ILLUSTRATION ID	COPYRIGHT
Cover	74956403	©Jon Feingersh
3	1085037	©iStockphoto.com/Deborah Wolfe
5	5912342	©iStockphoto.com/Alena Yaroslavtseva
21	Shiva	Photo courtesy of the author
22	4743031	©MKB/www.fotolia.com/
24	5022134	©MKB/www.fotolia.com/
43	5582547	©iStockphoto.com/Joan Loitz
51	1715899	©iStockphoto.com/Jeremy Edwards
54	Buddha	Photo courtesy of the author
59	Kuan Yin	Photo courtesy of the author
76	5Ks	Photo courtesy of Capt. Suresh Sharma/Green Frames
78	3857296	©iStockphoto.com/Wojciech Zwierzynski
91	The Red Cliff	National Palace Museum, Taiwan, Republic of China
99	3027036	©iStockphoto.com/Evgeny Kan
126	3837892	©iStockphoto.com/David Joyner
148	9359919	©iStockphoto.com/Eric Delmar
151	859723	©iStockphoto.com/Howard Sandler
152	3670758	©iStockphoto.com/Rafa Irusta
178	634570	©iStockphoto.com/BMPix
195	7507266	©iStockphoto.com/stockcam
198	2213316	©iStockphoto.com/winterling
211	ir1954	Painetworks.com
235	1766053	©iStockphoto.com/Damir Cudic
247	Wall Hanging	Photo courtesy of the author
262	Ring Stone	Illustration by Sandra Lindstrom
262	Nine-pointed Star	Illustration by Sandra Lindstrom

INDEX

Note: Page numbers in *italics* indicate photographs and illustrations.

A

B

C

D

E

F

G

H

I

J

K

N

O

P

Q

R

S

T

U

V

ABOUT THE AUTHOR

KIRK HERIOT EARNED BOTH an M.D. and a Ph.D. from Case Western Reserve University in Cleveland, Ohio, and is a practicing pathologist. *Understanding Each Other After 9-11* is his second book, following *Who We Are: A Chronicle of the Ideas That Shaped Our World,* and continues his lifelong exploration of the ideas that have shaped history and guided generations. Whereas *Who We Are* surveys ideas in all fields of intellectual activity, including religion, science, and artistic expression, *Understanding Each Other After 9-11* is a more focused and expanded discussion of the world's major religions. It reflects the author's deeply held belief that an understanding of the world's religions is critical to diminishing conflict among nations.